Communities of Kinship

Communities
of Kinship

*Antebellum Families
and the Settlement
of the Cotton Frontier*

Carolyn Earle Billingsley

*For Evelyn – the very
finest of examples –*
Carolyn Earle Billingsley

*The University of Georgia Press
Athens and London*

Credits for quoted material appear on page 216,
which constitutes an extension of the copyright page.

© 2004 by the University of Georgia Press
Athens, Georgia 30602
All rights reserved
Cartography by David Wasserboehr
Set in Adobe Caslon by G&S Typesetters
Printed and bound by Maple-Vail
The paper in this book meets the guidelines for permanence and
durability of the Committee on Production Guidelines for
Book Longevity of the Council on Library Resources.

Printed in the United States of America

08 07 06 05 04 c 5 4 3 2 1
08 07 06 05 04 P 5 4 3 2 1

Library of Congress Cataloging-in-Publication Data

Billingsley, Carolyn Earle.
Communities of kinship : antebellum families and the settlement
of the cotton frontier / Carolyn Earle Billingsley.
p. cm.
Includes bibliographical references and index.
ISBN 0-8203-2509-0 (hardcover : alk. paper) — ISBN 0-8203-2510-4 (pbk. : alk paper)
1. Kinship—Southern States—History.   2. Keesee family—History.   3. Patrilineal
kinship—Southern States—History.   4. Migration, Internal—Southern States—History.
5. Land settlement patterns—Southern States—History.   6. Southern States—Genealogy.
7. Southern States—History.   8. Southern States—Social life and customs.   I. Title.
GN560.U6B55 2004
306.83—dc22   2004003614

British Library Cataloguing-in-Publication Data available

CONTENTS

FIGURES

ACKNOWLEDGMENTS

The publication of this book represents a milestone of personal achievement I've been working toward all my life. For most of my life, I didn't even believe I'd ever get a college education, so I'm especially proud of earning a doctorate and having my dissertation deemed worthy of evolving into a book. The fact that these successes come when I am in my midfifties has allowed me to savor the emotions more intensely than I would have in my twenties. But that also means that there were quite a few decades during which friends, family, and colleagues sustained me and helped carry me onward toward my goals. I'd like to express my heartfelt gratitude here to all of those people in my life, both personally and professionally, who earned a share in my achievements.

My greatest debt of gratitude goes to my brother Robert J. Earle for his faith in my abilities and for his generous emotional and financial support— all of which constitute an apt demonstration of what kinship is really all about.

I owe a huge debt to my colleagues during graduate studies at Rice University, especially Bethany Leigh Johnson, Charles A. Israel, and Scott Preston Marler. They provided invaluable suggestions, inspiration, and insightful critiques of my work through two years of classes, three years of dissertation writing, and the writing of this book. Interactions with these and other colleagues constituted so much of my learning process, and I could not have had a better group of companions to accompany me through my graduate education and beyond.

Sincere thanks go to Dr. John B. Boles for his counsel and for his belief in this project but most of all for his example of excellence; to the entire group at the *Journal of Southern History* during my years of internship, particularly Evelyn Thomas Nolan and Patricia Bellis Bixel, who were superb exemplars and tutors during my time there; to Dr. Ira Gruber, an outstanding teacher, for his enthusiasm and learned critiques; to Dr. James D.

Faubion, who worked hard to enrich my understanding of anthropological kinship theory; to the members of the Houston Area Southern History (HASH) group and of the Works in Progress (WIP) seminars; and to Dr. Michael Winters of the Rice Counseling Center and the members of my group, without whom I'd never have sustained the courage or perseverance to accomplish my goals.

Thanks also to my professors at the University of Arkansas at Little Rock, who inspired me to continue my education—in particular, Drs. C. Fred Williams, Stephen L. Recken, S. Charles Bolton, James Miller, Gerald D. Hanson, and Earl Ramsey; and to the Fulbright Scholar Program for the two years I spent studying—and learning about life—at Karl-Franzens Universität in Graz, Austria.

I owe a debt of gratitude to Jim Billingsley, my children (Jimmy D. Billingsley, Amy E. Buquoi, Robert Earle Billingsley, and Sarah C. Wood), and my grandchildren (Jeffrey Aaron and Amber Michelle Billingsley, Carrie Elizabeth Bentley, Lillian Kaia Wood, and Trulie Ashcom Billingsley), all of whom I held in my heart to sustain me during difficult times.

A huge thanks to my friends, Desmond Walls Allen, Sondra Haile Curtis, and Henryetta Walls Vanaman, who have been an important part of my life for so many years, for being extraordinarily supportive in all areas of my life; Barbara Scott Wyche (who is also my fourth cousin twice removed through the Keesees presented in this work); and K. Diane Cain, the best person in the world for talking things over with. My friend Genevieve Meeker O'Neal died before I started this adventure, but it was our dream of going to college after we raised all our children that sparked everything that followed.

Thanks also to the many archivists, librarians, and county employees who facilitated my research time and time again, but especially to Susan Gore Knight, director of the Historical Foundation of the Cumberland Presbyterian Archives in Memphis, Tennessee; to Anita Poley, whose excellent work on the bibliography is much appreciated; to the Department of History and the Department of Humanities at Rice University for their ongoing financial support in the form of stipends, scholarships, research grants, and conference fees; to Paula Platt and Verva Densmore of the Rice history department for their unflagging support, good humor, dedication, and excellence.

Special thanks to the legions of genealogists, many of whom are my distant cousins, for the wealth of information they provided me, particularly the Reverend William M. Putman, Dr. Vincent Keesee, Teddie Sue Carter, Jeff Henson, William E. Bedinger, and Brigette Perkins.

I also appreciate the confidence placed in me by the University of Georgia Press, especially Nicole Mitchell, Derek Krissoff, and Sarah McKee, who worked with me to bring this project to fruition. Thanks also to Drs. Robert C. Kenzer (University of Richmond) and Edward Baptist (University of Miami) for their valuable suggestions on revisions.

All of the people mentioned deserve much of the praise for my achievements; the finger of blame for errors and missteps can only be pointed at me.

Communities of Kinship

A New Category of Analysis

Man is a knot, a web, a mesh into which relationships are tied.
Only those relationships matter.
—Antoine de Saint-Exupéry, *Flight to Arras*

As historians, our goal is to examine and analyze traces of the past in order to address the present meaningfully by placing it in context. In other words, we hope to understand what humankind and human society have become by comprehending the processes by which we as peoples evolved and constructed our varied cultures. This sentiment has been expressed so often as to become almost trite: William Shakespeare wrote, "What's past is prologue"; "Study the past, if you would divine the future" is attributed to Confucius; and "The past is never dead," according to William Faulkner. "It's not even past." To achieve the goal of mining the past for insights about the present and future, historians employ categories of analysis such as race, class, and gender, but they underutilize, overlook, or even reject a significant piece of the methodological puzzle—kinship.

This work will argue that kinship—particularly in the study of the antebellum South—should be considered a discrete category of analysis complementary to and potentially as powerful as race, class, and gender. Using kinship as a category of analysis and incorporating genealogical research methodology into traditional historical modes of inquiry can deepen insights into southern society in fresh and exciting ways. This study will demonstrate concretely the many ways family, defined broadly and comprehensively, made an impact on the public and private lives of antebellum southerners and how genealogical methodology can be used to tease out the underlying nuances of southern society. In the process, however, race, class, and gender are not rendered obsolete; rather, they are part and parcel of kinship, although, at times, they are subsumed by kinship as categories of analysis.

I also argue that we as a community of scholars need to arrive at a set of definitions of and an overarching theoretical base for this study of kinship in order to share our understanding of what kinship meant in the lives of antebellum southerners. Many studies offhandedly refer to the importance of kinship or family without ever unpacking it as a category. Scholars often present kinship as something we understand intuitively while leaving an interpretation of the term up in the air. Kinship is just *there,* we infer, like the oxygen we breathe. But, like other terms, it needs to be defined before we use it with any precision—and, it turns out, kinship is not as simple as it seems. This study will propose definitions and theories as a starting point for what I hope will become an ongoing discussion of the place of kinship in historical inquiry into the antebellum South. Since the discipline of anthropology has spent a great deal of time and effort theorizing about kinship, I see no need to reinvent the wheel. Thus here some of the insights of anthropology are integrated into a historical study of kinship. The acquisition of a common vocabulary and the construction of a theoretical base for kinship studies will enhance a historical reinterpretation of the social landscape in the antebellum South.

In advancing these views, I am cognizant that voluminous numbers of studies about the South have incorporated kinship to some extent in their data and analyses. What these studies have *not* done is to incorporate the methods of genealogy into the data and analyses to any significant degree, thereby leaving them incomplete. Seldom do historical studies of kinship go beyond basic surname matching or surveys of local marriage records, and this is not sufficient to study the tangled tapestry of family connections in a typical antebellum southern community or neighborhood. Therefore, the third element in my argument is a call for genealogical methodology to be recognized as a valid tool for historical investigation.

Genealogical methodology is, in reality, not so dissimilar to historical methodology. Students of history mine the past for nuggets of data in order to reconstruct that past—to create a plausible account of events or of the facts of particular lived experiences based on evidence gleaned preponderantly from primary sources. Along the way, they use secondary sources to take advantage of the accumulated knowledge and insights of previous researchers and thinkers. Modern genealogists have refined their sources even further to include making distinctions between original and derivative sources, primary and secondary information, and direct and indirect evidence.[1] Students of history with a capital *H* want to know "what *really* happened" and "why," even though we recognize the futility of thinking our conclusions are perfectly true to the original experiences. In genealogy, the research methodology is virtually the same; the difference lies in a somewhat different emphasis on the subject matter under investigation. Genealogists also want to re-create the facts of particular lives and experiences from the past, but their goal is to establish the kinship links between those lives. The aim of all this research is usually to better understand oneself through the explication of one's ancestors and relatives—the lives being researched have personal significance to the researcher. Historians may study the same lives and even, possibly, the same links of kinship, but their desired modality is disinterested objectivity, and their primary goals are explaining the past, making sense of the past, and putting the past in context in order to understand human societies of the present. Their aims have a broader purpose than self-knowledge and the satisfaction derived from a fascinating hobby. I contend that, by adopting genealogical methodology, scholars can facilitate their historical goals because the exploration of kinship ties often provides the desired explication of the past.

Moreover, historians can augment their research by taking advantage of genealogical sources rather than eschewing them. No matter what arguments one might make about the relative value of genealogy versus history, the fact remains that genealogy is the more popular pursuit. One result of this basic fact is that the marketplace of tools and sources for genealogical pursuits outstrips that for history.[2] Unfortunately, students of history too often either are not aware of these genealogical tools and sources or ignore them as irrelevant to their scholarly pursuits. One of the major goals in this study is to heighten awareness of the efficacy of genealogical sources for historical inquiry.

All of this is not to say that many historians have not already realized the value of investigating the common person and ordinary communities. Laurel Thatcher Ulrich's stellar recounting and analysis of Martha Ballard's life in *A Midwife's Tale* leaps immediately to mind. Brenda E. Stevenson's *Life in Black and White,* Orville Vernon Burton's *In My Father's House Are Many Mansions,* and Lois Green Carr, Russell R. Menard, and Lorena S. Walsh's *Robert Cole's World* are just three of the many other works that illuminate our knowledge of some aspect of the historical past through the lens of personal history. These are all premier examples of the rich patina of understanding that can develop from detailed investigations of single families or communities of ordinary groups of people.[3]

As another case in point, Darrett B. Rutman and Anita H. Rutman recognized the early development of kin networks in the South. They describe the process of increasing kin density over time in *A Place in Time:* "As late as 1687, more than half the families of the county had neither kin nor affinal ties to any other of the county's families, 43 percent had ties to between one and four families, and only a handful (4 percent) had ties to five or more. . . . By 1724 more than half of the county's families would be linked to five or more other families; the average household head would live in a milieu of thirty-one relatives." One popular newspaper columnist recently summed up this phenomenon in a nutshell: "The problem with relatives—unlike friends—is that, even without the slightest effort on our part, they still multiply with time."[4]

The idea that these networks of kin were significant to antebellum southerners is not a new one. Over half a century ago, the inimitable W. J. Cash wrote: "The degree of consanguinity among the population of the old Southern backcountry was very great. . . . Hence by 1800 any given individual was likely to be a cousin, in one degree or another, to practically everybody within a radius of thirty miles about him. And his circle of kin, of course, overlapped more or less with the next, and that in turn with the next beyond, and so on in an endless web, through the whole South."[5] Cash recognized long ago that "in the isolation of the plantation world the home was necessarily the center of everything; family ties acquired a strength and validity unknown in more closely settled communities."[6]

In *Kinship and Neighborhood in a Southern Community,* Robert C. Kenzer's conclusions are complementary to my own and reinforce many of my arguments. But, although he emphasizes neighborhoods "tied together by an extensive network of kinship," I would relocate the emphasis slightly to contend that neighborhoods were *composed* of kinship groups. Kenzer studied a community over time, both ante- and postbellum, whereas my study is of a kinship group diffusing through both time and space in the antebellum period. Yet his findings on the influence of kinship on class, economics, and politics are quite similar to the conclusions in this study: "By promoting cohesion and order, the network of kinship . . . shaped the county's economic, social, administrative, and political structure."[7]

Joan E. Cashin also closely reinforces certain of the claims presented here. In "The Structure of Antebellum Planter Families," she postulated a kinship group interaction far beyond the nuclear family or even the extended family. She, too, established that the nuclear family has dominated the traditional portrayal of southern families by historians but stated that the "borders [of the planter family] were permeable and its structure was elastic, including many other relatives—aunts, uncles, nieces, nephews, and cousins [broadly defined]—who were intimate members of the family" and who "fostered the intense bonds that historians associate with the nuclear family."[8]

Cashin further evidenced the broad scope of kinship when she cited the cases of Susan B. Eppes and J. W. Calvert, who had sixty-one and more than sixty first cousins, respectively.[9] When cousins to the second and third degree are added to kinship groups already including these first cousins, siblings, and aunts and uncles, the scope of such groups becomes huge and hard to dismiss as a contributory factor in shaping southern history. The sheer size of kinship groups points toward a complex web of family relationships and hints at the impact of those relationships on members of the extended family. Cashin stated forcefully in her conclusion:

> Historians should discard assumptions about the nuclear structure of the antebellum planter family and investigate further the nature of relationships among extranuclear kin. The study of such topics as political alliances and inheritance practices will no doubt yield more evidence of the importance of these relationships. Distinctions between nuclear relatives and other kinfolk were much less pronounced than scholars have assumed. Many individuals whom historians have considered to be marginal figures in the larger kinship network were actually significant members of the family.[10]

Other historians have made the case for the incorporation of kinship studies or genealogical methodology into the realm of historical scholarship. For example, in 1968 William Rundell Jr. wrote about the merits of using local sources of the type generally used by genealogists, and in 1981 Randolph B. Campbell claimed that using family history—"traditionally the province of a few 'little old lady' genealogists"—had "become an accepted way of studying our past."[11] The historical record, however, fails to reflect a revolution in attitudes following these articles.

These offerings about kinship, family, and genealogy from other scholars of the South are but a few to be found in the literature. Throughout this study I often directly quote the words of other historians to demonstrate that the recognition of kinship's significance in southern history has always been part of the historiography of the South. Using their own words on this subject acknowledges these scholars' insights into the role of kinship—insights that sparked my theories and that I synthesized. Although no cohesive theory of kinship emerged from these examples, these authors' words constitute many pieces of the puzzle used to create the cohesive theories presented here and are the words that lit the pathway to my own enlightenment about kinship theory and the South. This study is not the first to suggest the impact of kinship on southerners or the utility of genealogical methodology, yet it reveals the versatility of kinship studies in attacking traditional questions about the antebellum South by probing a variety of issues exclusively through the lens of kinship.

A caveat is needed: because the family studied here is white, this study does not address black southerners or race in any meaningful way, although I believe many of the theories and methods presented here have relevance to the study of race as well as to the study of black and mixed-race southerners and to slavery. Similarly, the study of women or of gender is beyond the scope of this study, although those concepts are implicit in any study of kinship and family.

To achieve these goals I conducted intensive genealogical research on a particular kinship group as it grew and changed through time and space and then used the accumulated data to demonstrate the power of kinship studies and genealogical methodology to answer some of the big questions posed by historians about the antebellum South. Chapter 1 introduces the kinship group, explains the methodology employed, and analyzes the database compiled. In addition, an interpretive framework and vocabulary, informed by anthropological kinship theory, are proposed as well as an argument for incorporating genealogical methodology into historical studies.

Chapter 2 demonstrates the intrinsic role of kinship in migration and settlement patterns. The evidence makes it clear that most of the migration in the South was driven by groups of kindred rather than rugged individuals seeking the proverbial elbowroom. Antebellum southerners communicated about new lands, made decisions about moving on or staying put, and settled communities through their engagement in their kinship groups. Marriages were the pivotal element in the formation of kinship groups, and since individuals overwhelmingly married neighbors, these kinship groups were continually being re-formed with each move. Without a basic understanding of kinship's role in antebellum southern society, studies of migration and settlement patterns are incomplete.

Chapter 3 addresses the issue of religious affiliation for antebellum southerners. I argue that the single largest predictor of their choice of religious affiliation was the religious affiliation of their parents. The largest nexus of change in religious affiliation was marriage; when two people married, they were often moved to reassess their religious ties, and it was not unusual for one or both to make a change at this time. Moreover, subscribing to the same religious denomination served as part of the glue that bound groups of kin together more tightly; conversely, when branches of kin were members of differing religious affiliations, the effect was distancing. Rather surprisingly, ministers were also intensely interrelated—not necessarily to the kinship groups to which they ministered but to each other. The fictive kinship of religious affiliation led a remarkable number of ministers to marry ministers' daughters and a remarkable number of ministers' daughters to marry other ministers, resulting in tightly bound castes of clergymen. The itinerant nature of the ministry also created lines of communication filtering back to congregations that in turn facilitated migration into new areas of the South.

Chapter 4 looks at the connections between kinship and economic and political power. In the absence of other strong institutions in the antebellum South, the family remained the primary organizing force of southern society. Migration to the frontier offered wide-open opportunities for advancement, both politically and economically. Individual members of a kinship group worked together to facilitate and consolidate their political and economic power by filling available government jobs at the county, state, and federal levels. At the same time, by selling more expensive land in established areas and moving to fresh, fertile land on the cotton frontier, which could be acquired cheaply from individuals and from the federal government, these individuals could increase their productivity and profit. Kinship group members used their economic largess as an entrée into political hegemony, helped other kin by backing them financially and politically, and consolidated their power through marriage connections with other well-connected kinship groups.

In chapter 5, the lives of some of the main members of the Keesee kinship group in the postbellum era are sketched out. The data on the family in the latter decades of the nineteenth century, although not nearly as complete as the research on the antebellum era, suggest that kinship studies have the potential to provide a new approach to the important debates about the nature of society in the postwar South, particularly regarding the continuity versus change discussion among southern historians.

The conclusion examines the role and efficacy of kinship studies in questions about migration, settlement patterns, religion, class structure, and economic and political power in the Old South. I argue for the value of the processes used in this study—that kinship studies assembled using genealogical methodology, examined through the lens of kinship theory gleaned from the discipline of anthropology, and organized using kinship as a category of analysis much like race, class, and gender can yield valuable insights into antebellum southern society.

Taken as a whole, this work argues forcefully for the explanatory power of kinship, informed by genealogical methodology, in the study of antebellum southern society. Kinship should be recognized as a category of analysis alongside race, class, and gender, to which it is complementary. With the incorporation of kinship studies, our analysis of the South becomes full-bodied and truer to that objective reality of the past we so assiduously seek.

CHAPTER ONE

Theory, Methodology, and Evidence

> Although genealogy can be used to justify privilege, it can also be
> used to impart values. While in certain eras it has appeared to be
> the preserver of society's elites, its universal application bespeaks
> the importance of origins for all humanity. It can be used to
> divide, yet the myriad relationships it uncovers imply the
> interconnectedness of the human race.
> —David Thackery, "Editor's Note"

In the fall of 1837 Thomas Keesee Sr., then almost sixty years old and the
veteran of at least four previous moves, gathered up his extended family, including slaves, and left Alabama, his home for the past sixteen years. The
kinship group formed a wagon train, bound for the newly created state of
Arkansas, following the kinsmen and -women who had immigrated there
the previous year. By 1840 the kinship group in Saline County, Arkansas,
numbered 131 individuals, along with their 140 black slaves, out of a total
white county population of 1,162 whites and 399 slaves; the families linked
to the Keesees by kinship comprised almost 8 percent of the white population and owned 35 percent of the slave population of Saline County at that
time.[1] As the years passed, the numbers increased, and the lives of Keesee
and his children and grandchildren were even more intricately enmeshed in
a web of kinship. These kin relationships factored heavily into the family's
social, religious, economic, and political endeavors. But what did that sig-
nify, to live as part of such an interconnected network of kin? And who were
the Keesees, and why are they the focus of this study? What exactly do we
mean when we invoke the term *kinship,* and how do we reckon these kinship links?

Before launching into an exegesis of the efficacy of kinship to explain significant elements of antebellum southern society such as migration, settlement patterns, religion, and economic and political power, it is important

to understand the basic elements underlying and informing the discussion. This chapter presents the four main elements that serve as a foundation for the rest of the study: the interpretive framework for kinship studies, which relies heavily on anthropological kinship theory; the argument for incorporating genealogical methodology into historical studies; a discussion of the origins, compilation, characteristics, and limits of the database that is used as evidence; and an introduction to the very extended family group that comprises the database.

The first step is to establish an interpretive framework. Historians of the South write often about kinship without ever defining it and without probing into the meanings of the terms they use. Perhaps this is not so surprising; the analysis of kinship has fallen most frequently within the purview of anthropologists, for whom kinship is central.[2] When historians use the term, they simply assume that readers have an intuitive understanding of kinship. On the face of it, kinship does, indeed, seem like a simple thing, easily grasped, but as is often the case, it is more fluid and complex than it first appears. Unpacking the term can lead to a deeper understanding of why it is important to the study of southern history. This work analyzes the concept of kinship much as other scholars have felt compelled to probe the terms *class, race,* and *gender* in their works.

Kinship is not something concrete that one can sense or touch. It is an abstraction and, as such, is always socially constructed, despite the fact that most people intuitively believe and act as if it were a biological fact. Anthropologists argue about whether or not kinship is a universal phenomenon, and most of their arguments swirl around the problems of constructing a definition capable of the universal applicability they are seeking. There seems little doubt that the notion of *blood* or shared biogenetic substance is most often at the heart of the meaning of kinship in the modern mind. Yet that is not universally the defining element of kinship—earlier peoples often had little knowledge of the biological facts of sexual union and very little if any conception of genetic inheritance. In some cultures, the biological father is not the socially recognized father, and in other times and places, more than one father was recognized, a belief not always at variance with modern biology, as demonstrated by "Biology: A Case of Twins with Different Fathers," a 1997 article in the *Washington Post.*[3]

Additionally, many cultures, including our own, consider those adopted to be kin, even though biologically they may not be related. Within the

American legal system, the father of a child is presumed to be the man married to the mother at the time of the child's birth, no matter who actually fathered the child and despite the knowledge that a significant percentage of children are not the offspring of their putative fathers. Although this legal presumption of paternity comes out of old English common law, it is still generally upheld as valid and useful even in light of modern DNA testing. In a 1999 article "Daddy No More: Ex-Husband Contests Presumption of Paternity with DNA Results Proving He Has No Biological Ties" by William C. Smith in the *American Bar Association Journal*, for example, the ex-husband was proven not to be the biological father of the child born during his marriage. In the lawsuit that followed this discovery, his case went to the state supreme court, and he was affirmed as the legal father of the child at each step, even though he was acknowledged not to be the biological father. "Temple University law professor Theresa Glennon says the presumption of paternity remains a vital family law doctrine. . . . Focusing on the social role of parenting may be especially important . . . in an age when reproductive technologies undermine traditional biological understandings of parenthood." [4]

Many U.S. laws reinforce the social over the biological definition of paternity. In Texas, for instance, "[a] man is presumed to be the biological father of a child if . . . he and the child's biological mother are or have been married to each other and the child is born during the marriage or not more than 300 days after the date the marriage is terminated by death, annulment, or divorce or by having been declared void." A great deal of evidence asserts that there are a significant percentage of children who were not fathered by the man who thinks himself the father, and the most often cited figure is about 10 percent of births. Robert Wright, in his 1998 article in *Time*, "Sin in the Global Village," cites statistics from Liverpool, England, showing that "1 in 4 kids had a biological father other than the father of record." In an entertaining look at this phenomenon, Desmond Walls Allen titled an article "Mama's Baby, Daddy's Maybe." [5]

If kinship were truly based on shared blood, then virtually every person would have to recognize his or her kinship with almost everybody else, for truly we are all one family in that sense. Thus, kinship is not necessarily dependent on a sharing of biogenetic material; rather, according to anthropologist R. Wagner, "the essence of kinship is *interpretation* of genealogy, rather than genealogy." [6] In short, as Wagner states, although "'consan-

guinity' [that is, relationship by blood] is sometimes used as an equivalent
of 'kinship' . . . [it] refers properly to a physical relationship, but in kinship
we have to deal with a specifically social relationship."[7]

On the other hand, David M. Schneider, in his seminal work *American
Kinship*, argues that the act of coitus is the "central symbol of American
kinship as a cultural system." That is to say, in the American cultural system, sexual intercourse is symbolically linked with marriage, with love, and
with unity; marriage produces children who, with the parents, compose a
family; and this family becomes part of networks of relationships linked by
both parents to the families into which they were born and to the families
their children in turn create. This web of linked relationships, although delimited by socio-emotional distance or degree of (socially perceived) consanguinity, explains in part what Americans mean by the word "kinship."
Schneider posits: "In American cultural conception, kinship is defined as
biogenetic. This definition says that kinship is whatever the biogenetic relationship is. If science discovers new facts about biogenetic relationship,
then that is what kinship is and was all along, although it may not have been
known at the time."[8]

Within this study, which deals with antebellum white southern society,
the central element of kinship is considered to be marriage, since identifying acts of coitus is problematic—and unnecessary. (If, however, research
into kinship implications regarding race were the focus, coitus would perforce be the symbolic center of kinship, as most interracial relationships in
the antebellum South were outside of marriage. In these instances, the act
of coitus, expressed via the birth of a child, creates the kinship link between
black and white individuals and groups.) For white antebellum southerners,
marriage produced alliances and was the basis of linking with other families. This is not to say that individuals necessarily married specifically to effect these alliances; these alliances, however, were the result of their marriages, whether or not that was a conscious consideration in their choice of
marriage partners.

Suffice it to say that there is no one agreed-upon universal definition of
kinship. It is a set of social relations concerned with a group's conception of
a commonality of identity based on the categories of biological connections
as known or *perceived* by that group, much like Benedict Anderson's theories in his *Imagined Communities*.[9] It is usually underpinned by concepts
such as obligation, constancy, and inalienability and some level of love or
affection.[10] In Schneider's words, kinship is a group of social relations char-

acterized by "enduring, diffuse solidarity." Kinship is enduring because family ties are inalienable—friends can be jettisoned if the relationship sours, but one is born with one's relatives and for the most part is stuck with them for life; kinship is diffuse throughout the group rather than being focused exclusively on one or two specific people; and solidarity is an all-purpose word that can mean love, affection, concern, responsibility—it means that "[t]he end to which family relations are conducted is the well-being of the family as a whole and of each of its members."[11]

The American kinship system shares certain elements with other systems and differs in other respects. For example, as anthropologist Ladislav Holy argues, one of the "basic assumptions" about kinship is that "kinship every-where is based on attributing social significance to the natural facts of pro-creation," and in this way American kinship is similar to other kinship sys-tems.[12] However, in the United States, kinship connections through both the maternal and paternal lines are valid, which is not and has not always been the case in every culture. Although American kinship retains some el-ements of an emphasis on paternal links such as the woman's assumption of the man's surname at marriage, bilateral kinship—that is, the reckoning of kinship through both the maternal and paternal lineage—is the norm both socially and legally. In the antebellum South, this was also the case.

The names we append to certain relatives, the roles these relatives play in our lives, and rules about whom one can and cannot marry are also socially constructed. In some cultures, a boy's maternal uncle plays a more signifi-cant role in the boy's life than his biologically and socially defined father does. There are cases in which every woman of one's mother's generation is called "mother" and every child of one's own generation is called the equiv-alent of "brother" or "sister." In other societies, now and in the past, mar-riages are often prescribed or proscribed on the basis of cousinship; that is, parallel cousins might be proscribed from marriage to one another, whereas cross-cousins may be prescribed or preferred mates. (As Ruth C. Busch ex-plains, "First cousins whose kinship is through their fathers [who are broth-ers] or their mothers [who are sisters], are parallel cousins; if the link is be-tween the mother of one and the father of the other [who are brother and sister] they are called 'cross cousins.'")[13]

During some eras in the United States, first-cousin marriages and other degrees of consanguineous or affinal marriage, namely, marriage to those related by blood or marriage, have been socially and/or legally proscribed. There is no compelling biological or even religious reason why this should be so—the taboo is purely socially constructed. The perception that first-cousin marriage is usually medically or biologically harmful is patently false, as any animal breeder can attest; it is as apt to be beneficial, biologically, as it is to be detrimental, as Martin Ottenheimer explains in his book *Forbidden Relatives*. Recent scientific studies have confirmed the overall genetic safety for children born of cousin marriages. There is even a website—*Cousin Couples: Support for Kissing Cousins*—for closely related people who are involved in romantic relationships "forbidden by society's erroneous stigma against marriages of consanguinity."[14]

In the antebellum South, cousin marriage was not at all unusual (and, in some families, was preferred), resulting in an even more tightly linked group of kin who were related to each other on several levels. As Peter W. Bardaglio states in his *Reconstructing the Household*, "Whereas New England Puritans strongly opposed first-cousin marriages, white southerners followed English tradition in accepting such unions." Although Lorri Glover seems to contradict Bardaglio regarding the acceptance of cousin marriages among English elites, in her study *All Our Relations* she asserts that "[l]owcountry elites routinely married their kin, including cousins."[15]

The conjugal family is recognized as the basic unit of kinship, and kinship is the interconnectedness of a group of such families. Before the twentieth century, family and kinship were more important elements in southern social organization than they are today. A partial explanation for this can be found in the low level of institutional organization in past southern society. Anthropologists recognize that in so-called primitive societies, "kinship is 'one of the irreducible principles on which . . . organized social life depends,' . . . in marked contrast to Western societies in which other institutions, particularly the workplace and the state, perform the wide-ranging functions which are performed by kinship groups in 'primitive' societies."[16] It is doubtful that even an anthropologist would classify the historical South as a "primitive society." Yet the point is salient to this discussion—the southern family remained the dominant mode of the organization of everyday life in the absence of higher order political institutions, which, although present, were less developed in the South than in other regions in the United States, especially in the nineteenth century and particularly on the forward edges of expanding cotton cultivation and settlement.[17] An argument can probably be made that family was the dominant mode of the organization of everyday life in the North as well, at least during the colonial and early republic eras. My contention is that at some point before the antebellum era the two regions began to diverge in character: the North developed a higher degree of institutionalization, probably related to urbanization and industrialization, while the South remained rural and agricultural; thus family and kinship retained their sway over social organization much longer in the South. This study, however, is not designed to be a comparative one and will leave a fuller discussion of this point for another day.

In the antebellum South, family groups rather than public institutions served most of the needs of individual citizens much as they had during the colonial era, when, as W. Wayne Carp has written, the family "was the cornerstone of church and state, the center of all institutional life, and the fundamental unit of society. As Lawrence Cremin has noted, the family 'provided food and clothing, succor and shelter; it conferred social standing, economic possibility, and religious affiliation; and it served from time to time as church, playground, factory, army, and court.'"[18] In southern society, characterized by patriarchy, agriculture, and rurality, the family maintained its power at the top of the social, political, and economic hierarchy through most of the nineteenth century. Modes of production remained centered in the household. For the majority of southerners, cash and credit were often available only from friends and family members due to the paucity and underdeveloped state of banking institutions.[19] Political power was often contingent on family connections (and remains so to some extent even today). Donn M. Kurtz II provides good examples of the impact of kinship on political office holding in his work *Kinship and Politics.* He finds that "[s]ixty percent of the Louisiana justices and 72 percent of the United States justices had at least one relative in public office before, during, or after the justice's public service." Edward Eugene Baptist's study of planter kinship in antebellum Florida "reveals wealthy planters who relied on their own large extended family networks in order to maintain and augment their power through migration to the Old Southwest."[20] President George W. Bush is a member of a political dynasty of at least three generations. Modern politics is replete with other such families, including the Kennedys and the Gores.

Only religion might be proffered as an institution rivaling the family in importance, yet religion served more as a prop to the family and to patriarchal values than as a rival. In many cases, church memberships and family memberships overlapped to the point where the two were often all but indistinguishable. Moreover, religious institutions were fragmented into a variety of denominations and congregations, which was somewhat of a check on their social authority.

Of course, kinship remained a potent force in the South long past the antebellum period. Eventually, as other institutional organizations became as entrenched in the South as they were elsewhere, the importance of extensive kinship groups waned. However, in *Arkansas and the New South*, Carl H. Moneyhon assesses the role of the family in New South Arkansas; he asserts that for the 97 percent of Arkansans who were considered rural, three major social institutions—family, class, and race—became central to life. Each of these helped define the lives of rural folks. These institutions also sustained the status quo and served as checks to change. Family, often extending beyond the nuclear unit and at times even including servants and laborers, was clearly the most important social organization. It not only filled conventional biological and educational functions but was also the primary economic unit in the agricultural economy.[21]

Once Arkansas society became "more intricate with the development of new institutions," Moneyhon states, the role of the family changed in an increasingly urban environment; although family "remained an important institution, . . . it lost many of its traditional functions." Economic functions were no longer centered in the home; education became more the responsibility of institutions outside the family; and women's work and roles changed, as did the roles of children when their labor became less significant.[22] Anthropologists recognize this same effect: in *Sex, Gender, and Kinship*, Burton Pasternak, Carol R. Ember, and Melvin Ember write that "descent groups lose viability in complex state-organized, commercial-industrial societies because non-kin agencies or the state assume many kin functions (e.g., defense, education, welfare, adjudication)."[23]

Some historians have addressed the changing significance of family and kinship within the context of modernization theory. Joan E. Cashin offers a simple definition of modernization, worth quoting here in its entirety:

> [Modernization is] the transformation from a hierarchical, deferential society in which kinship ties largely determine status, to a dynamic, open society, in which status is a function of occupation, achievement, or some other ascriptive trait. This transformation also involves a change in outlook on the world, from one that is localistic, religious or mystical, and noncommercial to one that is cosmopolitan, rational, and commercial. Patterns of geographic mobility also change, from circulation in familiar routes near home to movement over vast distances. Finally, modernization involves a change in attitudes to-

ward a change itself: in a premodern society people value stability and see change as threatening, while innovation in all phases of life characterizes a modern society.[24]

While scholars will no doubt continue their discussion about whether or not the antebellum or postbellum South was a premodern society or when, if ever, it became modern, the role of family and kinship plays a key part in any analysis of the merits of the various arguments.

Furthermore, it must be noted that the importance of family and kinship to southern whites was augmented by the antebellum South's idiosyncratic racial ideology. In a society that consigned people to a stigmatized caste based on race, it became important to ensure the "proper" categorization of people by knowing one's own lineage and the lineages of others. As Barbara J. Fields so aptly argues, it is false to assume that "race is an observable physical fact, a thing, rather than a notion that is profoundly and in its very essence ideological."[25] Since race is not "an observable physical fact," dividing people into race at times became dependent on social memory. That memory required a working knowledge of one's own pedigree and the pedigree of those in one's social orbit, hence an emphasis on the genealogy of families.

It is crucial to realize that, although kinship in the American South in the seventeenth through nineteenth centuries may have had many similarities to a present-day perception of kinship, there were nuances of difference that are significant. Three points especially that have relevance to this study need to be reiterated here: (1) the socially defined roles of kin beyond the nuclear family were closer or more personal and were qualitatively more intense, and therefore these more distant ties were more meaningful than they are today; (2) the family was a more substantial element in social organization than it is today; and (3) marriage was the nexus of change and the locus of kinship alliances and was therefore a major determinant in social, political, and economic power.

To ensure a common vocabulary in the discussion of kinship in the antebellum South, a discussion of some of the important terms critical to the proffered arguments is germane.

The evidence for this book mainly comes from the Keesee family *descent group*, that is, a group of people who share a common ancestor and who are, therefore, descended from the same individual. In reality, the entire human species might be considered a part of one very large descent group; however, anthropologists use the term to refer "to groups of kin that behave or function collectively, as groups."[26] This study primarily focuses on the descent group(s) of Thomas Keesee Sr. by examining the ways in which various offshoots of his descendants group together and function at diverse levels of interaction.

Family refers, in some instances, to the nuclear or conjugal family, that is, parents with their children; but in the antebellum South, the degree of relationships that might be included in the term *family* were often more distant and might include any range of kinship—biological, legal, or fictive. Within this study it refers most often to the entire group of people who considered themselves kin, and I use the word to denote the larger meaning except where nuclear or natal family is specifically invoked or implied.

Kinship refers to a structure of family connections either by blood, marriage, adoption, or social fiction. It comes with the understanding that kinship, to the modern researcher, is socially constructed and that it, without a doubt, was more widely constructed in the antebellum South than it is today. James Casey describes family "as one part of the hierarchical ordering of pre-industrial communities" in *The History of the Family*. Here I assert that family—or kinship—was the *primary* influence on day-to-day life for antebellum southerners. Kinship groups are aggregate groups of people who share kinship to any degree, even distantly. In this study, the main kinship group is all the descendants and spouses of descendants of Thomas Keesee Sr. "But family structures are not self-contained institutions," states Casey; "rather, they are imperfect, ramshackle adaptations of the human psyche to the culture and ecology of a particular area." A kinship group's parameters are anything but static; they adapt to circumstances over time and space, as the evidence from the Keesee kinship group illuminates.[27]

Cousins are those related through mutual descent from siblings. Although in modern society only first cousins (that is, the children of siblings) and, less often, second cousins (that is, the children of first cousins) are generally acknowledged as or considered to be kin on a meaningful basis, to antebellum southerners cousins of both blood and marriage of a greater range and degree were acknowledged as kin and more integrated into an effective kinship group.

Figuring cousin relationship is usually confusing, especially when relationships veer into the "removed" category. Succinctly, parallel generations descending from siblings are counted as first cousins, second cousins, third cousins, and so forth, with third cousins, for example, being of the same generation, all being the great-great-grandchildren of a common ancestor and the great-grandchildren of siblings. When the generations are not parallel, then the term *removed* comes into play. If Mary and Tom are second cousins, then the relationship of Tom's children to Mary's children is that of third cousins, but Tom's children's relationship to Mary herself is that of second cousin, once removed; that is, the nearest parallel relationship is second cousin (between Tom and Mary), and Tom's children are one generation removed from that relationship vis-à-vis their relationship with Mary. A term used in the South to denote a familial relationship that acknowledges a kinship tie the exact nature of which in all probability is too distant to reconstruct is *kissing cousins*. The connotation is that, since these two people are somehow kin, they would greet one another affectionately with a kiss rather than with the more formal greeting given a stranger or acquaintance. There are times this appellation is used when, in fact, there is no actual blood or marriage kin relationship, but the two people know that a relationship of some warmth has existed between their families for some time, and the line between kinship and friendship has been blurred over time. A similar term is *shirttail cousins*, meaning a kinship tie is acknowledged but just barely, perhaps a relationship so distant that the details have been forgotten.

When siblings of one family marry siblings of another family, their children are not only first cousins but also double first cousins, that is, first cousins through both parents. "Double" also refers to any other degree of cousinry, that is, second cousins, third cousins, and so forth, where the cousin relationship exists through both parents rather than through only one parent. This closer relationship in double first cousins is almost as close as if they were siblings rather than cousins, and genetically, these double cousins are more alike than cousins but less similar than siblings.

This double cousinry was unexceptional in the antebellum South and is not uncommon even today. My mother and her sister, for example, were double first cousins to another pair of sisters; these cousins had fathers who were brothers and mothers who were sisters. The four have always been almost as close as sisters and resemble each other as much as if they were, indeed, all sisters. These cousins were closer to each other than they were to other first cousins, no doubt because their parents had double the impetus to interact socially. *Sibling exchange* is the term used when siblings of one family marry siblings of another family; for example, two brothers marry two sisters, or a brother and a sister from one family marry a sister and a brother from another family, creating even closer ties of kinship between two families. The result is a larger aggregate group of grandchildren shared between the two families and a group of children who are double first cousins. Sibling exchange, at times, extends to three or more siblings from each family intermarrying.

In making a case for the significance of kinship in the lives of antebellum southerners, determining the range of *effective kinship* is a key factor. The range of effective kinship refers to the extent to which a genealogical connection played a role in the lives of antebellum southerners. If the family connection was not acknowledged, considered, or known or did not act as a factor in the decisions or activities of the two related individuals, then these individuals' relationship did not fall into the range of effective kinship. This is not a clear-cut issue; there are varying degrees and shades of importance. Second or third cousins, though they might not play an important role in everyday life, might still exert influence to some degree, and thus they would be included in the effective range of kinship. The most salient point is that the range of effective kinship was fluid: as members of the kinship group died, were born, married, or relocated, the boundaries of effective kinship flexed or constricted with the changing circumstances. To look at kinship as a whole tells us little, since every person is technically related to every other person; only by studying the range of effective kinship can we delimit family relationships in a meaningful way.

Fictive kin refers to those whose kinship ties are not biologically or legally based but who, for a variety of reasons, are treated and named as kin. Slave kinship group members often fell into this category. When slaves were sold away from their families, they usually found a place within a family unit in their new home that functioned as a kinship group. Slaves who were called "uncle," "aunt," or "mammy" by whites might also conceivably be examples of fictive kin, but generally one would have to believe that the white person using these titles felt some tie of kinship rather than what was probably the case in general, that these appellations were a social fiction to avoid giving African American slaves the respect that "Mr." or "Mrs." would bestow. Church members can constitute another form of fictive kin; people often genuinely feel as though they are brothers and sisters in the church, all children of God. Another example of fictive kin is an unrelated person taken into a family because of circumstance: an unattached woman who becomes part of a family group and functions as and earns the title of a grandmother or aunt to the children she helps raise; an older man who becomes part of an unrelated family group and has a relationship and title as if he were truly kin; a child who is taken into an unrelated family group and, although not legally adopted, becomes indistinguishable from the other biological children of the family. Sometimes it can even refer to a close friend or neighbor whose relationship with another individual becomes so close that they consider themselves as if they were actually biologically kin, often with the children in the family addressing them honorifically as "aunt" or "uncle." Although these categories are labeled "fictive," the individuals included can and often do fall within the range of effective kinship.

In summary, historical scholars often use kinship in their analyses, but they lack a defined theoretical interpretive framework and a shared defined universe of terminology. An understanding of the meaning of the terms *kinship* and *family* is usually taken for granted. It is assumed that we all inherently know exactly what these referents symbolize—that they need no definition. And yet one has but to examine the panoply of ways in which these words are used and the meanings they transmit in thousands of different cultures all over the world as well as within a single culture to realize how slippery and fluid they really are. Ponder the many nuances within the various word symbols for kinship: we speak of the family of man; members of a church call one another brother and sister; our colleagues at work and school are often referred to as our second family; people refer to God as the father, and we are all God's children; nuns are sisters, and the head of the order is the mother superior; gang members regard the group as their family; some African Americans call each other "brother" or "sister" to denote their shared racial identity; feminists evoke gender by referring to their "sisterhood"; we talk about Father Time and Mother Nature.

Yet, even so, most people, called upon to provide a definition of kinship, would instinctively assert that kinship was based upon a "blood" relationship, biologically determined. The many exceptions to that widely held view, however, render it virtually unusable as a true definition. In short, if we are to be able to engage in a communal discourse about family and kinship, it is imperative to discuss and define the parameters of these culturally constructed concepts. Moreover and perhaps more importantly, to make sense of and extract meaning from the lives of antebellum southerners, we must discuss and define the parameters of these culturally constructed concepts within the context of the *past* rather than embedded in a modern perspective. This study attempts to reconstruct antebellum southerners' understanding of the referents "family" and "kinship" by looking at the tangible effects of family and kinship on their lives, that is, performatively. Only then can we begin to fully comprehend the impact of kinship on this particular society.

This is not to say that kinship does not exist in the world as an actual phenomenal thing, insofar as it is the concrete relationship of people to one another—relationships defined by ties of blood or marriage or created in a legal sense. There are explicit referents matching terms of kinship; when the term *aunt* is invoked, for instance, there is a one-to-one correspondence between the word and a specific person or set of persons. Yet we cannot afford to forget that in a more abstract sense kinship only exists in a noumenal way, somehow implicit instead of explicit, in the way it is played out in the lives of human beings. In this sense, it is performatively constructed based on the needs and desires of the individual. These can consist of but are not limited to the need or desire for being part of a group, for approval, for love, for support, for friendship, for economic facilitation, or for political support. During the lifetimes of antebellum southerners, they constructed their concepts of kinship and family through their actions—by showing concern for, by being responsible for, by living close to, and by being involved in the social, religious, economic, and legal lives of their families. As this study will demonstrate, it is apparent that for antebellum southerners, the definition of kinship was deep and broad indeed and constituted the most important single factor in their daily lives.

So although kinship has not been overlooked or genealogy totally scorned as a relevant methodology, this book's primary goal is to put kinship under the microscope, bringing its every aspect into clear relief in order to hammer home its potential for redefining some aspects of historical inquiry into antebellum southern society, and to use genealogical methodology to accomplish this goal. The discussion in each chapter demonstrates the importance of kinship studies to historians of the South. The connections forged in the name of kinship and the social, economic, and political power it engendered in that place and time are worthy subjects for scholarly investigation. It should become obvious that we as a community of scholars need to begin a process of collective reflection on this topic in a more meaningful way than has been done thus far. In doing so, we may find that kinship is the link forging a connection between the somewhat disparate fields of social history, economic history, and political history. Furthermore, the members of the beloved triad of race, class, and gender lose none of their status as analytical categories par excellence; indeed, they are enhanced and complemented by the addition of kinship as a category of analysis and by the interplay between them.

The key to accomplishing all this is determining the range of effective kinship. Merely proving genealogical connections adds little to our understanding of antebellum southern society. To reveal the significance of kinship, we must be able to identify the realm of meaningful or effective kinship. With written records such as letters or diaries, that task is fairly simple; visiting patterns, social activities, mentions of names in a diary on a regular basis, business records, gossip about certain people in a letter to one's sister—these types of writings speak to us clearly about who was important in an individual's life. Few documents of this sort exist within the Keesee kinship group, and the range of effective kinship must be ascertained in more indirect ways. People's actions have to substitute for words to reveal the significant ties in their lives.

The most evident way people expressed their ties to specific groups of kin was by living close to each other. If one family moved to a new location and another related family moved with them and then settled within hailing distance despite having thousands of acres to choose from, the two families obviously had a meaningful relationship. Similarly, county records indicating a pattern of business or legal activity between two or more men are evidence of instrumental ties, as is the witnessing of deeds for a relative or the posting of a security bond for him when he applies for letters of administration on an estate or runs for sheriff. Joining the same church, changing religious affiliation, or receiving a letter of dismissal from a church at the same time can also serve as indicators.

Naming patterns are particularly significant manifestations of close personal ties and can be used to delimit the parameters of effective kinship. As stated by Mary Jo Maynes, Ann Waltner, Birgitte Soland, and Ulrike Strasser, editors of *Gender, Kinship, Power*, "Naming—perhaps the primal act of culture—is a conceptual act that is central to the mapping of people into kinship relationships. . . . [It is] an important dimension of power."[28] When choosing a name for their children, parents seek names that are meaningful to them in some context. Jane Turner Censer also notes the pattern of naming children for close relatives within families and states: "[N]aming could strengthen ties among family members . . . by the esteem it signified." By bestowing family names upon them, "children could also carry memories of the past into the future." Even more importantly, "naming practices firmly placed the infant in the conjugal family by identifying it with an important relative from a parent's family of origin."[29]

In *All Our Relations,* Glover found that "[t]o repay the debt owed relatives and symbolize the importance of the kinship network, parents honored their most valued living kin by naming children after them." Glover, however, found that South Carolina low-country parents of the gentry preferred naming children after siblings or close kin rather than after themselves or their parents—a pattern not replicated in the Keesee kinship group.[30] Study of the Keesee kinship group demonstrates how naming patterns situated children within a web of familial relationships and thereby constantly reinforced and extended the bonds of kinship.

Sometimes the context of naming a child was religious: there was a plentitude of eighteenth- and nineteenth-century males, for example, whose given names are "Finis Ewing," "Francis Asbury," or "Martin Luther," each a prominent religious figure.[31] In another context, parents honored the founders of the country by choosing names for their sons such as "George Washington," "Thomas Jefferson," and "Benjamin Franklin." They also chose the names of political and military figures they admired—"Andrew Jackson" and "Oliver Hazard Perry" became quite common given names after these men rose to prominence, and in virtually all eras, biblical and classical names like "Moses," "James," "John," and "Marcus Aurelius" were popular. For girls, family and Bible names were most common, but many daughters were named for states—"Virginia" and "Alabama" were quite fashionable as female names. When Thomas Keesee Sr. named his last daughter Virginia, he was no doubt honoring his fondly remembered natal state.

In their detailed study of colonial Middlesex County, Virginia, Darrett B. Rutman and Anita H. Rutman point out that "analyses of naming patterns . . . can highlight differences and similarities, secular trends and, potentially, human constants [in different cultures and in different time periods]." They found an overwhelming tendency to name children for family members. Their data indicate 90 percent of first and second sons named for fathers, grandfathers, and uncles and 80 percent of first and second daughters named for mothers, grandmothers, and aunts. "Instances of shared names are highly suggestive of a familial rather than individual view of children," the authors conclude, although "not definitive[ly]." Furthermore, the naming patterns found in Middlesex County, Virginia, are indicative of "the strong family orientation of the society in question" and are "suggestive" of a familial rather than an individualistic point of view, although there is no way of knowing what parents had in mind when naming their children.[32]

When the Rutmans investigated whether or not there was a "proscriptive rule" for male cousins (meaning that two sons would not both give their own sons the name of their father), they found no such rule in effect. In contrast, Daniel Scott Smith's data on Hingham, Massachusetts, indicated such a proscription, indicating that children were seen as distinct individuals. In Middlesex County, two or more coexisting male cousins often carried the name of their paternal grandfather. The Rutmans reiterate that the duplication of names for first cousins was a further indication that children were seen less as individuals and more as parts of a family group. Although the Keesee kinship group examined here lived in an era considerably later than the Rutmans' study, this tendency to duplicate (or even triplicate) names for first cousins was still prevalent, perhaps pointing to a less individualistic view of children, much as the Rutmans posit for the time and place of their own study and in contrast to Smith's study of Massachusetts family naming practices. The Rutmans also briefly discuss a pattern comparison of both New England and the Chesapeake with the originating culture—England. The given data support the idea that Middlesex patterns were more conforming to the mother culture and that New England was the variant. But the data are much too skimpy to support such a broad assertion, as the authors readily admit.[33]

In a test group, the Rutmans found 63 percent of sets of patrilineally related male cousins (those related through their fathers' lineage) shared the name of their paternal grandfather, and 53 percent of sets of female cousins shared names. This high percentage of cousins with the same names is one of the many factors that make southern family history research so difficult. Real differences existed between Virginia and Massachusetts, at least insofar as naming patterns and their implications are concerned: Daniel Scott Smith argues for a higher degree of child individualization, and the Rutmans argue "for a higher degree of familialization [in the Chesapeake]." Stated simply in Smith's terms, colonial New England culture seems to reflect latent but developing modern attitudes toward family, while southern family culture retained its premodern character.[34]

As the authors discussed in the foregoing narrative have amply demonstrated, the examination of naming patterns can provide insights into the interior lives of people by revealing what or whom they found significant. When parents named their children after kin, we can assume that those kin were emotionally important to the name-givers. Whether parents give their children the names of biblical figures, grandparents, or famous personages tells us the signified person is in some respect relevant to the name-giver, and determining whether namesakes are grandparents, siblings, or more distant kin can locate the boundaries of effective kinship. In this study, naming patterns as well as residential propinquity, migration patterns, economic and political interactions, and religious affiliations are used to identify the family members who were part of the Keesee family kinship group and help pull new implications from the lives of antebellum southerners.

To accomplish the goals of integrating kinship studies into southern history, scholars of the South need to be convinced of the need for genealogically oriented kinship studies and to get over the fairly prevalent disdain for genealogy in general within the academic world. My life experiences and academic qualifications allow me to observe the gulf between academic history and genealogy with some authority and, I hope, with some objectivity. I have been researching my own family history for over twenty-five years and, for many of those years, worked as a professional genealogist, doing client research in both history and genealogy.[35] Like the mother of two feuding siblings, my aim is to settle the differences between history and genealogy—to reconcile the two and, in doing so, to midwife a more fruitful synergy for both.

So, having viewed the issues between historians and genealogists from both sides of the metaphorical fence, I understand the myriad reasons why professional historians tend to ignore and look down on family history research, that is, genealogy.[36] Professionals of any ilk are often intolerant toward those they consider amateurs and dilettantes, and genealogists often strike "real" historians as incompetent researchers with only an antiquarian interest in the past and a hagiographic mindset. William Rundell Jr. remarks on the "disparagement" of genealogists' work by historians due to the "quality of much genealogical work and the unfortunate impressions created by those who pursue genealogy to qualify for membership in exclusive patriotic and hereditary organizations" in addition to the "Brahmin attitudes" displayed by some genealogists.[37]

There is at least a grain of truth to this opinion: there are still and will probably always be a significant number of genealogists who have sloppy research techniques—those who surf the Internet, for example, trolling for somebody, anybody, with the same name and date of birth as their great-grandfather so they can plug these data into their own family tree without ever setting foot in a library or archive to confirm the unsubstantiated facts they have grabbed so greedily, literally out of thin air. There are also old-style local historians in small towns all over America who gather the oral lore of kith and kin, add a little dash of information from tombstones and county courthouses, and are then content never to think beyond how "interesting" it all is. Family-proud individuals who whitewash the sins of their foreparents in order to glorify their antecedents will always be with us. And, truth be told, there is nothing wrong with what these genealogists and local historians do or with how they do it as long as it meets their own needs. The problem, of course, comes when their flawed or incomplete work misleads others—or when it turns others away from a useful interpretive tool.

So let us not tar the whole bunch with the same brush. Not every work produced by bona fide academics turns out to be something the historical community points to with pride. It should be noted that there are incredibly meticulous genealogical researchers and local historians working today who would meet any historian's most stringent standards. These are the students of the craft of genealogical research of whom historians should take particular note. A true scholar learns to be discerning, to examine and analyze critically, to sift through the evidence presented, and to embrace or dismiss the theses argued in tomes published by the university presses. One must critically examine genealogical works with the potential to aid the quest for "real" history. Just as we do not throw the baby out with the bathwater when confronted with bad history, we cannot ignore the work of all genealogists merely because the work of some is less than stellar. Genealogy is not per se a bastardization or trivialization of history but, rather, often functions as a complement to history as practiced by academia.

Although by no means universal, the trend in genealogy during the past few decades has been toward delight in the full range of human nature enacted in the lives of one's ancestors and away from hagiography. There are even genealogy websites dedicated to flaunting families' less reputable members. A society called the International Black Sheep Society of Genealogists (IBSSG) "includes all those who have a dastardly, infamous individual of public knowledge and ill-repute in their family . . . within 1 degree of consanguinity of their direct lines. This individual must have been pilloried in disgrace for acts of a significantly anti-social nature." More and more often, individual researchers are thrilled to find something a bit interestingly naughty in an ancestor's background, and, when they do, they do not mind writing about it for the general public. Many genealogists have become advocates for humanizing our ancestors. Living up to a legacy of family sainthood is impossible, and to construe past lives as perfect renders genealogy empty of meaning; narratives of real but imperfect lives speak to our own humanity. The very fact that our great-great-grandparents persevered and overcame obstacles despite personal imperfections and sometimes even downright criminality can make their stories all the more grand and awe inspiring—or at least instructive. This new attitude is obviously indicative of the broadening of genealogists' focus to achieve an understanding of flesh-and-blood people of the past rather than a glorification of themselves in the reflective glow from saintly and illustrative ancestors.[38]

At any rate, even if there are those who continue to assert that the practitioners of genealogy can or should be dismissed in whole or in part, the soundness of the discipline's methodology remains. In general, genealogical theory is much less fixated on lineage to the exclusion of all else. The modern standard is to construct a historical context for each ancestor, much as a historian might do, and to go beyond mere names and dates. Any mainstream genealogical methodology book hammers home the importance of fleshing out the skeletons of names and dates to create whole and actualized people.[39] Moreover, the standards for documentation in genealogy are, in some regards, even more stringent that those for scholars. Genealogists, for example, are expected to document each statement of fact as it occurs in the text rather than providing a blanket citation at the end of a paragraph in order to maintain pristine clarity as to the source of each piece of data. In genealogical research, it is considered critical to note alternate facts and sources, because genealogical conclusions rely so heavily on a weighing of conflicting evidence from a variety of sources unequal in reliability. Genealogists are also encouraged to use footnotes rather than endnotes so photocopies of individual pages cannot be severed from their appropriate source citations. According to the basic precepts of the discipline, facts divorced from source documentation are all but worthless. Even more to the point, rules for standards of proof are explicitly laid out for the genealogist. Elizabeth Shown Mills's *Evidence! Citation and Analysis for the Family Historian* is a well-used reference on the shelves of top-notch genealogists, who are ever striving to make their documentation clearer and more precise not just as an academic exercise but as part and parcel of doing solid genealogical research. Moreover, virtually all genealogy computer programs now include a variety of functions for sourcing data and produce reports with either endnotes or footnotes, offering a variety of styles for citations.[40]

The perspectives presented here constitute a persuasive argument why serious scholars should not routinely discount anything and everything bearing the label of genealogy. But another reason a few historians tend to reject genealogy is because some still do not see the value in personal histories of ordinary people. While it is true that the story of one individual does not embrace the scope of southern history, the aggregate compilations and analyses of individual and group stories can and do layer our understanding of the past. While there seems to be little question among historical scholars about the value of a deep reading of the lives and activities of someone like Jefferson Davis and his circle, for example, there is still a handful who may be more dubious about investigating the lives and activities of undistinguished yeoman farmers and their families in the antebellum South, although the validity of this type of social history has been more recognized in recent times. I would argue that, although Davis's actions may have affected more people and put the scholar's finger on the pulse of momentous events, the lives of that ordinary farmer and his family are more revelatory of the realities of the past for the majority of people and equally as valid to the discipline of historical inquiry. Moreover, when a kinship group is defined as broadly as construed in this study, arguments about genealogical research being narrow, personal, or anecdotal lose their relevance. The utility of genealogical methodology is illustrated in this study by the insights into southern society provided by the Keesee family research.[41]

A comprehensive database of information on the Keesee extended family kinship group is the keystone of this study. The illustrative vignettes, the examples, the narrative, the assertions, and the arguments—in short, the evidentiary data and derived conclusions—rest on this considerable assemblage of research. This fact alone creates a compelling reason for a full discussion and clarification of this important body of evidence. Moreover, the multitudinous family ties and intertwined family trees are not easily accessible to the reader because of their inherent complexity. For these reasons, it seems both sensible and prudent to begin with a full explication of the background and scope of this database and to provide here a discussion of its strengths and weaknesses.

A primary concern was choosing an extended kinship group to serve as a database of evidence providing the underpinning for my arguments.[42] My first inclination was to choose a family for which there was a wealth of primary sources, but that seemed too much like stacking the deck. I wanted to prove that genealogical research has a broad application to the issues of southern history, but handpicking a family with unusually rich documentation would only prove my thesis in a restricted and narrower range of cases. The family chosen should demonstrate the efficacy of using genealogical methodology on lesser-known and -documented individuals. If this method of research is valid, it needs to be valid for just about any group of people, not just the elites or other narrow groups of southerners. It seems that so many of the studies we rely upon include the caveat that the data apply only to the upper class, as the other classes left no records of their activities or thoughts. This work is meant to dispel the notion that we have no way of studying most such groups that left no letters, diaries, and other personal records.

For a brief time I toyed with the idea of randomly picking a family group. That, however, seemed like folly. Not only would I be forced to start from square one, but there was a distinct possibility I would strike out completely and be forced to start over if this randomly chosen family turned out to originate in the North or to have recently immigrated to America.[43] Or, by a total fluke, I might end up with a kinship group that was, for some reason, inherently difficult to reconstruct or essentially unrepresentative of the South as a whole; for example, the group might be descended from Native Americans or triracial isolate groups,[44] thereby rendering productive research into early history improbable and complicating a thesis striving to achieve relevance for a broader range of southerners.

The solution seemed apparent. I had on hand case files on hundreds of families from research into my own family origins as well as from client files, and from among these files, I felt, I could find an appropriately representative family, one without particular distinction or sources of unusual depth.[45] There were several considerations to be weighed in the final decision. The family chosen should, of course, not by any means have been previously or completely researched throughout the collateral lines—the scope of the investigation I foresaw for this study was beyond what I had done delving into my own or clients' families.[46] Yet enough of the bare bones of the family should be apparent to ensure representation of general southern society—a family group that was unique and yet if not typical then not atypical.

I decided to pass on several promising client families because of the potential difficulties of being so involved in and possibly compromised by digging into someone else's family. While poking around in family history, it would not be altogether surprising to find skeletons in the closet that a former client might not want exposed.[47] Moreover, the involvement of someone else in the process had the distinct potential for unforeseen complications and influences. In short, I decided, if I were going to defame, embarrass, or disprove the cherished illusions of a group of family members, it seemed most prudent to make sure they belonged to my family rather than to a stranger's family—at least my family is used to this sort of thing and thus less likely to threaten me with a lawsuit. Turning my eye toward my own genealogical background, I considered then rejected several interesting family lines. The Boones, for example, are one of my maternal lines but are too famous and too well researched; another maternal line, the Wittenburgs, were Germans who only came to the South in the late nineteenth century and were part of an atypical (for the South) immigrant community.

I finally settled on one of my paternal lines—the Keesee family. My paternal great-grandmother (my father's father's mother) was Sarah Jane Elizabeth Keesee, who married Jesse Augustus Haywood Earle. She was the great-great-granddaughter of Thomas Keesee Sr., the principal focus of this study. I knew the Keesees to be a virtually all-southern group; the immigrant ancestor arrived in Virginia about 1700, and his children and their descendants fanned out across the upper and lower South. As my research into the kinship group expanded, I discovered several members of the extended family group who were somewhat wealthy or somewhat distinctive, although no one could be considered famous or unusual on much more than a local level. As far as I know, there are no manuscript collections, diaries, plantation records, or elaborate biographies of anyone in the Keesee kinship group. Yet, because of their membership in the wealthier small planter class (in the aggregate), wills and probate records, deeds, tax records, and biographical sketches are somewhat more abundant than is often the case for antebellum southerners, making it easier to flesh out the life histories of the individuals studied and making my arguments more vivid.

The genealogical database of this extended Keesee family forms the bedrock of my analysis of kinship in the antebellum South.[48] This database has grown to over seven thousand individuals who lived from the early 1700s through the present. The people in the database are virtually all white, although I did not set out to create an all-white database. Unfortunately, I have not yet located records that tie named nonwhite individuals to the white extended Keesee kinship group in any meaningful way during the antebellum period. When I discovered black families with the kinship group's surnames who lived near the Keesee kinship group, I added them to the database as unlinked individuals, hoping that I would be able at some point to link them. As yet, that hope has been unrealized. On the other hand, uncovering these connections has not been one of the principal goals of my research. Moreover, neither the book nor the database focuses on women except peripherally by their association with men and inherently as members and propagators of families. So although perforce the database contains nearly equal numbers of men and women, the data for the men overwhelmingly predominate. Almost all of the pre-twentieth-century individuals were southerners (the South being defined here as the Confederate states), but some of the later generations spread into other areas of the country. The families in this database are neither wholly typical nor wholly unique but constitute a range of lifestyles.

Based on my experience in doing genealogical research on a wide variety of southern families, I find the Keesee kinship group to have a higher than average incidence of wealth and slave ownership and of education and literacy. They are more typical of the planter classes and cotton farmers engaged in a market economy than of the yeomen and common classes engaged in subsistence agriculture or of southerners on average. But the scope of the study is large and contains some branches composed of those who were not wealthy and who did not own any slaves or who owned only a handful of slaves. Nevertheless, the main thrust of this study pertains to planter and slave-owning families, especially to ones who kept moving to the cotton frontier. Although "frontier" can be a highly contested term, in this book the idea of the "cotton frontier" refers to areas of the South where planters took advantage of cheap land and fertile soils previously untouched by cotton cultivation, usually in areas recently vacated by Native Americans and opened to white settlers, where they could maximize their assets to produce cotton through plantation slavery in a generally westward migration pattern.

The database itself has been and continues to be compiled from a variety of sources. Much of the data come from my own research in archives, libraries, and courthouses, that is, deeds, probate records, wills, marriage records, court documents, tax records, census records, federal land records, biographical sketches, family Bibles, family papers, birth and death records, Social Security records, newspapers, manuscript collections, and other traditional types of both primary and secondary sources.

A good portion of the data has been collected from other researchers. For the most part these are genealogists researching their own families, using many of the sources mentioned above to supplement private sources and personal knowledge within the family. Data from these researchers are uneven in quality: while most of these genealogists' work seems to be accurate based on spot checks, it is often undocumented or documented improperly. Often the data from family genealogists were used to supply information that allowed my own investigations to progress by providing clues to the location and names of groups of people. In general, the genealogical work by hobbyists seems to be most accurate when it concerns the generations closest in time to the researcher; that is, more confidence can be placed in data personally gathered from relatives and from cemeteries and courthouses close to home. And, it must be remembered, the past is with us longer than we think—many of the older people with whom I corresponded remembered grandparents and great-grandparents who were born in the antebellum South. The farther the research goes into the past, the more its accuracy depends on research skills with complicated and unfamiliar data and thus the less it can be trusted, particularly since inaccurate data, once published, can be passed back and forth for decades between genealogists who do not verify the accuracy of the printed word. The explosion in Internet sources has magnified the problem, as more people rely on gleanings from websites without ever setting foot in an actual archive. In cases where someone did not provide documentation for his or her facts, I have cited the individual providing the information as the source and evaluated the accuracy of those data before incorporating them into my database. However, the major portions of the study—those based on case studies of individuals— are almost fully derived from verified documentation.

When I refer to the Keesee extended kinship group database, I am speaking generally of the individuals who descend from George Keesee I, the immigrant ancestor who arrived in Virginia about 1700, possibly as an indentured servant. He was reputedly a Huguenot, and at least one of his sons was a Quaker. No evidence of his marriage or of his wife's name has surfaced, but four sons can be tied to him. He died in King George County, Virginia, in 1741. Each individual in the database either descended from George Keesee I or married a descendant or, in some cases, was the ancestor of someone who married one of George's descendants. The database, however, is not confined to the eighteenth and nineteenth centuries; many of the lines are brought down to the present and/or go back into the seventeenth century. Identifying and finding living descendants was an important part of the data-gathering process, since I could gather data more effectively from descendants who had already done research on their particular lines rather than through personally researching all the records myself to recover the family connections.[49]

More specifically, this database concentrates on George's great-grandson Thomas Keesee Sr. and his descendants. Not every descendant has been tracked. Indeed, this would be virtually impossible. If one couple, as George Keesee and his unknown wife did, had four children, and if each of those children grew to adulthood and had four children of his or her own who survived to adulthood, and if this continued in each succeeding generation, then the resulting geometric progression produces an amazing number of descendants in just twelve generations, or three hundred years, if the average generation is twenty-five years. Employing a calculator, one finds that, theoretically at least but by no means impossibly, this one couple would have 4,194,304 descendants in the twelfth generation. When the descendants in each of those twelve generations are tallied, the descendants of the original couple number a staggering 5,592,404.[50]

Of course, real life doesn't operate in the neat and objective world of mathematics: there were wars and epidemics, and not every couple raised four children to adulthood. Yet, prior to the twentieth century, many couples raised more than four children to adulthood, and many of those who died in wartime or of disease were already adults who left their full complement of offspring. Nevertheless, the end result is seemingly incomprehensible. If we looked at the imagined progeny of one thousand married couples in this country in 1700, by the year 2000 the descendants of those couples theoretically would account for a population in the United States of over 4 billion if each generation married outside the family.[51]

There are, no doubt, many reasons why those numbers don't hold up. For one thing, when two people have offspring, those children combine the two separate ancestral lines into one. Another reason of interest in the context of this study is intermarriage; simply stated, when cousins married, they reduced the number of potential descendants in later generations significantly. For example, if two first cousins among the sixteen first cousins in the third generation married each other instead of marrying out of the family, then the final tally in the year 2000 is reduced by over a quarter of a million descendants even with no further intermarriage. Significant numbers of southerners have the same ancestors showing up more than once in their pedigrees. It is not uncommon for southerners (and probably those from other regions) to be virtually related to themselves in a manner of speaking, often in more than one way. A recent posting to an email list was written by a man who sought help with the "bug" in his genealogy computer program. When he produced a personal kinship report (that is, he invoked the program that lists all the individuals in the database and labels them as to their relationship to the indicated person), he had the following labels beside his own name: self, sixth cousin, and seventh cousin. Quite a few list responders wrote to tell him there was no bug and that this situation was quite common; many of us are related to ourselves due to cousin marriages in our ancestry.[52]

Conversely, looking backward over that same three hundred years, each person alive today has 2,048 direct ancestors just in that twelfth generation of the past: in the second generation back, there are two direct ancestors (one's parents); in the third generation, each person has four direct ancestors (their grandparents); in the fourth generation, each person has eight great-grandparents. This continues back to 2,048 ninth great-grandparents. Obviously, the population three hundred years ago was not 2,048 times larger than it is today. On the one hand, the answer to this conundrum can be explained by factoring in siblings. In other words, not every single person has a distinct set of ancestors; most people share ancestors with one or more siblings. On the other hand, that still leaves us with a posited greater population in the past than we have today. The explanation is, of course, that most of us shared the same ancestors; at some point in the past we were closer kin, but over the years the relationship became so distant that it ceased to be relevant in any meaningful way.

Even with the lessened number of descendants that are the result of intermarriage, it is apparent from the numbers that the Keesee database is far from a complete accounting of all branches. Furthermore, it is important to remember that even where some information is provided about a particular person or groups of individuals, rarely have all the life events or all the documents pertaining to those people been gathered. In other words, this is a broad base of data that is not consistently deep.

In considering the merits of the overall data, it should also be pointed out that the realities of historical research lead to more data being gathered on the most prominent and the wealthiest. Those who did not hold political office, those who owned little in the way of land or slaves, those without descendants to reminisce about the activities of their family in manuscript or print, those who preferred not to preserve the scandals of their forebears, and those without public voices in a white patriarchal society are inevitably less visible in a work such as this one, despite the compiler's best efforts to tease out the voices of those who were underrepresented in the records.

Nevertheless, the data for the Keesees are complete enough to more than hint at the complexities of kinship ties in the antebellum South. The family entanglements, ranging widely over social, political, economic, and religious spheres, are quite clear even within this limited reconstruction of a kinship group. The large size of the database creates a more diverse view than could be accomplished by focusing on a single individual or a single nuclear family group. An overarching view of the Keesee kinship group reveals nonslaveholders as well as slaveholders, wealthy planters and cash-poor subsistence farmers, public-minded (or ambitious) officeholders as well as less prominent ordinary citizens, the bonds of kinship in the private sphere of women as well as that of men, and Baptists as well as Presbyterians. In short, the overall group in its totality can be seen as representational of antebellum southerners at large.

Furthermore, the reconstruction of so much of their lives without the rich source materials so often used in historical studies serves to demonstrate the efficacy of genealogical techniques paired with historical analysis. Thus virtually any group can be studied, even one whose members left no diaries, letters, or written sources. Although the thoughts, dreams, and desires of so many antebellum southerners cannot be divined or recovered, scholars of the South can retrieve many of their actions, subject them to analysis, and make educated guesses about motivation and intent.

This study re-creates the meaningful bonds of kinship that existed in the antebellum South and demonstrates the effect of that kinship on the everyday lives of southerners. For the most part, we tend to take our understanding of kinship from its meaning in our own lives. But the lives of antebellum southerners were demonstrably different from our lives today: in a less mobile and smaller population of people who had little institutional support systems other than the family, kinship was a deeper and more meaningful concept.

For the purposes of this work, investigations focus most intently on Thomas Keesee Sr., his kinship group, and his descendants. Thomas Keesee's life began during the war that led to the founding of his nation and ended as the war that threatened to fracture the bonds of that nation started. He was born in 1778 in Pittsylvania County, Virginia, and he died in Ashley County, Arkansas, in December 1861. During the eighty-three years of his life he moved many times and lived out the archetype of the southern planter on the cotton frontier. As a young man he and much of his nuclear family left Virginia in the waning years of the eighteenth century to relocate in Spartanburgh District, South Carolina. He probably married there, as his first children were born there. Less than a decade later, the bulk of the kinship group pulled up stakes and migrated to Sumner County, Tennessee. Little is known of Thomas's life during these years, but his father became a prosperous planter and slave owner who distributed his wealth to his children at his death in 1825. By that time, Thomas had joined other kin in yet another relocation to Franklin County, Tennessee. During his stay there in the 1810s and early 1820s, his oldest son married and presented him with his first grandson. And, although no official record of service has been found, his grandchildren later claimed he had been a soldier with Andrew Jackson during the War of 1812 and had fought at the Battle of New Orleans.

Perhaps during this service Thomas Keesee Sr. first glimpsed the lands of Alabama. At any rate, by 1821 he and his extended kinship group were living in the newly opened lands along the Black Warrior River near the boundary between Tuscaloosa and Bibb Counties, Alabama. Presumably, he fetched the six slaves his father had willed him in 1825 to add to his own growing group of slaves, who were an integral factor in growing his cotton crops. Thomas bought tracts of government land, became an overseer of the poor in his district, and watched his children marry and have children of their own.

By 1837, however, fifteen years of cotton crops had no doubt worn out the land that was needed to produce wealth for him and his ever-expanding family. The panic of 1837 hit everyone in Alabama hard, and the fertile, cheap lands of the new state of Arkansas beckoned. His son Milton and son-in-law Robert Calvert picked up and moved to central Arkansas in 1836 and must have relayed a thumbs-up message back to Alabama—the following year, the extended kinship group and other neighbors and members of the same church congregations formed a wagon train to join their kinsmen in Saline County, Arkansas. Once in Arkansas, Thomas Keesee, a ruling elder in the Cumberland Presbyterian Church, knit together the threads of his religious life once again. One of the first things he did, along with others who were mostly relatives, was to found a new Cumberland Presbyterian church in Saline County. One of his sons, a staunch Baptist, helped establish a Baptist congregation in the newly settled area.

Thomas Keesee's wife apparently died before or shortly after the move to

Arkansas, possibly after giving birth to her last child. In 1840 the sixty-two-year-old Thomas married the twenty-year-old daughter of a fellow planter and, before another two years had gone by, added two more children to his family. He and the extended family prospered: in 1840 he was the largest slave owner in the county, with thirty-one slaves. He and seven other members of the kinship group—eight men out of a total white population of 2,061—held over 30 percent of the slave population of Saline County. As befitting their financial prominence, many of the men in the family held positions of responsibility in local affairs: among the offices they held were road overseer, captain of the slave patrol, sheriff, county judge, and state legislator.

Yet again, however, once-fertile lands lost their ability to grow cotton after a decade of use. By 1848 much of the kinship group had moved south into Union County, Arkansas, where they engaged in the familiar processes of involvement in county affairs, buying land from the federal government, and growing cotton. At the time of the 1850 census, Thomas Keesee was seventy-two and still prospering: he owned forty slaves. Before the decade was out, he moved one last time to the adjacent county of Ashley.

Thomas was eighty in 1858 and, being "in a low state of health" although "in perfect mind and memory," felt moved to write his will.[53] In this will, having already given assets to many of his children, he distributed the rest of his worldly accumulations acquired during a lifetime as a southern planter: 636 acres of land, 11 slaves, $37,000 in cash, a carriage, a bay horse, and household and kitchen furniture. Three years later, age eighty-two, Thomas died on the first day of December 1861. In the following years, the Civil War wreaked havoc on his family as it did on the remainder of the South. Sons and grandsons served and died in the war, crops suffered, slaves were emancipated, and much of the kinship group's basis for wealth and social standing was dissipated. But a level of family solidarity endured. There were pockets of Thomas Keesee's descendants in Ellis, Washington, and Robertson Counties, Texas; in Columbia and Union Counties, Arkansas; and across the state line in Union Parish, Louisiana, as well as a group who chose not to leave Saline County, Arkansas, when the others moved on.

This, in short, is the narrative of Thomas Keesee's life. But in the larger study here, I propose to enhance the story of a southern small planter by exploring his life as well as the lives of his kin as a kinship group. This genealogical investigation will, I believe, flesh out the story of one individual's life and, by extension, expand our understanding of kin relations among southerners in the social, political, economic, and religious aspects of their lives. Keesee was part of a copious assemblage of kin, and a large proportion of his kin remained an integral part of his long life as he moved from the time of the Revolution to the time of the Civil War, from Virginia to South Carolina, to Tennessee, to Alabama, and, finally, to Arkansas. As John Donne wrote, "No man is an island, entire of itself." Thomas Keesee and his fellow antebellum southerners were not and did not attempt to be "islands" and thus cannot be separated from the context of their kinship groups if the broader story of antebellum southerners is to be told and understood.

CHAPTER TWO

Kinship, Migration, and Settlement Patterns

Call it a clan, call it a network, call it a tribe,
call it a family. Whatever you call it,
whoever you are, you need one.
—Jane Howard, *Families*

When Thomas Keesee Sr. arrived in Tuscaloosa County, Alabama, in 1821, he was a mature man of about forty-three, with a passel of children just entering adulthood. Although his status as a planter and slave owner is unclear in the preceding years, he was plainly a slave-owning small planter during his years in Alabama. Seeking economic opportunity, he was surely drawn to the newly opened area by the fertile lands in the Black Warrior River valley. He, like many others, might have become acquainted with Alabama during the War of 1812 campaigns against the Creeks.[1] The Creeks and the Choctaws were forced to cede their lands between 1814 and 1816, the territory of Alabama was created in 1817, both Tuscaloosa and Bibb Counties were formed in 1818, and Alabama became a state in 1819.[2] Tuscaloosa sat at the head of the Black Warrior River, a major transportation route from upper Alabama to the Alabama-Tombigbee Rivers, which drain into Mobile Bay on the Gulf of Mexico. Tuscaloosa became a principal market for cotton because of the convenient steamboat transportation via the rivers. Cotton prices were extremely high after the War of 1812, reaching their peak about 1819. This propelled many planters like Thomas Keesee toward the fresh soils of the newly opened territory of Alabama, especially with land available for purchase from the federal government at low prices.[3]

The story of the antebellum South is incomplete without an understandable narrative of migrations like Thomas Keesee's. What became known as "the South" began with sparse settlements of Europeans and Africans along the eastern seaboard and Gulf coast and, over the course of almost 250 years, diffused to include Texas, the westernmost reaches of the region as usually defined. During the course of this population redistribution and growth, Europeans, African Americans, and Native Americans blended and interacted to create a distinctive southern culture.[4]

Scholars of the South continue to debate the merits of the various causative factors behind and the effects of the westward migration of whites, often accompanied by their black and mulatto slaves.[5] This study asserts that kinship strongly shaped migratory and settlement patterns in the antebellum South and that we must therefore include kinship as a category of analysis when debating these issues. Moreover, by adding genealogical methodology as a research tool, scholars will be able to unveil the power of kinship as one of the primary forces influencing migration and settlement and thus reveal the social scaffolding of antebellum southern communities more completely and precisely.

The main issues in migration boil down to motive: what combinations of push-pull factors affected some individuals', families', and groups' decisions to remain where they were and others to relocate? What factors affected their choices of destinations? But although the issues can be stated relatively simply, migration is nevertheless quite complex, encompassing a myriad of questions about economics, demographics, geography, agriculture, religion, politics, family dynamics, slavery, race, class, and gender. Unfortunately, scholars cannot read the minds of these antebellum southerners to discover their reasons for moving, and the majority of migrants did not leave written evidence addressing these issues comprehensively. Even if we were able to interrogate them, antebellum southerners, like most humans, were probably not fully conscious of all the subtle thought processes involved in evaluating the factors pushing them to leave one location and pulling them to a new location.

In this book, however, I have used the information from the Keesee kinship group database to examine the actions of a representative group of southerners on the move in the belief that actions truly speak louder than words. Scrutiny of their actions over time and throughout the South indicates that kin relations were a driving factor in choices about migration and settlement and a key element in establishing a community. This study draws on an anthropological approach to families that regards "[a] system of kinship and marriage . . . as an arrangement which enables persons to live together and co-operate with one another in an orderly social life."[6] Finally, this chapter reveals the efficacy of using genealogical methodology to investigate the antebellum South.

Naturally, kinship was not the only force affecting migration. The study of the Keesee kinship group reveals that economic advancement was the motivation for most moves, particularly for the segment of the group classified as planters (almost universally understood to be those engaged in plantation agriculture and owning twenty or more slaves).[7] This is not a new idea—many historians have presented effective cases for economic motivation. Scholars have expressed this in a number of ways: a desire to exchange worn-out soils for fertile new lands; a lack of available land for sons coming of age; the desire to exploit profitable crops such as indigo, tobacco, cotton, and sugar; or a desire to move west to newly opened lands where landownership was possible for very little investment.[8] Ulrich Bonnell Phillips largely equated migration in the South with land and cotton culture, which implicitly offered the chance for wealth. The most significant factor in migration into Arkansas, declares Robert Bradshaw Walz in his dissertation on the subject, was "the desire for cheap, fresh land."[9] "Migration was a prerequisite to success," according to James Oakes, and many southerners like Thomas Keesee were desirous of a chance at that success.[10] Robert Hughes writes that "[t]he metaphor of all wealth production is gambling." Similarly, Ray Allen Billington asserts that "in every pioneer there was a touch of the gambler," and the ones who chose to stay put were "the contented, the cautious, and the secure."[11] The Keesees and kin were a mixture of those seeking something more and those comfortable with what they had; in every generation there were some who moved on and some who remained behind.

But whatever the motivation—whether an individual was pushed out of an established area by escalating land prices or by the poverty of the soil or by a need to provide a maturing family of children with land of their own, or whether he was pulled to the borderlands by a hunger for fertile and cheaper land or by the chance to make his fortune—when an individual moved, it was virtually always in the company of a host of kin. In a world where political and economic power frequently was contingent on a network of kin, where having a baby was a dangerous business, and where a trip by wagon to a new territory was a long and arduous venture, and in a society where family was the main organization of everyday life, kinship groups stuck together.

In the antebellum South, society was institutionally less complex than it

was in the North (or than it is in the United States today) and thus more
dependent on kinship groups; as Burton Pasternak, Carol R. Ember, and
Melvin Ember state: "In complex societies, it is individuals (not families or
larger kinship groups) who take advantage of economic or occupational opportunities; [today] when someone moves to a new job, parents and siblings
are not likely to go along (and cousins and aunts and uncles even less
likely)."[12] Conversely, in less institutionally complex societies, like the antebellum South, individuals aligned with kinship groups were the ones who
were able to take advantage of economic opportunities. The road to success
was traveled by groups of related families, and their cohesiveness was often
the basis of that success. Social capital was the surest route to prosperity if
not survival, and kinship groups were the source of the greatest social capital in the antebellum South.

Thomas Keesee's six relocations, from Virginia to South Carolina, to
Tennessee, to Alabama, to central Arkansas, to southern Arkansas, and to
southeastern Arkansas, along with the fluctuating formations of his kinship
group that ebbed and flowed in conjunction with these moves are illustrative of some of the common migration experiences of antebellum southerners. By decoding the behavior of Keesee and his kin, we can infer many
of their motivations and beliefs.

After his migration to Alabama, Thomas Keesee took full advantage of
federal land offerings in that state: from 1825 to 1837 he bought a total of
1,161.805 acres of federal land. (See figure 1 for a complete list of the parcels
of land Keesee acquired from the federal government, all cash purchases.
Figure 2 is a reproduction of one of the actual land patents Keesee received.)
If Keesee had been a simple farmer engaged in diversified agriculture, he
would not have needed this much land, and he would not have had the financial wherewithal to pay for it. Although the number of slaves he owned
at this time cannot be verified from any record yet found, Thomas Keesee
would have had to own quite a few slaves to make use of even a part of this
amount of land (although his purchase of much of the land must have been
speculative in nature).

What is known is that neither Keesee nor his father owned slaves in 1790
or 1800; that in 1825 Thomas Keesee Sr. acquired six slaves (Booker, Big
Isram, Clock, Minnie, Gabriel, and China), part of his inheritance from the
estate of his father, George, who died in Sumner County, Tennessee; and
that he had clearly moved into the planter class later in life—in 1840 he
owned thirty-one slaves, making him the largest slave owner in his county
of residence. Moreover, his father, George Keesee, had also moved into the

Figure 1. Thomas Keesee's U.S. Land Patents in Alabama

Signature Date	Document Number	Land Location	Number of Acres
15 July 1825	3897	Sec. 6, T22S, R6W	80.01
15 July 1825	3905	Sec. 7, T22S, R6W	79.91
15 July 1825	3922	Sec. 1, T22S, R7W	80.19
15 July 1825	3923	Sec. 2, T22S, R7W	80.07
15 July 1825	3924	Sec. 1, T22S, R7W	80.19
15 July 1825	3925	Sec. 1, T22S, R7W	80.19
15 July 1825	3926	Sec. 1, T22S, R7W	80.19
15 July 1825	3927	Sec. 1, T22S, R7W	80.19
15 July 1825	3928	Sec. 1, T22S, R7W	80.19
15 July 1825	3929	Sec. 2, T22S, R7W	80.07
1 September 1825	4323	Sec. 1, T22S, R7W	80.19
1 September 1825	4379	Sec. 2, T22S, R7W	80.07
1 October 1835	10804	Sec. 3, T22S, R7W	40.035
1 April 1837	14407	Sec. 1, T22S, R7W	80.19
1 April 1837	14408	Sec. 3, T22S, R7W	80.12

1,161.805 acres total. From U.S. Government Land Office Records, showing the Alabama lands Thomas Keesee Sr. acquired from the federal government. This does not include any private land purchases.

planter class by the time he died in 1825; his will distributed to his heirs fifty slaves, land and a "plantation" (total 570 acres, in Sumner County), a cotton gin, livestock of every description, farming equipment, a riding carriage, furniture, one hundred barrels of corn, one hundred pounds of picked cotton, ten bushels of wheat, and a crop of tobacco.[13]

The two decades previous to Thomas Keesee's move to Alabama are hazy due to the paucity of records in Tennessee during this period—the 1810 census is not extant for Tennessee except for two counties, and many of the courthouses burned or were destroyed and lost many of their earliest records. He was probably in Sumner County with his parents and siblings, but he has not been found on any records placing him there. That he was in Tennessee at this time is confirmed by later census records of his children, stating they were born in Tennessee during these years. He emerged in Franklin County in 1811, where he entered a Tennessee land grant of three hundred acres that year.[14] During the ten years he remained in

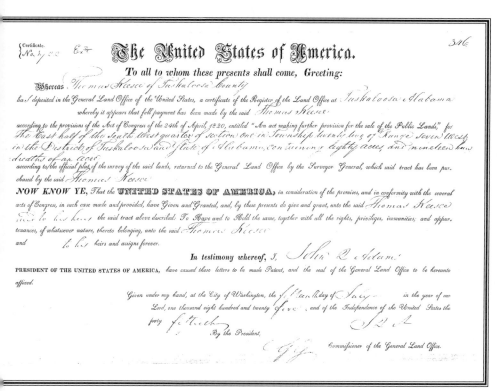

Figure 2. Thomas Keesee Cash Entry
From U.S. Government Land Office Records, Tuscaloosa County, Alabama, 1825.

Franklin County, he participated in the War of 1812, and his children grew up. His oldest child, named George for Thomas's father, married in that county and presented Thomas with his first grandchild in 1817. Although the marriage records for Franklin County are not extant for this period, the Keesees were in this county at the time George married, and his daughter Elizabeth was born there on 4 November 1817, according to her tombstone in Magnolia City Cemetery, Columbia County, Arkansas.

Thomas Keesee's life begins to unfold more clearly after 1821, when he moved to Tuscaloosa County, Alabama. There a new network of kin evolved. It is possible, even probable, that Keesee arrived in Alabama in company with a wider range of kin than is presented here. I have chosen, however, to begin the narrative with the formation of new ties of kin in Alabama in order to illustrate the evolution of kinship groups in a clearer and more complete way. Keesee's residence in Tennessee during parts of the first

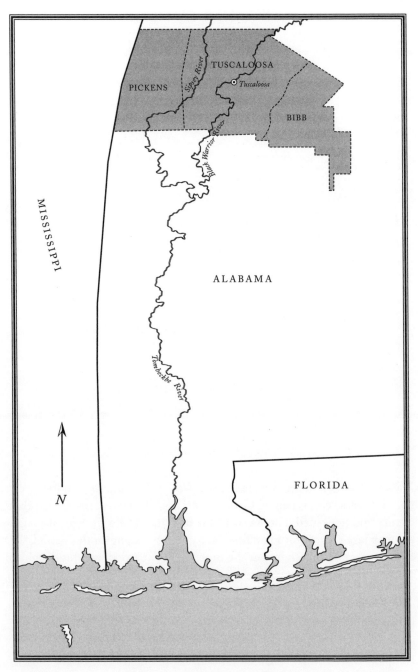

Figure 3. Selected Counties in Alabama, 1834
Map source: "Parts of Louisiana, Arkansas, Mississippi, Alabama, and Florida: North American,
Sheet XIII," Society for the Diffusion of Useful Knowledge, 1834.

two decades of the 1800s is difficult to flesh out due to the paucity of records in Tennessee for this time period and to the lack of emphasis in my research. One thing that seems clear, however, is that he apparently did not come to Alabama with any of his siblings, which is fairly unusual.

Although his oldest son married in Tennessee, Thomas's other children married during their residence in Alabama and formed alliances with many local families. These marriages are the tangible evidence of the creation of a new kinship group or, perhaps more precisely, the natural development of Thomas Keesee Sr.'s kinship group. A study of the reconstruction of Thomas Keesee Sr.'s neighborhood (see figure 4) along the Tuscaloosa-Bibb county line illustrates a prime tenet of marriage connections in the antebellum South: people must meet to marry, and, given the narrow range of everyday mobility in this era, chances are that the persons of the opposite sex whom an antebellum southerner would meet would be neighbors, relatives, and fellow church members. As Robert C. Kenzer has so ably demonstrated in his own work, propinquity was the key factor in selecting a mate.[15]

The area in which the Keesees settled came to be called Hill's Settlement or Mars, and it was located near the Tuscaloosa-Bibb county line. In *Bibb County, Alabama: The First Hundred Years, 1818–1918,* Rhonda Coleman Ellison discusses the origins and location of the community and the fluctuating county lines that affected it during the early years of settlement. The inhabitants of this area as named by Ellison have a high correspondence to the names of men shown on the neighborhood reconstruction illustrated in figure 4. This is the center of the neighborhood where the Keesee kinship group was residing during the period when the kinship group was evolving.

> Throughout the years, the exact position of the line between this county [Bibb] and Tuscaloosa has often been debated. An act approved by the state legislature on January 15, 1828, ordered the boundary to be established so as to leave Captain James *Hill* in Tuscaloosa County, but three years later, a new law reversed this decision: Edward *Calvert,* Grief *Ragsdale* [married a *Hill*], Benjamin *Hubbert* [was married to a *Calvert*], John A. *Bagby* [married a *Hill*], Robert *Hill,* Hamilton *Kile* [married a *Hill*], and James *Hill,* at their present residences, or as many of them as can be so included, without taking any others, shall, by this act, be taken from the county of Tuscaloosa and be added to the county of Bibb. . . .

> Hill's Settlement, which grew up at the headwaters of Hill's and Schultz

Figure 4. Thomas Keesee's Alabama Neighborhood, Tuscaloosa/Bibb Counties, Alabama

S34, T21S, R7W	S35, T21S, R7W	S36, T21S, R7W	S31, T21S, R6W	S32, T21S, R6W
		Benj. *Clardy* Saml. Falkner Danl. Rowland David Lindley	Danl. *Canterberry* Blake Falkner Wm. James	
S3, T22S, R7W Robt. L. Boyd Wm. James Thos. *Keesee* Luke Williams	S2, T22S, R7W Benj. *Clardy* Robert *Hill* Thos. *Keesee* Edward Sims	S1, T22S, R7W Thos. *Keesee*	S6, T22S, R6W Robt. *Calvert* Isaac James Wm. Jemison Geo. *Keesee* Thos. *Keesee*	S5, T22S, R6W Lucy *Calvert* Robt. *Calvert* Flm. Heathcock Edward Sims John A. Woods
S10, T22S, R7W Pleasant *Hill* Robert *Hill* John James Wm. James	S11, T22S, R7W Benj. *Clardy* Robert *Hill* John James Sol. Johnson George *Keesee*	S12, T22S, R7W William Brown Pharoah *Hill* Robert *Hill* Milton *Keesee*	S7, T22S, R6W Jno.A. Goodson George *Hill* Milton *Keesee* Thos. *Keesee*	S8, T22S, R6W Willis Banks Lucy *Calvert* Jno.A. Goodson Berryman McDaniel
S15, T22S, R7W Robert *Hill*	S14, T22S, R7W Hardy Clements Jesse *Hill* Robert *Hill* Adam James	S13, T22S, R7W Jesse *Hill* John *Hill* Pharoah *Hill* Robt. C. *Hill* Milton *Keesee*	S18, T22S, R6W James *Hill* David Scott Phillip Shuttlesworth	S17, T22S, R6W Joseph Acre James *Hill* Ismi Kellum David C. McDaniel
S22, T22S, R7W	S23, T22S, R7W Francis *Hicks* Robert *Hill*	S24, T22S, R7W James *Hill* Jesse *Hill* John *Hill* Robert *Hill*	S19, T22S, R6W Alexander *Hill* James *Hill* Robert C. *Hill* Richard Hogan	S20, T22S, R6W

This neighborhood is reconstructed from records at General Land Office. These landowners are drawn from government land records only and do not reflect private land purchases. The individuals charted are ones who patented land during the years of Thomas Keesee's residence in the area. Names emphasized are those who were, or became, part of the Keesee kinship group. For those unfamiliar with the rectangular survey system used in public land states, a section is 1 mile square and contains 640 acres; there are 36 sections in a township. Thus the grid above represents an area 5 miles wide and 5 miles long. Compiled by author from U.S. Government Land Office Land Patents.

creeks near the Tuscaloosa line, not far from Johntown today. In 1825, John ("Jake") *Hill* received a patent to an entire section (around 640 acres). Farmlands of this large settlement were cleared not only by the *Hill* family but also by others, including John Goodson, *William Calvert*, Jackson Caffee, Robert Woods, and *Thomas* and *Milton Keesee*. In the Hill-Oldham Cemetery, the oldest marked grave is that of William Green *Hill*, the two-year-old son of James and Jane *Calvert Hill*, who died in 1823. The early importance of Hill's Settlement is documented by the establishment of the Mars post office in 1823; James *Hill* was the first postmaster.[16]

Many of the families in this neighborhood would come to have family ties to Thomas Keesee Sr. through the marriages his children made. There were also, however, families listed in the neighborhood description above and the reconstructed neighborhood in figure 4 with no kin ties to the Keesees, making it clear that there were choices for marriage partners as well as for those with whom the Keesee kinship group interacted socially and legally. Although there was a limited selection available, there *was* a selection.

Viewing Keesee's children's marriages in the context of their proximity and settlement patterns in Alabama is enlightening:[17]

1. George Polk Keesee married Elizabeth (?) (Harrison?) in Tennessee, probably in Franklin County, where their oldest child was born. George owned land in the neighborhood after his marriage. ("Neighborhood" indicates the area within the five-mile-square grid illustrated in figure 4.)

2. Milton Keesee married William and Lucy Calvert's daughter Mary, known as Polly, on 4 August 1823; Milton was just short of twenty-four at the time of his marriage to his seventeen-year-old wife. His sister Mary, also known as Polly, married his wife's brother Robert Calvert (Mary Calvert became Mary Keesee; Mary Keesee became Mary Calvert)—a classic case of sibling exchange. The Calverts were neighbors and were closely related to the Hills, also of the neighborhood. Milton owned land nearby.

3. Agnes Keesee married Benjamin Clardy III; they owned land in the neighborhood. Oral history from descendants states that before he married Agnes, Benjamin Clardy worked for her father, Thomas Keesee Sr., on Keesee's farm. Some of Clardy's family lived near Keesee in Bedford and Franklin Counties, Tennessee, so the story is plausible.

4. Thomas Keesee Jr. married Jane Caroline Green on 7 July 1826 when he

Figure 5. Thomas Keesee Sr.'s Family

Children of Thomas Keesee Sr. and Mary (McKnight?):
George Polk Keesee
    B: 1797, Spartanburgh County, South Carolina
    M: (1) Elizabeth? Harrison? ca. 1817
         (2) Unity Leech 2 November 1840
    D: 1 August 1864, Saline County, Arkansas
Milton Keesee
    B: 31 August 1799, Spartanburgh County, South Carolina
    M: Mary "Polly" Calvert, 4 August 1823
    D: 10 March 1860, Washington County, Texas
Agnes Keesee
    B: ca. 1801 in South Carolina
    M: Benjamin Clardy III, 1822
    D: bef. 21 December 1859, Hot Spring County, Arkansas
Thomas Keesee Jr.
    B: 5 February 1804, Sumner County, Tennessee
    M: Jane Caroline Green, 27 July 1826
    D: 26 November 1879, Ovilla, Ellis County, Texas
Mary "Polly" Keesee
    B: 11 October 1807, Sumner County, Tennessee
    M: Robert Calvert, 28 October 1823
    D: 16 December 1873, Robertson County, Texas
William Keesee Sr.
    B: 8 April 1809, Sumner County, Tennessee
    M: (1) Mary Jane Chappell, 14 August 1828
         (2) Emiline Howth, 15 March 1854
    D: 28 September 1864, in Washington County, Texas
Jane Keesee
    B: ca. 1811–15, in Tennessee
    M: Elias Jenkins, 22 December 1831
    D: ca. 1850–52 in Choctaw County, Mississippi
Gideon Keesee
    B: ca. 1816, (Franklin County?), Tennessee
    M: Martha Wooding Hargrove, ca. 1838
    D: after 1875, probably in Texas
Children of Thomas Keesee Sr. and Malinda Bond are:
Virginia Keesee
    B: ca. 1841, Saline County, Arkansas
    M: David H. Thornton, 18 December 1855
Benton Keesee
    B: ca. 1842
    D: 1862, Antietam, Maryland

Thomas Keesee Sr., son of George Faris and Agnes Keesee, was born in 1778 in Pittsylvania County, Virginia, and died 1 December 1861, in Ashley County, Arkansas. He married Mary (McKnight?) ca. 1796 in South Carolina, and Malinda Bond 10 May 1840, in Saline County, Arkansas.

was twenty-two and she was fifteen. There is no proof the Greens lived in the neighborhood, but her parents, Jonathan E. and Jane (Kerr) Green, did live in Bibb County; Jonathan Green died there in 1837, and Jane died there in 1855. In 1839 Thomas Keesee Sr.'s granddaughter Mary Ann Clardy married Jane Caroline (Green) Keesee's brother George Sidney Green.

5. Mary Keesee married William and Lucy Calvert's son Robert on 27 August 1823; Robert Calvert, who had just become her brother-in-law earlier in the month, was twenty-one when he married Mary, who was fifteen. The families lived within one mile of each other at the time the two couples married. Both Robert and his mother owned land in the neighborhood.

6. William Keesee married Mary Jane Chappell, daughter of Robert Wooding Chappell, on 14 August 1828 when he was nineteen and she was seventeen. The Chappells lived less than two miles northwest of Thomas Keesee Sr.'s land shown on the neighborhood grid in figure 4.[18]

7. Jane Keesee married Elias Jenkins on 20 December 1831 when she was in her late teens and he was twenty-nine. He had no known connection to the neighborhood, but he was the sheriff of Tuscaloosa County when they married and had been involved in legal transactions with the Hill family in the neighborhood, thus making it probable that he was well known to the Keesees.

8. Gideon Keesee, youngest child of Thomas and Mary, married Martha Wooding Hargrove. Although Martha's brother's autobiography states that the couple was married in Alabama, no marriage record has yet been located. Her family is not known to be of the neighborhood, but she was the granddaughter of Robert Wooding Chappell and the niece of Gideon's sister-in-law Mary Jane (Chappell) Keesee, who was the daughter of Robert Wooding Chappell.

Without question, propinquity was a strong factor in choosing a spouse, and this proved true in the Alabama neighborhood in which the Keesees resided during the 1820s and 1830s; for the most part, Thomas Keesee Sr.'s children married neighbors. The larger question, however, is whether or not the kinship connections forged by these marriages translated to something of significance; in other words, did the marriage of two people create an *effective* bond of kinship between the two families thus united? As anthropologists A. R. Radcliffe-Brown and Daryll Forde phrase it: "The first determining factor of a kinship system is provided by the range over which these relationships are effectively recognized for social purposes of all kinds."[19] To determine the strength of the effective bonds or the extent of social recognition, we can examine the local records for evidence of instrumental ties between the Keesees and the families into which their children married.

Tuscaloosa County records are not complete for the early years but nevertheless provide some evidence of ties between the families. In 1825, when Milton Keesee got into trouble with the law ("for committing an affray on the County of Tuskaloosa aforesaid against the peace and dignity of the State"), he was hauled into circuit court and required to post a two-hundred-dollar appearance bond. His security on that bond was Pharough Hill. Pledging security on a bond was not something taken lightly. The financial penalty would fall on the person acting as security if the principal failed to perform the act guaranteed in the bond. Hill also pledged security on an appearance bond at the same time for his younger brother George W. Hill, indicating that, whatever kind of trouble Milton Keesee had found, George Hill was in it with him. Justice of the Peace Jesse Hill witnessed these bonds. The cases were "continued from day to day and from term to term" until finally a nolle prosequi was entered. There is no further information on the nature of the crime. Although Pharough Hill was not related to Keesee by blood, the wife of one of Hill's brothers was Keesee's wife's aunt, and the wife of another of his brothers was Keesee's wife's sister.[20]

Few things demonstrate strong bonds between individuals as well as the willingness to risk a rather large amount of money together. In 1826 and 1827 a group of men from the extended kinship group were willing to post a security bond in the amount of $5,122.07 for Claibourn Harris, who had a judgment against him in the Tuscaloosa County Circuit Court that he was appealing to the Alabama Supreme Court. Among those involved in the transaction were Robert Hill, John Hill, Claibourn Hill, Milton Keesee, Jesse Hill, Thomas Keesee, John Hill, Robert Calvert, and James Moore, who married Robert Calvert's mother after she was widowed. John L. Purdy had sued Claiborne Harris for slander perpetrated during a previous lawsuit between them in which Harris accused Purdy of lying. In order to appeal, Harris had to post a bond and provide men willing to serve as securities for that bond. To protect his securities against a potentially huge financial loss, Harris executed a deed of trust, conveying several tracts of land along with appurtenances, eight slaves (and their increase), a wagon and harness, four geldings, twenty-three head of cattle, twenty-eight sheep, one hundred hogs, and all his household goods to his securities if he failed to satisfy the judgment against him. The judgment against Harris was affirmed, but apparently he paid his debt, relieving his securities of their obligation. If there was a kin relationship between Harris and the men serving as his securities, it is not known at this time.[21] All of the men involved, except the principal, had close ties of kinship. The neighborhood construction makes it clear that there were other families nearby outside of the kinship group but that these men chose to bind themselves legally with kin instead of with men who were merely neighbors, possibly friends, or even fellow church members.

Another type of legal record that demonstrates the effective ties of kinship between these families is probate. As with marriage, probate is a civil matter, with laws designed to designate legal heirs for the protection and orderly transference of property, and the role of guardianship was created for the purpose of protecting the property rights of minor heirs. In fact, guardianship had little or nothing to do with physical custody of minors — a mother often remained the main caregiver of her children who were minor heirs, while a trusted relative or close friend (usually male) held legal guardianship over the child or children. Guardians were chosen with care because a guardian's malfeasance could have serious financial consequences for the minor heir and, by extension, for the family. The man chosen administrator or executor of the estate of a deceased person was also a trusted family member or friend for the same reason.[22] The death of William Calvert, father of Robert and Mary, on 23 August 1823 began a series of interactions that were played out in the Tuscaloosa County Orphans Court (the court that handled probate matters in Alabama) between relatives and family connections.[23] William Calvert's probate is an exemplar of the role of family in legal matters of property and of the range of family involved.

Calvert was about forty-eight years of age when he died and left a widow, Lucy, and seven children, two of them already married — Jane, who had married George Hill the previous year, and Mary, who had married Milton Keesee less than three weeks before her father's death. Within days of William Calvert's death, his eldest son, Robert, married his recently acquired sister-in-law Mary Keesee. Since William Calvert left property, an estate to be probated, and no will, his remaining children, still minors, needed guardians to safeguard their interests. At first, their mother, Lucy, applied for and was granted status as the guardian of William, Nancy, and Paulina (often spelled Polina), while son-in-law George Hill served as guardian for James Calvert, who at fifteen was the oldest of the children left at home.

On 6 January 1825, about sixteen months after her husband's death, the widow married James Moore and lost her briefly held status as a *femme sole*.[24] Perhaps believing a stepfather would not make the best of guardians for her offspring (or perhaps following the wishes of her sons, who might dislike having her new husband control family assets), she went to court the following month and asked to be released from her guardianship. At the same session of the court, her son Robert Calvert applied for appointment as guardian of his brother William, posting a twenty-five-hundred-dollar bond to ensure proper performance of his duties; Jesse and John Hill were his securities on the bond. At the same time, Milton Keesee was appointed guardian of his sister-in-law Paulina and posted a similar bond with the same securities.

Less than a month later, Nancy Calvert, now fourteen, was legally able to choose her guardian and in testimony before Jesse Hill, the local justice of the peace (and relative), chose her brother Robert Calvert. This time, *James* and Jesse Hill were his securities. Her mother, Lucy Calvert, now Lucy Moore, formally turned over Nancy's assets—$100.00 from the hire of a slave (or slaves) the previous year—to the new guardian. At the same time, she turned over $50.00 to Milton Keesee as Paulina's share in the hiring out of "property" the previous year; $109.50 to Robert Calvert for William Calvert (Jr.), representing "the Bond Executed by George Keesee for . . . the hire of [William's] property for the current year"; $111.00 to Robert Calvert as Nancy's share; and $93.00 to Milton Keesee (presumably for Paulina), representing "the bond of Lucy Calvert for which the property of Polina Calvert hired for the Year 1825."

Meanwhile, James Hill, who held a sale of property from the estate as part of his duties, was administering the estate of the deceased William Calvert. In February 1827 the court ordered Robert Calvert to pay Robert Hill, who had recently married Calvert's ward Nancy, her share of her deceased father's estate. Although part of the entry in the court minute book is marked out, it appears that Calvert turned over to Hill $832.00 "and two negroes named Henry & Violet." Robert Calvert continued as William Calvert's guardian, George Hill continued as James Calvert's guardian, and Milton Keesee continued as Paulina Calvert's guardian.

At the January session of the county court in 1830, Jessee E. Hill and John Hill petitioned the orphans court to release them as securities on both Robert Calvert's and Milton Keesee's guardianship bonds. They claimed to be "fearful" that Calvert and Keesee would "mismanage" the estates of their wards. The court issued an order for Calvert and Keesee to appear, and on 30 August and 4 October 1830, respectively, they did so. Both released Jessee E. Hill and John Hill and filed new bonds; Calvert's new securities were James Hill and Blake Falkner, and Keesee's were his father, Thomas Keesee Sr., and his brother-in-law James Calvert. The underlying reason for the Hills' concerns about the guardians is unknown, but it was probably a disagreement over some element concerning the disposition of property. Although the closeness of kinship groups was often a benefit, this may be an example of the sometimes bitter disagreements that can erupt within families.

It is important to reiterate that, during all the actions in probating William Calvert's estate and in creating guardianships for his minor heirs, the bottom line was not physical custody of the minor heirs but, rather, was all about the protection of property. The guardian's job was to protect the financial interests of the minor children and, to some extent, to protect the financial interests of the family. Guardians, administrators, and executors also personally benefited from their appointments, partially from fees paid to such agents out of an estate but also from their temporary control of the property and their elevation in social status.[25] Thus the men involved in the administration of the estate were always drawn from within the family or were very close friends so as to safeguard the property. The appointment of James Hill as administrator of the estate is an indication he was included within the range of effective kinship for the Calvert family—not surprising, since he was married to the deceased's sister. The widow's new husband was apparently *not* deemed part of the range of effective kinship at that point in time, possibly because it was not uncommon for a new husband, who upon the marriage controlled his wife's assets, to fritter away or mismanage the property. The details of Calvert's probate are evidence of a family's use of the legal framework to conserve the assets of the family and to protect them from being siphoned away from the family. Every person involved in the Calvert estate but one (Blake Falkner, security on a guardianship bond) was related to William Calvert's family; their service in the probating of his estate demonstrates their membership within the range of effective kinship. In other words, they were not just kin but were kin in a meaningful way.

An example of the importance of kin in matters of probate from outside the Keesee kinship group can be found in the will of Elizabeth R. Craft of Amite County, Mississippi, dated 1853. In her will she named her brother guardian of her son rather than appointing either her second husband (the son's stepfather) or any of the son's paternal relatives. She apparently put more trust in blood kin than in her husband or former in-laws when it came to protecting her son's inheritance.[26]

Naming patterns are another significant manifestation of close personal ties and can be used to locate the boundaries of effective kinship. There is no question that naming children for grandparents, parents, and aunts and uncles was the predominant pattern in the antebellum South—and in the Keesee kinship group. Milton and Mary (Calvert) Keesee, for instance, named their first son Thomas, presumably for Milton's father, and their second son William Calvert Keesee for Mary's father. Other names given their children were Jane Hill Keesee (probably for Mary's paternal aunt), Lucy Rogers Keesee (for Mary's mother), and Mary McKnight Keesee (for Milton's mother). (Note that the children were given the relatives' full names, including surnames—not just Jane but Jane Hill.) Their other children were named Franklin, Nancy Caroline, and Louise Virginia Keesee. If these names were patterned on kin, I have yet to uncover their namesakes; Franklin may have been Benjamin Franklin, and Virginia may have been in honor of the Keesees' state of origin, as it was not uncommon to name girls for states, for example, Tennessee, Alabama, and Louisiana. Thus there is evidence that the parents' nuclear families of origin were of primary importance but that other kin (or family connections) also fell within the range of effective kinship for them.

Thomas Keesee Jr. and his wife, Jane Caroline Green, named their oldest son Robert C. Keesee (presumably Robert Calvert Keesee, for Thomas's brother-in-law), and among their other children were Milton Keesee (for Thomas's brother), Thomas J. Keesee (his father's and grandfather's name), William Fortenberry Keesee, John Hill Keesee (for one of the many John Hills who were neighbors and family connections of the Keesees in Alabama and Arkansas), and George Keesee (for Thomas's brother George, although with a different middle name). Thomas and Jane evidently felt especially strong ties to their brother-in-law Robert Calvert and to Thomas's brothers Milton and George. But we can infer an emotional bond with John Hill, someone outside of Thomas's immediate family. Although it is not clear who William Fortenberry Keesee was named for, Absolom Fortenberry was a Cumberland Presbyterian minister who lived near the kinship group members in Saline County and Union County, Arkansas, in 1840 and 1850, respectively. Perhaps Thomas and Jane combined Thomas's brother's given name with a respected minister's surname, or perhaps there was a William Fortenberry known and respected by the Keesees. Thomas and Jane had other children, but their names cannot be tied to specific namesakes at this time.

Mary (Keesee) Calvert and her husband, Robert, had the following children for whom namesakes can be ascertained with reasonable certainty: Mary M. (for her mother and grandmother and/or for Robert's sister; her middle name might have been McKnight), Lucy (for Robert's mother), William (for Robert's father), Paulina (for Robert's sister), and Sarah Agnes (the Agnes might have been for Mary's paternal grandmother, the mother of Thomas Keesee Sr., or for Mary's sister Agnes). Each of their known children was apparently named for close kin.

An examination of the naming patterns throughout the kinship group would yield similar results. Although the most explicit message derived from these naming patterns is that parents, siblings, and grandparents had the tightest of bonds with an individual, there is evidence that other more distant kin were often significant in their lives—significant enough to name a child after them. Furthermore, there are occasional clues that individuals who would not seem to be that close, based on the available evidence, must have maintained meaningful ties. For example, William Keesee Sr., son of Thomas Keesee Sr., and his sister Jane, married to Elias Jenkins, had not lived in the same state since about 1836, and yet when William had another son in 1848 he named him Elias Jenkins Keesee. Benjamin and Agnes (Keesee) Clardy named a son Smith Clardy after the *maiden* name of his maternal grandmother. This and other such occurrences raise the question of how much contact family members maintained when they lived far apart and leads to the possibility that communication and possibly even visits were more frequent than previously believed—or it could merely indicate an affection for and fond remembrance of certain relatives who were no longer part of parents' everyday lives.

Another interesting facet of names given to children in this era is the widespread custom of incorporating the given name *and* surname of the namesake into the names of both males and females. George West Murphy and his wife, Mary Elizabeth (Clardy) Murphy, named their first son Robert Calvert Murphy, born in 1842, after Elizabeth's uncle by marriage, Robert Calvert. They did not merely name him Robert but, rather, gave him the full name of his great-uncle. Similarly, when James Moore and his wife, Saryan (Clardy) Moore, had a son born about 1851, they named him Thomas Keesee Moore for Saryan's grandfather. Daughters, too, received full names as given names: William Dudley Hargrove and his wife, Charlotte (Chappell) Hargrove, named a daughter Martha Wooding Hargrove in 1821 for Charlotte's father's mother, whose maiden name was Martha Wooding; Caleb Frayser and Elizabeth (Keesee) Frayser named their daughter Martha Burton Frayser after Elizabeth's mother's mother, whose maiden name was Martha Burton; and Etta Murphy Harrell was given not only her mother's given name but also her maiden name. This custom makes it crystal clear that the names given to children were in honor of a specific person in the family and that the honored name was not chosen merely for its harmonious sound. This usage was probably even more extensive than can be shown here due to the difficulty of ascertaining a full name for each member of the kinship group.

There is not sufficient evidence for me to claim this as a distinctively southern naming pattern, although at least it is perceived so by some; when NBC reporter Campbell Brown explained the origin of her name, she replied, "My full name is Alma Dale Campbell Brown. . . . Alma Dale was my great-grandmother's name, and Campbell is my mother's maiden name. It's all very Southern."[27]

These legal documents and naming patterns illustrate the intricate ways in which the lives of these kinfolk were intertwined, even in the nascent phase of the kinship network studied here. When it came time to post a bond, to choose a guardian, to administer an estate, or even to get in trouble with the law (as was the case with Milton Keesee and George W. Hill), relations and connections were preferred. Although there were others living in the same neighborhood, as illustrated by the plat of the area in figure 4, the important roles were almost exclusively filled by those within the family as defined by antebellum southerners.

After a fifteen-year residence in Tuscaloosa County, Alabama, the Keesees were ready to move again. Arkansas had just become a state in 1836, and the federal government was offering land cheaply. The combination of worn-out cotton lands in the family's present location, the availability of cheap fertile land in the new location, and the panic of 1837 were no doubt determining factors in the Keesees' and others' decision to relocate. During this time, Thomas Keesee's son Milton and his son-in-law Robert Calvert headed to Arkansas to scout out conditions there. They apparently found what they wanted in Saline County, which had just been cut from Pulaski County the year before, was located just west of the capital city of Little Rock on the Old Southwest Trail (also known as the Military Road), necessitating only a short haul to ship cotton down the Arkansas River to the Mississippi and thence to New Orleans, and had plenty of good, well-watered bottomland along the Saline River. It was just the type of land they seemed to prefer for growing cotton and, perhaps most importantly, was much like the soil, topography, and climate in Tuscaloosa County, Alabama. Antebellum southerners showed a marked propensity for moving to areas similar to their previous area of residence.[28]

Milton Keesee and Robert Calvert either sent word or traveled back to the rest of the family in Tuscaloosa to let them know about the promise of this new area. By 1838 Thomas Keesee Sr. had arrived in Saline County, Arkansas, along with much of his extended family, many of his Alabama neighbors, and his Cumberland Presbyterian minister. Many other residents of Tuscaloosa and Bibb Counties followed in two large wagon trains in 1841 and 1843 after economic conditions worsened, and they settled in Saline County among their former neighbors.

At the same time Thomas Keesee and most of his family were migrating to Saline County, Arkansas, son William Keesee migrated to Texas with the Chappells and Hargroves (his wife's family), and Thomas's daughter remained behind in Alabama with her husband, Elias Jenkins, then later migrated to Mississippi. This split in the Keesee family provides us with clear corroboration of the essential nature of kinship groups—their boundaries are fluid, expanding and contracting depending upon time and circumstance and upon the strength of emotional ties between the members.

Determining causality for the splitting of the kinship group is difficult without personal testimony from the family members, but some speculation can be proffered. If one element was decisive, religion was probably that element. From the time William married into the Chappell-Hargrove family, he resided among his wife's kin rather than his own. Although his own family group was, for the most part, strongly Cumberland Presbyterian, it seems likely that William became a Methodist at the time or near the time of his marriage into that intensely Methodist family. Religion was often a major influence in the lives of antebellum southerners like William Keesee, and as his wife's kin converged with the fictive kinship group of his religious affiliation, the bond with them intensified, simultaneously loosening his ties to his birth family.

That is not to say that William Keesee never again had contact with his own family. After he moved to Washington County, Texas, he had fairly frequent interaction with some of his brothers. Brother Milton Keesee's

death in 1860, for example, occurred in Washington County, presumably
amongst his kin, although his wife and children were living at that time in
Falls County and Milton's probate was administered in Robertson County,
Texas, by his brother-in-law Robert Calvert.[29] William's brother Gideon
Keesee murdered a man in Washington County in 1871, was sought out in
Ellis County, Texas (where his brother Thomas lived), and returned to
Washington County to serve his prison term.[30]

   In Saline County, Arkansas, a major contingent of the kinship group
settled and began to establish themselves. But even so, the Keesees and
their kindred spread out over the landscape in several groups. George Polk
Keesee settled in Davis Township with some of his Alabama neighbors,
and they established a Baptist church. Edward Calvert also settled in this
neighborhood; although he was clearly closely related to Robert Calvert,
George P. Keesee's brother-in-law, the exact relationship has not yet been
established. In Saline Township, the 1840 manuscript census lists Benjamin
Clardy, Milton Keesee, James Moore, Thomas Keesee Jr., James Hicks,
Robert Calvert, and William Wharton, the Cumberland Presbyterian minister who migrated to Arkansas from Alabama with the Keesees and
Calverts. Thomas Keesee Sr. was living in Owen Township, next door to
his granddaughter Maryann Clardy and her new husband, George S.
Green. Earlier that same year, Thomas, a sixty-two-year-old widower,
married Malinda Bond, age twenty, the daughter of Richard Bond, a
neighbor of Thomas's relatives in Saline Township. The next year, Thomas
and Malinda had a daughter they named Virginia and the following year a
son named Benton (no doubt named after the Saline County seat of Benton, Arkansas). Gideon Keesee, Thomas's youngest son by his first wife,
along with Gideon's wife and baby daughter, were living with Thomas and
Malinda at the time of the 1840 census. Although the 1840 census only provided the names of the head of the household, the ages and genders of the
additional people in Thomas Keesee Sr.'s household match those of his son
Gideon's family. Moreover, Gideon does not appear elsewhere in this census as a head of household, although he was definitely in Saline County. He
was listed as a captain of the Second Battalion, Eighteenth Regiment,
Saline County, Arkansas State Militia, in November 1842, with a notation
that he had "removed from county."[31]

   Another method of determining the Saline County Keesee kinship
group's pattern of settlement across the landscape is by making use of
county and federal land records. Figure 7 illustrates where some of the ma-

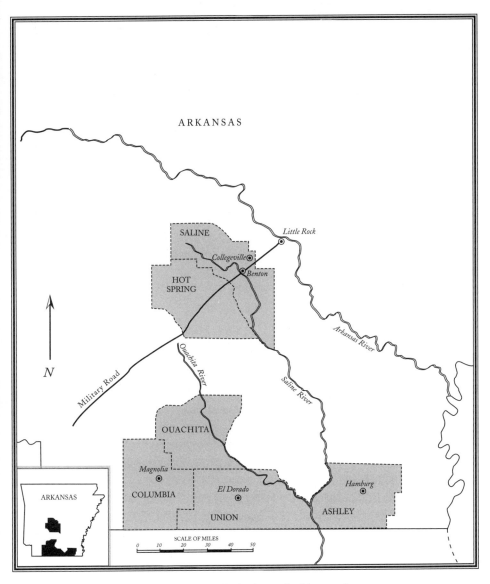

ARKANSAS

SALINE

Little Rock

Collegeville

Benton

HOT
SPRING

Arkansas River

N

Ouachita River

Saline River

OUACHITA

Military Road

Magnolia

Hamburg

COLUMBIA

El Dorado

ARKANSAS

UNION

ASHLEY

SCALE OF MILES

0   10   20   30   40   50

Figure 6. Keesee Family Settlements in Arkansas, 1850s
Map source: "A New Map of Arkansas," Thomas Cowperthwait and Company, 1850;
Morse and Gaston Map of Arkansas (1857), published in Charles Colby's
American Diamond Atlas.

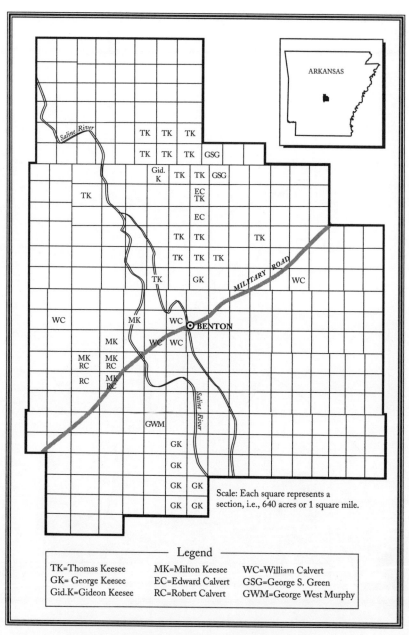

ARKANSAS

Saline River

TK | TK | TK
TK | TK | TK | GSG
Gid. K | TK | TK | GSG
TK | | EC TK
| | EC
| TK | TK | | TK
| TK | TK | TK
| TK | GK | MILITARY ROAD | WC
WC | | MK | WC ⊙ BENTON
| MK | WC | WC
MK RC | MK RC
RC | MK RC
Saline River
GWM
GK
GK
GK | GK
GK | GK

Scale: Each square represents a
section, i.e., 640 acres or 1 square mile.

Legend

TK=Thomas Keesee	MK=Milton Keesee	WC=William Calvert
GK= George Keesee	EC=Edward Calvert	GSG=George S. Green
Gid.K=Gideon Keesee	RC=Robert Calvert	GWM=George West Murphy

Figure 7. Settlement Locations, Saline County, Arkansas, 1837–43

This is a portion of the Saline County map from Blaisdell's 1919 *Atlas of Arkansas*.
The locations indicated are approximate within each section of land; the owner did not
necessarily own the entire section. The data are drawn from Saline County, Arkansas, Deed
Record Indexes, Benton, Arkansas, and from Allen and McLane's *Arkansas Land Patents:
Grant and Saline Counties.*

jor figures in the kinship group owned land purchased during their early years of settlement in Saline County, Arkansas. Many families belonging to the kinship group moved about four hundred miles distant from their former homes in Alabama and then settled within a few miles of one another in Arkansas. And, just as they had in Alabama, they settled on the fertile lands near rivers and creeks where cotton could be grown profitably.

Over the decade of the 1840s, the Saline County kinship group's boundaries continued to grow and change: established groups lost members and new clusters of kin were created; there were births and deaths; marriages created new alliances. During this decade, some members of the kinship group began to look for new frontiers, and their gazes were drawn southward to Union County, Arkansas. They had passed through this area in the 1830s on their way to Saline County, and, moreover, their kinspeople and neighbors who followed them to Saline County in the early 1840s had also passed through the territory. They had seen the potential of the fertile soils and the river access. At that time, however, the county had been too undeveloped and underpopulated to facilitate their success as cotton planters.

Besides their own experience and the experience of their neighbors, there was another significant line of communication at work in acquainting kinship groups with new areas: the network of religious communities. We tend to think of people in the antebellum era as cut off from knowledge of the wider world, especially in contrast to modern methods of communication, but antebellum southerners had access to significant sources of information through ministers and elders as well as through social and political leaders. These groups, particularly ministers and elders, traveled more than we might think and brought home to their communities information about potential areas of settlement at the periphery. The Keesees' experiences in relocating to Union County, Arkansas, are a good example of the many potential lines of communication.

Many of the kinship group attended church together at Saline Congregation, a Cumberland Presbyterian church where William Wharton was the minister. In fact, the church was on Elder Robert Calvert's land, and presbytery meetings were occasionally held at his house.[32] In the organizational structure of the Cumberland Presbyterian Church, churches were under the direction of presbyteries, presbyteries were grouped into synods, and synods met in the General Assembly of the entire church. Wharton first appears in Cumberland Presbyterian Church records in 1840, when he appeared at the Arkansas Presbytery, held at Van Buren in Crawford

County, Arkansas (about 150 miles northwest of Saline County); his min-
isterial credentials were accepted, and Saline Congregation was brought
into the presbytery.[33] Over the next few years, Wharton attended meetings
of the presbytery in Hempstead County (1842, 1844, and 1848), Hot Spring
County (twice in 1843), Sevier County (1845), Ouachita County (1846, 1847,
and 1848), and Union County (1847). Moreover, Wharton, like most ministers, held camp meetings over a large area, and he was appointed commissioner to the General Assembly in Lebanon, Ohio, in 1847. Robert
Calvert attended a meeting of the presbytery in Dallas County, Arkansas
(1845), as an elder representing his congregation and was appointed as an alternate to the 1848 General Assembly in Memphis, Tennessee. This small
sample from the records of one presbytery demonstrates how widely traveled some antebellum southerners were.[34]

In much the same way, Masons visited other lodges and Masonic gath-
erings, while legislators and politicians traveled far and wide in fulfilling
their duties. Ministers and lay leaders, members of fraternal organizations,
and politicians were able to bring knowledge of other areas gained from
their travels—and from their conversations with other travelers—back
home to the community, where word of mouth distributed it far and wide.
Before a group migrated, they no doubt gathered intelligence about their
planned destination from a variety of sources.

Gideon Keesee might have been the first to move with his family to
Union County in southern Arkansas, and many of his siblings and other kin
followed him there. And, although the Hills did not migrate to Saline
County, Arkansas, when the Keesees did in the late 1830s, they were
once again neighbors of the Keesees and the Calverts in Union County,
Arkansas, in 1850 and in Ashley County, Arkansas, in 1860.[35] The families
were apparently still closely associated, as Thomas Keesee and John Hill
posted a twenty-thousand-dollar bond together when they were cosecuri-
ties for Union County Sheriff S. D. Drennan in 1850.[36] It seems unlikely
that the Keesees, Calverts, and Hills appeared simultaneously in a new area
totally by coincidence; it seems more likely they were in contact and mutu-
ally considered this move. Appendix A lists members of the kinship group
taken from one contiguous section of the 1850 census of Union County,
Arkansas. Their coresidence in the same county and in the same neighborhood cannot be ascribed to a fluke; through more than thirty years and at
least three moves, these families maintained their connections because these

connections were important to them and because they were a significant component of their quality of life, both emotionally and socially.

But not all members of the overall Keesee kinship group migrated to southern Arkansas. Evidently, George Polk Keesee was happy where he was and remained in Saline County, Arkansas.[37] His father, Thomas Keesee Sr., sold his son 1,520 acres of land when he left the county.[38] George died in 1864, intestate, with a large estate to be settled. Thomas Keesee's son-in-law and daughter Benjamin Clardy and his wife, Agnes (Keesee), moved a few miles southwest of Saline County into Hot Spring County, Arkansas, and never again migrated. George Polk Keesee's daughter Elizabeth, who had married James A. Hicks in Tuscaloosa County, Alabama, then migrated to Saline County, Arkansas, with the rest of the family, moved south into Columbia County, Arkansas (contiguous to Union County), as did her sister Emelia Manda Keesee, who had married Daniel Leech in 1840 in Saline County. Once again, the kinship group evolved and was reconfigured.

George West Murphy and his wife, Mary Elizabeth Clardy, who was Thomas Keesee Sr.'s granddaughter, briefly moved to Union County, Arkansas, with the kinship group. Murphy joined the Union County Masonic Lodge with his relatives, Hamilton G. Quarles, George W. Rutherford, Gideon Keesee, George S. Green, Milton Keesee, and William Calvert.[39] Later he settled directly across the state line in Union Parish, Louisiana, as did his brother-in-law James Moore, who was married to Mary's sister Saryan Clardy. They maintained ties with the larger family, however, naming their children for family members: Murphy's first child, a son, was named Robert Calvert Murphy, and Moore named sons Thomas Keesee Moore and William Calvert Moore.

William Calvert, a young man not yet of age, the son of Robert and Mary (Keesee) Calvert, went to Union County in company with many of his relatives, taking a group of his father's slaves with him to help him establish himself. There, in 1849, he married Alabama Cottingham, the sixteen-year-old daughter of a local small planter. His parents, however, moved directly to the Brazos River bottoms in Robertson County, Texas, from Saline County, Arkansas, about 1852, and their son William along with his young family soon joined them there. Also accompanying the Calverts to Robertson County were their son-in-law George Washington Rutherford and his four young children (the Calverts' daughter and Rutherford's wife, Lucy Ellen, died in Saline County in 1851); their daughter Paulina Jane, her husband, Joseph Tom Garrett, and their young children; and their daughter Mary M. with her husband, Dr. Peter H. Smith, and their first child. The Calvert kinship group settled just up the Brazos River from Mary (Keesee) Calvert's brother William Keesee, who had been in Washington County, Texas, since 1837. Brother Milton Keesee and his wife, Mary (Calvert) Keesee, along with their children moved to Robertson County also, leaving Union County, Arkansas, behind. Before long, Milton bought land on the west side of the Brazos, across from his brother-in-law, in Milam County. The Cumberland Presbyterian minister William H. Wharton, who had ministered to the family since their residence in Alabama, also moved with Robert Calvert to Robertson County, where he preached at a church built by Calvert's slaves on Calvert's land.[40] A portion of the Saline County kinship group had separated from the main body but by the mid-1850s in Robertson County, Texas, had formed a good-sized group of kin centered around Robert Calvert.

In 1864, toward the end of the Civil War, another of Thomas Keesee Sr.'s sons, Thomas Keesee Jr., moved his entire family to Robertson County, Texas, joining his brother-in-law and sister, Robert and Mary Calvert, there. Family lore, related to me by John Hill Keesee's great-granddaughter Barbara Scott Wyche, describes how Thomas Jr.'s sixteen-year-old son, John Hill Keesee, in order to escape conscription into the Confederate Army, hid under a big wash pot artfully placed upside down at the top of goods stowed in the wagon. Evidently, he was hidden because of his young age rather than any antipathy toward the Confederacy; his father, Thomas Keesee Jr., was a private in the Johnson Township (Union County, Arkansas) Confederate Home Guard, and, according to the Confederate pension application of John Hill Keesee's brother Thomas J. Keesee, both Thomas J. and brother Milton S. Keesee served together in Company G, First Arkansas Mounted Rifles, C.S.A., during the Civil War. (The wash pot is still in the family.)[41] At least in part, the move was probably an effort to protect the family's slave property. After two years, when the war was over, they moved northward into Ellis County, Texas. On 14 July 1867, according to the records of the Shiloh Cumberland Presbyterian Church in Ellis County, the church "[r]eceived into cong. Bro. Thomas Kesee [*sic*] and his wife sister Kesee by Recomm. C. P. C. Texas."[42]

Robert Calvert's daughter Mary M. (Calvert) Smith was widowed in 1861 and married again in 1864 to the Reverend W. G. L. Quaite, a Cum-

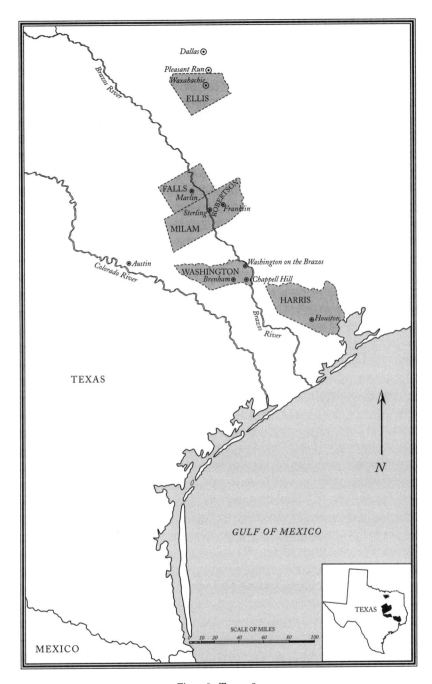

Figure 8. Texas, 1854
Map source: "Cerographic Map of Texas," Sidney E. Morse, 1854.

berland Presbyterian minister. In 1867, after the death of Robert Calvert, her father, she, along with her new husband and children, went with her maternal uncle Thomas Keesee Jr. to Ellis County, even though her mother remained in Robertson County and lived out her life among her other children and grandchildren. Mary M. and the Reverend Quaite had one child, then divorced; she married a third and final time in Ellis County and died there in Waxahachie in 1889. During her life and through three marriages, Mary M. was never far from close kin.

At about the same time the Thomas Keesee Jr. family moved into Ellis County, Texas, Jesse Ellis Clardy and family also moved there. He was the first cousin twice removed of Thomas Keesee Jr.'s sister's husband, Benjamin Clardy III. Jesse Ellis Clardy had taken a completely different migration path: from South Carolina (where the Keesees and Clardys lived before moving to Tennessee, Alabama, and Arkansas), Jesse had moved to Florida. There is not adequate evidence at this time to ascertain whether or not Jesse Ellis Clardy had contact with family and family connections that prompted him to choose Ellis County, Texas, as a residence at the same time as his kin did, but it seems unlikely that there would not have been some contact between them.

Thomas Keesee Sr.'s youngest child from his first marriage, Gideon, born about 1816, began life in Tennessee, came to adulthood and marriage in Alabama, and followed his family to Saline County, Arkansas. By 1842 he had migrated to Union County, Arkansas, with his family and his slaves. After his wife died in 1859, he and his children all joined their relatives in Washington County, Texas—Gideon's brother William and his family were living there, as were Gideon's deceased wife's Hargrove and Chappell relatives. In 1874 Gideon was imprisoned for murder; the trial took place in Washington County, although he had been arrested in Ellis County, where his brother Thomas Keesee Jr. lived. Due to "the ill health and extreme age of the convict, and doubts existing as to the correctness of his conviction," Gideon Keesee was pardoned by the governor and discharged the following year, on 5 May 1875. In his record it is also noted that his left arm was paralyzed. Nothing is known of his whereabouts after his release, but he probably died shortly thereafter.[43] Each move or event in Gideon's life took place alongside or in the vicinity of kin; although he had a wide-open field of choices, he always chose to live his life within (and even to hide out with, when he was in trouble with the law) the kinship group.

The county and federal records, the patterns of migration and settle-

Figure 9. Gideon Keesee
Born ca. 1816, died after 1875.
Son of Thomas Keesee Sr. and Mary [McKnight?].
Photographic image provided by Kathy McMaster,
a descendant of Gideon Keesee.

ment, and the naming patterns demonstrate some of the ties of kinship at work in the lives of the Keesee family and demarcate the shifting borders of effective kinship. Moreover, these instrumental ties of kinship multiplied exponentially to include the families whose children married into the families into which the Keesees married. The Hills, for example, who were related to the Calverts in several different ways, had no direct ties of kinship to the Keesees in any record yet found, yet the two families' actions were those of members in a common kinship group because both the Hills and the Keesees shared a mutual kinship with the Calverts. The Hills were bound tightly to the Calverts, and the Calverts were bound tightly to the Keesees—the result was a commingling of all three families in their every-

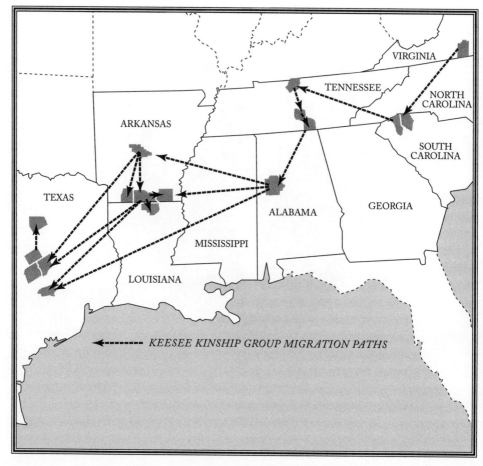

Figure 10. Keesee Kinship Group Migrations, 1778–1870

day lives. For antebellum southerners, the range of effective kinship was broad enough to encompass family connections beyond those defined merely by blood or by marriage relationships.

This study begins when Thomas Keesee Sr. and his children moved into the Tuscaloosa and Bibb Counties, Alabama, area, and the kinship group can be fairly well defined as it developed in the neighborhood where they settled and lived for almost two decades. As they migrated and as Thomas Keesee Sr.'s children married and had children and grandchildren of their own, the boundaries of the kinship group proved permeable and flexible. As his children married and formed their own nuclear families, more connections were forged with other kinship groups; some of these connections proved meaningful, while others were less so. At the same time, some portions of the group remained in place as other parts moved on, sometimes breaking the bonds of kinship but, more often, merely attenuating them somewhat. Some members of the group chose a different religious affiliation and moved away from segments of their previous kinship group as they formed closer bonds with other groups.

But although the Alabama kinship group split and re-formed over time and space, none of their moves or changes took place outside of a group of kindred. Their lives virtually always played out within the context of a kinship group. The boundaries of each group were affected by proximity, by interdependence within the group, by births, deaths, and marriages, and by religious and economic choices. These metamorphosing boundaries were not always obvious or entirely clear or completely discernable, either to the present-day researcher or to the contemporary members of the group. As the needs of the individuals comprising the group shifted, so too did the parameter of each group; for each individual, a group parameter was erected according to the needs of that particular individual. Clearly, the identity of each member of the kinship group had its foundation in a kinship group membership.

The conclusions drawn by this study clearly oppose those of Jane Turner Censer in her study of antebellum southern migration. She posited that the primary impediment to western migration by elite North Carolinians tempted by the "almost unparalleled economic opportunities" to be found in the West "was the threat to an institution they highly prized—the family, especially the extended family. Generally they decried the attenuation of kinship ties that migration would cause." It seems evident that the family was just as important to the Keesee kinship group studied here as it was to Censer's North Carolina planters; rather than eschewing emigration, how-

ever, the Calvert-Keesee group demonstrates that many planters kept the
family largely intact by migrating as a group. On the other hand, Censer
found that when migrations did take place, although economics rather than
family might have been the motivation, the migrations were "built upon a
network of friends and family already established in the West." [44] The
Calvert-Keesee kinship group certainly can serve as a prime exemplar of
that insight. However, although Censer never actually defined what she
considered "family," she mentioned only parents, children, and siblings,
with an occasional reference to "other kin." [45] The Calvert-Keesee kinship
group demonstrates an interest and involvement in family beyond parents,
children, and siblings.

Similarly, Joan E. Cashin misses the mark in her book *A Family Venture*,
which is advertised as a work "[s]ensitive to questions of gender, race, and
class." Cashin might have deepened her insights considerably had she chosen to incorporate kinship into her categories of analysis. Instead she inves-
tigates family roles and argues that young men redefined "the male sex
role . . . [to emphasize] the fulfillment of a man's personal goals at the ex-
pense of his obligations to other human beings"; thus they "ensure[d] their
independence" by escaping the family rather than by being "submerged in
it." She found the "kinship networks of the Southwest [to be] . . . imperfect
and incomplete," and "nuclear households became the norm." "In contrast
to seaboard families who lived surrounded by kinfolk, Southwestern families lived near a few relatives or none at all. The planter family was reduced
to its nuclear core." [46]

Although families might very well indeed have been living in nuclear
households in the antebellum South, the spin Cashin puts on this fact fails
to hold up in the face of the large numbers of kin who were neighbors on
the southern frontier no matter how far or how often a family moved.
Cashin writes of the distances households on the frontier were from one another and backs this up with evidence showing that an Alabama planter's
neighbors "lived at least a mile from their new plantation." A mile is not a
significant distance at all; it can be walked in less than fifteen minutes and,
on a horse or mule, ridden in far less time. It is the size of the width of one
section of land—a common tract for one person to own. On a good day, if
the wind and terrain are favorable, an individual can holler loud enough to
be heard a mile away, especially in the incredibly quiet days before modern
background noise from airplanes, electric appliances, and traffic. Neighbors
but a mile distant from one another would have heard the comforting

sounds of nearby homesteads, from the lowing of the cattle to the rever-berating ring of wood being split on a chopping block. If the ground was fairly open, covered perhaps by cotton fields, a person could see another house a mile away—or at least the smoke from the chimney of that house.

The neighborhood studies presented here, in conjunction with analyses of the records, demonstrate the close ties maintained by members of the kinship group even while living dispersed across a neighborhood in pre-dominately nuclear family units. This chapter and subsequent chapters sub-vert Cashin's thesis conclusively; the evidence proves quite forcefully that while the men described in this study "saw migration as a shortcut to wealth," they obviously were not "try[ing] to escape the intricate kinship networks of the seaboard."[47] To the contrary, they recognized that their success was dependent on their inclusion within a group of kin.

Nor were young men the only heads of families migrating to the cotton frontier. As this study shows, Thomas Keesee Sr. was about forty-three when he moved to Alabama, fifty-nine when he moved to Saline County, Arkansas, seventy when he moved to Union County, Arkansas, and almost eighty when he moved to Ashley County, Arkansas. Similarly, Robert Calvert was a fairly young man of thirty-four when he blazed the migration trail from Alabama to Saline County and fifty when he moved to Robert-son County, Texas. And Thomas Keesee Jr. was sixty-three when he made his final move from Robertson County, Texas, to Ellis County, Texas. Many more examples could be proffered to show that migration was not ex-clusively or even mostly a young man's venture.

The complicated pattern of migration for the kinship group as a whole is difficult to comprehend in its entirety. A "splinter" group might move away from the main cluster of kin, from location A to location B; ten years later, another splinter from the main group in location A might join the original splinter group in location B; at the same time or a few years later, yet an-other splinter group might join with members of the first splinter group in location C. This splintering and re-forming occurred many times, while at the same time births, deaths, and marriages continued to change the con-tours of the overall kinship group. While most of a kinship group eventu-ally migrated to another location, there was usually a part of the family that chose to stay behind.

The story of another family's constantly fluctuating kin boundaries can be found in Edward Ball's *Slaves in the Family*, which gives an excellent sense of the grand sweep of the ebb and flow of the Ball family kinship group—the group that stayed in one location as other segments moved on. The Ball family of South Carolina are descendants of an Elias Ball who emigrated from England in 1698 and became the progenitor of a large family of prosperous rice planters. They persisted as a kinship group, many remaining in the same area, well into the twentieth century. They intermarried (with a distinct preference for first cousins), tightening the bonds between many members of the family; as some were born, others died. Some groups moved away, particularly at the time of the American Revolution, when the Tory members of the family fled to England after residence in America became untenable for them; but there was always a group that remained. As the cast of characters changed over the generations, the essential element—the kinship group—remained, conscious of their Ball identity and reinforcing it through intermarriage as well as stories, letters, documents, and family portraits passed down through the generations. At the same time, as the author reveals, the black slaves on those Ball family rice plantations formed kinship groups that fluctuated over time, subject not only to births and deaths but to forced relocation—and, as the title of Ball's book makes clear, to mingling with the white kinship group. The entire narrative sweep of the book reveals the changing composition of the kinship group vis-à-vis its persisting nature over centuries in a striking fashion.[48]

The boundaries of subgroups of kin expand and contract, forming and re-forming according to a myriad of factors, including migration and resettlement. This complexity is the main factor that obscures underlying kin relationships from researchers of the antebellum South. Without reconstructing the genealogy of neighbors in a particular area for previous generations, it is all but impossible to comprehend that so many permutations, migrations, and marriages from decades or even a century or more in the past have all but obscured the fundamental ties between apparently unrelated people. By connecting only those who share a surname, historians miss the bulk of the kinship group. For example, to know who was a part of the Keesee kinship group, one has to study Calverts, Clardys, Greens, Cottinghams, Rutherfords, Garretts, Chappells, Hargroves, Hills, and many others. Once those ties of kinship are revealed, migration as well as settlement patterns can be examined in a new light.

Just as kinship groups were not static entities, they were also not deterministic—members of kinship groups were not passive participants. They had agency in their choice of a marriage partner, in their decisions about where to live, in their options for religious affiliation, and in their political and economic arrangements. When Thomas Keesee Sr.'s son William became a Methodist and married into the Chappell family, he chose a closer relationship with his wife's family over his own. He demonstrated this by migrating and settling close to his in-laws, even though his blood kin migrated at about the same time to similar land. And, although he still had contact with his own kin, he lived among and attended church with the kinship group to which he had shifted his loyalty. The various decisions made by antebellum southerners determined the parameters of their own group of effective kin, but life decisions were virtually always affected by their membership in a group of kin.

And, conversely, the kinship group was not a collective enterprise. The emphasis of the members was, for the most part, on individual success or gain, not on the needs of the whole as if it were some type of socialist collective. In his seminal work *The Elementary Structures of Kinship,* Claude Lévi-Strauss extended M. Mauss's theories of reciprocity. In "The Gift" ("Essai sur le don: Forme et raison de l'échange dans les sociétés archaïques"), Mauss theorized that the basis of human society was an absence of war, and, to maintain that state, groups exchanged goods and services (gifts) in a system of reciprocity. Lévi-Strauss extended that theory to include marriage as the exchange of women between groups as a way of cementing alliances. Although marriage in the antebellum South certainly was not as ritualized as in the societies Lévi-Strauss used as illustrations, the basic principle still holds — once two families have exchanged children via marriage between the two offspring, an alliance is perforce created between those two families. Since most families had more than one child, the result of the marriages of all their children is an interconnected grid of kinship between groups of families, that is, a kinship group.[49] That does not mean, however, that the needs of the group take precedence over the needs of individual members of the group; it means that members of the alliance, that is, the kinship group, privilege insiders over outsiders in many ways.

Given the membership of antebellum southerners in these kinship groups, it is impossible to truly examine either migration or settlement patterns without taking kinship into account. Even that intrepid individualist Daniel Boone, "the embodiment of American possibility," was accompanied by kin on his initial foray into the wilderness of Kentucky and brought his wife and children, members of his kinship group, and even members of his wife's kinship group to settle on the new lands. His most esteemed biographer describes Boone's life as "enmeshed in relationships of extended family."⁵⁰ The story of southern migration and the resultant settlement patterns is the story of groups rather than individuals, relocating the stereotypical rugged individual seeking "elbow room" largely to the category of myth. Telling the story completely calls for using genealogical methodology to identify groups whose dynamics were based on kinship, the locus of which, at least in antebellum southern society, was marriage—the exchange of children between families. These bonds between families formed the social capital that facilitated successful migration, settlement, prosperity, and even at times survival.

CHAPTER THREE

Kinship and Religion

[Human beings] look separate because you see them
walking about separately. But then, we are so made that
we can see only the present moment. If we could see the
past, then of course it would look different. For there
was a time when every man was part of his mother, and
(earlier still) part of his father as well, and when they
were part of his grandparents. If you could see humanity
spread out in time, as God sees it, it would look . . . like
one single growing thing—rather like a very
complicated tree. Every individual would appear
connected with every other.
—C. S. Lewis, *Mere Christianity*

The incorporation of religion into studies of the antebellum South has always been essential. Religion and church membership were major influences on individuals, on families, on communities, and on southern society as a whole. As John B. Boles has explained, the Great Revival, which swept through the South between 1800 and 1805, launched "[a]n evangelical pietism [that] came to characterize southern religion and as such contributed significantly to that perhaps amorphous outlook labeled 'the southern mind.'"[1] Combining kinship studies with investigations of religion can bolster our understanding of antebellum southern society by complicating and enriching our comprehension of religion, its intrinsic meaning in the lives of individuals, and its effects on southern culture. Kinship played a causative role in the religious lives of antebellum southerners.

Churches challenged the family as the leading organizational factor in the lives of antebellum southerners.[2] Yet in many ways church and family were often so interwoven as to be all but indistinguishable and, therefore, reinforced one another rather than vying for control of society. Churches were most often neighborhood oriented, and these neighborhoods were composed of a tangled array of kinspeople; the result was that the local congregation and the local kinship group had an overlapping constituency. Moreover, an individual's choice of religious affiliation was often based on the religious affiliation of his or her family, perpetuating the admixture and commingling of congregation and family group.

A more surprising situation revealed by my research is that the ministry of the various Protestant denominations was also tremendously interconnected by family ties, which increased the blurring of the lines between the sacred family and the secular family. Church membership can be seen, in fact, as yet another type of kinship. The individual members of a congregation consider themselves fictive kin—brothers and sisters through the shared paternity of a common God. This fictive kinship is further demonstrated through religious terminology: nuns become the "brides" of Christ and are called "sisters," they are led by a "mother superior," monks are called "brother," and priests are called "father." Baptists call their ministers "brother," and southern evangelical denominations often refer to fellow congregants as "brother" and "sister." Religious groups often refer to themselves as "children of God," and God is referred to as "our Father, who art in Heaven."

This sacred kinship, acting in combination with the secular kinship of the biological and social family, adds another overlay of connection in some instances and in others all but supplants family kinship. And because family ties and church ties are often congruent overlapping groups, it is sometimes difficult to separate the two. In antebellum southern society, the tapestry of kinship was woven throughout virtually every sphere (economics, politics, and community composition), but perhaps nowhere was it integrated as completely as in the realm of religion because of the synergy between sacred and secular kinship.

Based on my study of the Keesee kinship group, the denominational affiliation of a person's family is one of the most significant determinants of that individual's choice of denomination; that is, for antebellum southerners, an individual's choice of denominational affiliation is most often predicated on his or her parents' denominational affiliation. It is ironic that what seems to be one of the most personal of decisions might, in reality, be somewhat predetermined. Yet common sense dictates that the denominational beliefs and form of worship introduced to people as children and reinforced throughout their adolescence would become the denomination most transparent and comfortable for the adult. Although I am trying to avoid the more polemical term "indoctrination" here, the fact of the matter is that most of the "choices" made in one's life are dictated to a certain degree by culture and environment rather than rational, conscious thought. This is not to say, however, that many people did not and do not break out of these molds to make their own individual choices. If we grow up eating southern cooking, more than likely that is the type of food we will continue to eat and be most comfortable with, but this does not mean we will never try Chinese or Mexican food or that we will not make a conscious choice to find another style of cooking as our default mode. The family unit, however, powerfully combines the two most significant influences in the development of an individual: genetic predispositions and environmental influences, or, in the shorthand of modern psychology, nature and nurture.[3]

But although antebellum southerners had a *tendency* to retain the religious affiliation of their nuclear families, it was not at all unusual for some catalyst to intervene and effect a change. A clergyman's powerful preaching at a camp meeting, for example, was often a fomenter of change. An individual who was Methodist might move to an area where the only organized church was Baptist and thus might join the church at hand. Marriage, however, was probably the most common catalyst. Two people of different religious affiliations marrying created an intersection of change. In keeping with the general paternalistic environment of the antebellum South, we would perhaps expect to find that the wife was more likely to follow her husband's lead, even in such a profoundly personal issue as religion. Cornelia Pond Jones, a woman of the planter aristocracy and the subject of Lucinda H. MacKethan's *Recollections of a Southern Daughter,* changed her life-long affiliation with the Presbyterian Church to the Episcopal Church when her husband converted. In recounting the events of her life to her daughter, she explained her own conversion: "Your father having decided to leave the Presbyterian Church, I thought it best to go with him by Dr. Axson's advice. . . . This was a most important step in our life, and we have always been glad we took it, and that we had the opportunity of bringing up our children in the Church." (Dr. Axson was Cornelia's former minister, officiated at Pond's wedding to her husband about seven years previously, and was related to her by marriage.) It is fairly clear that Pond was willing to entrust the status of her immortal soul to her husband's judgment (after consulting her kinsman and minister) despite the fact that the church she was leaving had been her family's church for quite some time, although we do not know what prompted her husband's change of churches. It seems evident that Pond placed great weight on a unified front for the sake of her marriage and for her children.[4]

In another example, Methodist preacher John Haynie was baptized in 1786 as an infant in the Virginia Episcopal Church of his parents. His family moved to Tennessee when he was a boy,

> and subsequently his parents united with the Methodist Church. In his twentieth year he was married to Elizabeth Brooks. "On the 9th of August, 1809 [at the age of twenty-three]," Haynie says, "I rode out to the field to shoot some squirrels, and while trying to get a shot at one suddenly this thought struck me with force—'There is one who watches all your actions with more care than you watch that squirrel.' Instantly all my sins passed in review before me. I had at the same moment such a view of the holiness of God as I never had before. My limbs trembled; immediately I clasped my hands together and cried for mercy." He returned home in such great distress of mind that a fever ensued which threatened to cut short his life. He was at one time tempted to commit suicide. Soon thereafter while in the field on his knees in an agony of prayer he was gloriously converted. *In the same year while attending church he joined and had his wife's name put down, "as we always go the same way," he said.* He went home and told her what he had done. She was struck with conviction and about a week later was converted while the family were at prayer. In June, 1811, Haynie was licensed to preach.[5]

Husbands and wives who "always [went] the same way" in matters of religion were no doubt common, but it was not always the wife who followed the husband's lead. In Margaret Jones Bolsterli's work *A Remembrance of Eden*, Charles Lewis Bullock, an Arkansas planter, "was a strong Presbyterian but [his wife, Sara Jane Shepard] was a great Methodist. . . . [Bullock] attended the Methodist church regularly while he lived in Tennessee and when he reached Arkansas, joined Manchester Church of that denomination until he could 'do better,' as he said." (Bullock's parents were not members of any church, although his mother had been baptized in the Episcopal Church, but two cousins with whom he had a close relationship were Presbyterians, and perhaps this influence led Bullock to join the Presbyterian Church.) Later Bullock helped build a new Methodist church, which he attended with his family. Although seemingly content to attend a church of a denomination different from his chosen one, which might indicate that his religious views were not that strongly held, he was, in fact, a very religious man—his daughter recalls him having "family prayers" for the family and slaves every morning and night. Obviously, there were cases where circumstances influenced a man to join his wife's denomination rather than the other way around.[6]

The marriage of John H. Vincent and Mary Raser, discussed in Anson West's *History of Methodism in Alabama,* completes the pattern of possible permutations. Vincent, a descendant of a French Huguenot family, was born in 1798 in Pennsylvania and came to Alabama as a teenager with his family. Mary Raser was born in Philadelphia, Pennsylvania, the daughter of a sea captain who died in the West Indies when she was two and of a mother who died when Mary was ten. Mary came south with her two brothers and met Vincent through one of her brothers. Although Vincent had been raised a Presbyterian and Mary a Lutheran, they married in 1821 in Tuscaloosa County, Alabama, and then joined the Methodist Episcopal Church of Tuscaloosa, where they were involved members for many years. In 1837 they returned to Pennsylvania, where their son, also named John H. Vincent, was licensed by the Methodist Church in 1849 to exhort and in 1850 to preach. He eventually became a Methodist bishop. Another son, B. F. Vincent, also became a Methodist preacher in Pueblo, Colorado. For some reason, John H. and Mary (Raser) Vincent both surrendered the denominations of their childhoods and together became committed Methodists, launching two sons into the Methodist ministry.[7]

Drawing from the Keesee kinship group data, we find a situation similar to that of Cornelia Pond Jones. Martha Wooding Hargrove was born on 21 December 1821 in Tuscaloosa County, Alabama, the daughter of William Hargrove and Charlotte Chappell, both resolute Methodists, and she was the granddaughter of the Reverend Dudley Hargrove, a prominent Methodist minister. According to Martha's obituary, she became a member of the Methodist Church of her family when she was sixteen, but when she married she "joined her husband in the Cumberland Presbyterian church."[8] Martha's family background in Methodism could not have been more pronounced, and yet she switched denominations upon her marriage to "go the same way" as her husband and form a united family unit.

Martha's husband, Gideon Keesee, was the youngest son of Thomas Keesee Sr. and his first wife, Mary, and he was probably raised in the Cumberland Presbyterian faith of his parents. The first evidence of the Keesee family's religious affiliations are records pertaining to their arrival in Saline County, Arkansas, between 1836 and 1838, after the kinship group left Tuscaloosa and Bibb Counties, Alabama:

The Presbyterians began church work [in Saline County] in 1838, and in that year founded an organization four miles south of Benton. Rev. William Harland [*sic,* Wharton] was pastor, and Robert Calvert, Thomas Keesee Jr., and Gideon Keesee, ruling elders. The society was called "Saline Congregation," and for a time flourished, but finally went down. It was reorganized at Benton, in 1851, by Rev. John F. King, pastor, and F. Leech, Robert Calvert and John Lindsey, ruling elders.[9]

Members Thomas Keesee Jr. and Gideon Keesee were brothers, both sons of Thomas Keesee Sr., and Robert Calvert was their brother-in-law, married to their sister Mary "Polly" Keesee; Finis Leech was a brother of George Polk Keesee's second wife. The ruling elders at the time of the church's first organization were all close kin—not surprising, since it was an in-migrating group of kin that prompted the creation of the new Cumberland Presbyterian Church, an example of the frequent overlapping of kinship group and church memberships.

William Wharton, the Cumberland Presbyterian minister mentioned above, was not related to the Keesees or Calverts (at least insofar as can be determined), but his spiritual kinship with Robert Calvert was evidently as strong as if it were a blood relationship. Wharton was in Bibb County, Alabama, with the Keesees and Calverts, traveled to Saline County, Arkansas, with them, pastored their church, and ended up with Robert Calvert and kin in Robertson County, Texas. Wharton wrote his will in 1861, "commend[ing his] soul to the great Architect of the Universe, and [his] body to the hope of a glorious resurrection," and he appointed his lifelong "friend," his fellow Mason, and member of his congregation Robert Calvert as his executor. His secondary and tertiary choices for executor were "some responsible brother" selected by their church or "the three principal officers of the Masonic lodge nearest to the place of [his] domicile at the time of [his] death."[10] Wharton's decision to choose Robert Calvert to carry out the important duties for his family at the time of his death makes it clear that Robert Calvert was within Wharton's range of effective kinship, although Calvert was not a "real" relative. Wharton and Calvert's lifelong association as friends, leaders of their church, and Masons created a kinship between them, and, although it was a form of fictive kinship, its effects were robust and real to the two men.

The Masonic ties deduced from Wharton's will are indicative of yet another type of fictive kinship at work in the lives of antebellum southerners:

fraternal organizations. In almost every case, the men of the Keesee kinship group belonged to Masonic groups, usually the same lodge, and often were the founders of lodges in their new residences. In Union County, Arkansas, for example, Polk Lodge, Ancient Free & Accepted Masons (AF&AM), located in Hillsboro and organized on 7 November 1849, included the following roster of officers and charter members: "Hamilton G. Quarles, J.W.; G. W. Rutherford, Sec.; Gideon Reese [*sic*, Keesee], Treas.; H. C. Pratt, G. S. Green, M. Reese [*sic*, Keesee], W. Calvert, G. W. Murphy."[11] Milton and Gideon Keesee were brothers, William Calvert was their nephew by blood, and George W. Rutherford and George West Murphy were their nephews by marriage. Their exact relationship to Hamilton G. Quarles is unknown, but one of William Calvert's aunts was a Quarles. The Pratt and Green families were with the Keesees and Calverts in Tuscaloosa County, Alabama, moved also to Saline County, and then moved into Union County, Arkansas, with them as well. Joab Pratt was the Baptist minister who brought most of his congregation to Arkansas with him and pastored the church of which George Polk Keesee was a member. Hillary Cole Pratt—the H. C. Pratt above—was the grandfather of Mary Cole Pratt, who married one of George West Murphy's sons in 1903 in this same county. George S. Green—the G. S. Green above—was married to a granddaughter of Thomas Keesee Sr. who was also a niece of Milton and Gideon Keesee and a cousin of William Calvert. Eight men with seven different surnames founded the Masonic lodge in Union County, but all were united by ties of kinship.

Some members of the Keesee kinship group were Baptists. In December 1837, shortly after their arrival in Saline County, James A. Hicks and his wife, Elizabeth (Keesee) Hicks, joined Spring Creek Baptist Church, and seven months later, Elizabeth's father, George Polk Keesee (a son of Thomas Keesee Sr.), along with three of his other children and the father-in-law of one of his daughters, joined the same church. In 1841 a huge wagon train composed of many of the Keesees' kin and former neighbors from Alabama arrived in Saline County, Arkansas, along with their pastor, Joab B. Pratt, a Baptist minister. They settled near the Keesees and founded Philadelphia Baptist Church. In 1842 George Keesee and his family moved their membership from Spring Creek Baptist Church to join their old friends and neighbors (and, often, kin) in the new church in their neighborhood. Descendants of George Keesee are still being buried in the Philadelphia Baptist Church Cemetery.[12]

Benjamin Clardy III, usually pronounced "CLAIR-a-dee," was also part of the Keesee kinship group. (The designations I, II, and III were not used by the men named Benjamin Clardy but were adopted by researchers in order to differentiate the generations.) He was born about 1797 in Pendleton District, South Carolina, and married Thomas Keesee Sr.'s daughter Agnes about 1822 in Alabama, probably in Pickens County, which was cut from Tuscaloosa County in this time period (marriage records there are not extant for this time period).

The Clardys and the Keesees might have known each other since the colonial era. Both families have a tradition of immigrant ancestors who were Huguenots, and both lived in the same vicinity in Virginia and then moved to South Carolina shortly before 1790, George Faris Keesee along with his son Thomas to Greenville and Spartanburgh Counties and Benjamin Clardy II's family to adjacent Pendleton County (all three counties were in the Ninety-Six District of South Carolina). Deeds indicate Benjamin Clardy II owned land on the Saluda River as early as 1789. Benjamin Clardy II was also enumerated in Pendleton District, South Carolina, in 1790. George Faris Keesee was in Greenville District, South Carolina, in 1790, and his son Thomas Keesee Sr., now married and in his own household, was enumerated in Spartanburgh District, South Carolina, in 1800. Note that the county lines were changing during this period—Thomas Keesee was living on his father's farm, which he bought when his father moved to Tennessee, but the land that was in Greenville County in 1790 was in Spartanburgh County in 1800.[13] By 1817 Thomas Keesee Sr. lived on property adjacent to Richard Smith Clardy, one of Benjamin Clardy III's brothers, in Franklin County, Tennessee. Family tradition says Benjamin worked for Keesee as a farm laborer before marrying Keesee's daughter Agnes about 1822. When Thomas Keesee's family moved to Tuscaloosa and Bibb Counties, Alabama, he and Benjamin patented adjacent tracts of land on the same date. Clardy continued to follow his father-in-law when the kinship group moved to Saline County, Arkansas, in 1837. But about 1838, Benjamin Clardy—now a mature man in his forties—separated somewhat from his father-in-law; the Clardys relocated to Hot Spring County, just a few miles southwest of Saline, and in the 1840s Thomas Keesee Sr. moved into southern Arkansas, while Benjamin Clardy and family remained behind.

Now a resident of Hot Spring County, Arkansas, Benjamin Clardy donated land to establish a Baptist church in his new location.

According to research and reference given by descendants, Francois Baptist Church is . . . about five (5) miles north of Malvern. The land was owned by Benjamin Clardy and upon request of his young daughter, Jennie Clardy who asked her father to have a Baptist Church erected and a Cemetery site given, he carried out her wishes by taking his slaves and clearing four (4) acres for this purpose. Jennie passed away in 1843 and was buried in this, then new, cemetery. The slaves later on were buried in here too. Her father, Benjamin died 1875. He is also buried there.

The cemetery was given the same name as the Church, and has been kept through the church from the beginning to the present time.

With a presbytery of three men, Samuel T. Cobb, William G. Frost, and Davidson Cunningham and thirteen (13) members, they gave the Church the name Sardis. In 1859 the name was changed to Franceway, later on was spelled Francois [pronounced Franceway].[14]

Clardy's separation from the Keesee kinship group provides yet another example of how the boundaries of kinship groups constantly changed. If every individual related by kinship remained closely bound to all the other relatives, kinship groups would become unwieldy and too large to be meaningful. Instead, the boundaries were delimited by the needs and desires of individual members—they maintained connections with those who fell within their range of effective kinship at the time or created new offshoots as circumstances changed. For whatever reasons, Clardy split from the main kinship groups examined in this study. The most likely reason is his religious affiliation; since Clardy was Baptist, he might have become closer to the fictive kin of his Baptist congregation than to his wife's true kin, who were mostly Cumberland Presbyterian.

The decision of George Polk Keesee, eldest son of Thomas Keesee Sr. and Clardy's brother-in-law, to remain in Saline County when other kin left might have also been motivated, at least in part, by the difference in religious affiliation. Like Clardy, Keesee was Baptist and formed a close association with other Baptists from Tuscaloosa and Bibb Counties who moved into Saline County, especially after his children intermarried with fellow congregants. A secondary reason for both Clardy and Keesee might have been a conscious decision to abandon the life of planters on the make. Unlike other members of the kinship group who constantly moved to the cotton frontier, seeking wealth through cotton and slavery, both Clardy and Keesee chose to remain in the same area when their relatives moved on. Although they were both slave owners, they were evidently content with their status as yeoman farmers, raising cotton and other crops with only a few slaves.

Clardy's brother-in-law William Keesee, the sixth of eight children born to Thomas Keesee Sr. and his wife, Mary, was—or became—Methodist. He was probably raised in the Cumberland Presbyterian faith of his parents and converted at the time of his marriage. Born in 1809 in Tennessee, he moved as a boy with his family to Tuscaloosa County, Alabama. In 1828 in Tuscaloosa County he married Mary Jane Chappell, born in 1810 in Tennessee, the daughter of Robert Wooding Chappell and Mary Tittle. The Chappells, like the Keesees, were in Halifax County, Virginia, during the colonial and early republic eras and migrated to Tennessee in the early 1800s. By the 1820s they too were in Tuscaloosa County, Alabama, where Mary Jane married William Keesee. Her sister Charlotte "Lottie" Chappell married William Dudley Hargrove, the son of Dudley Hargrove, a Methodist minister, in 1820, probably in Pickens County, which was carved out of Tuscaloosa County that same year.[15] William and Lottie Hargrove's daughter Martha Wooding Hargrove married William Keesee's brother Gideon, mentioned above.[16] In other words, Gideon Keesee married his brother William's niece by marriage, the niece of Gideon's sister-in-law.

But whereas Gideon's Methodist wife converted to Cumberland Presbyterianism when she married him, William Keesee became Methodist, probably when he married into the Methodist Chappells and Hargroves. In 1837, when his own family moved to Arkansas, William instead migrated with his wife's family to Washington County in the Republic of Texas. It could be argued that the religious ties William and Mary (Chappell) Keesee had in common with her family trumped his ties to his own family, none of whom were Methodist.

During the early years, when Texas was part of Mexico, Anglo settlers were forbidden to practice Protestant religions, although there were sporadic incursions by ministers of Protestant denominations. Macum Phelan, in his *History of Early Methodism in Texas, 1817–1866*, claims that William Stevenson, a Methodist minister, was "the first preacher to enter Texas."[17] In 1837, just after Texas independence, a host of members of the Keesee kinship group—more properly, perhaps, members of the Chappell kinship group, which included an offshoot of the Keesee kinship group—moved to Washington and Austin Counties, Texas (part of the original Austin Colony). The leader of the kinship group was Robert Wooding Chappell, whose daughter was married to William Keesee, son of Thomas Keesee Sr.[18] Chappell and Keesee both entered claims for land in the new republic. Certificate 68, issued to William Keesee on 5 July 1838, stated that Keesee "appeared before us the board of land commissioners, for [Washington County], and proved to our satisfaction that he arrived in this Republic, subsequent to the Declaration of independence, and previous to the 1st October 1837, that he is a married man and entitled to twelve hundred and eighty acres of land to be surveyed after the first day of August 1838."[19] Of little relevance but of interest is the fact that William Keesee transacted the business of buying other land on Christmas Day, which might hint that antebellum southerners' feelings about the holiday differed from our modern sensibilities in some ways.

Despite the assertions of some southern historians that those who migrated to the cotton frontier were usually younger men escaping the tight bonds of family or, as Joan E. Cashin asserts, that "individual nuclear families became isolated on the frontier" and that "women were left without the sustenance of their female kinfolk," here is yet another example of a family patriarch leading the move of a large kinship group, replete with female kinsfolk, which my study shows to be the norm. Robert Wooding Chappell was about fifty-five when he moved to Texas with his large extended family—and he even brought his elderly widowed mother with him.[20]

There was activity by Methodists in this area even before the Chappells and Keesees arrived, but the kinship group participated in religious life from their earliest years of settlement in Washington County. An Austin County deed dated 26 April 1839 records the purchase of some land on the "[north] bank of Piney Creek below the campground" to the "Trustees of the Methodist Episcopal Church (John Wesley, Henry James Stephison, *Robert W. Chappell,* Henry Metthews, Ralph Graves, Junr., Josiah Crosby, Wm. Gant, Edward S. Coblee, and Madison M. Davis."[21]

In 1843 there was a "great camp-meeting" at Cedar Creek, probably on Robert Wooding Chappell's land. This meeting

marked the beginning of the rise of the church there, which was destined soon to become one of the most important appointments in Texas. Among the first settlers of that community were the families of Stevenson, Hubert, *Chappell, Hargrove, Kesee* [sic], Reavill, King, and others, all Methodists. The great camp-meeting of 1843 commenced at Cedar Creek, the then name of the place [near what would later be the town of Chappell Hill], on October 19. There were eleven preachers present, among whom were Clark, presiding elder, [John Wesley] Kenney, [Chauncey] Richardson, [Robert] Alexander, [John] Haynie, [Orceneth] Fisher, [Josiah W.] Whipple, [John W.] DeVilbiss and [Homer S.] Thrall. Nearly all of the giants of that day were there, and of the preaching 'we have never heard it excelled,' says Thrall.[22]

Cedar Hill, later supplanted by the nearby town of Chappell Hill when it came into existence, was often referred to as a "center" of Methodism for the area. When the eighth session of the Texas Conference of the Methodist Episcopal Church met from 29 December 1847 through 3 January 1848, "[t]he sessions were held in the second story of Father Chappell's new house, three miles distant from Cedar Creek."[23]

The kinship group continued to worship in the Methodist faith and along with others set up the Chappell Hill Male and Female Institute in 1850 on land donated by Jacob and Mary Elizabeth (Hargrove) Haller, a granddaughter of Robert Wooding Chappell. William Keesee was a member of the first board of trustees for the institute and, along with nephews Alexander Hargrove and Jacob Haller, was also a trustee of the church.[24] After the Methodist Church acquired another adjacent lot in 1852, the female students were housed separately in a new building, and the school was reorganized as Chappell Hill College. In 1853 a correspondent reported that the school was prospering, with "about ninety pupils," and that a "new church [was] expected to be completed before the end of the year."[25] Although the school's original charter stipulated a nondenominational school, the Methodist Episcopal Church, South took control of the school in 1854. Soule University was established in Chappell Hill in 1856, and the female half of the former institute became the Chappell Hill Female College.[26]

In 1853 a membership list for Chappell Hill Methodist Church registered fifty-two white male members, fifty-six white female members, and eighty-nine "Coloured Members." Of the fifty-two white male members, the nine listed here were close kin:

William Keesee (a widower, who served as class leader and steward); son-in-law of Robert Wooding Chappell

George W. [sic, Marion] Keesee; son of William and Mary Jane (Chappell) Keesee; grandson of Robert Wooding Chappell

Robert W[ooding] Keesee; son of William and Mary Jane (Chappell) Keesee; grandson of Robert Wooding Chappell

Thomas [Milton] Keesee (probationer); son of William and Mary Jane (Chappell) Keesee; grandson of Robert Wooding Chappell

Gideon Keesee (probationer); son of William and Mary Jane (Chappell) Keesee; grandson of Robert Wooding Chappell

William Keesee Jr. (probationer); son of William and Mary Jane (Chappell) Keesee; grandson of Robert Wooding Chappell

J. A. Hargrove (single and a steward); son of William Dudley and Charlotte (Chappell) Hargrove; grandson of Robert Wooding Chappell

James Chappell; son of Robert Wooding Chappell

Six other members were slaves belonging to William Keesee: Cubit (who "drinks"), Franky, Jimmy, Sarah, Joe, and Missouri (probationer).[27]

Although Chappell Hill also had Baptist, Episcopal, and Presbyterian churches during the antebellum era, none of the brief histories mention any of the familiar names of the Chappell-Keesee kinship group except for a mention of Robert W. Hargrove, one of the sons of William Dudley Hargrove and a grandson of Robert Wooding Chappell, who was a trustee of the Episcopal Church in 1851.[28] This reinforces the argument that the secular and the sacred family were often all but indistinguishable from one another because of their synergistic qualities. Moreover, it demonstrates that the Chappells, Keesees, and Hargroves in Washington County, Texas, had choices about which church to attend but most often were influenced by kinship in their decisions about religion.

This tangled conflation of church and family is wonderfully illustrated in William Oates Ragsdale's *They Sought a Land*. Ragsdale describes the founding of the Pisgah community in Pope County, Arkansas, by two groups of members of the Associate Reformed Presbyterian (ARP) Church, most of whom were Scottish or Scotch-Irish. The families in these groups "were remarkably homogeneous" and were "bound by many ties of family kinship." In fact, "[s]ome of the families had known each other and had ties before they came to America, for the most part in the eighteenth century. Here, their kinship lines became inextricably mixed as a result of the families' long close association on the Carolina and other frontiers." Over a thirty-year period, the church members, who had formed a dissenting sect after 1789, emigrated from the historical center of the ARP Church— adjoining counties on the border of North Carolina and South Carolina— and joined friends, relations, and other members of their church in Arkansas. Although their major motivations centered on acquiring fertile new lands in sufficient quantities to ensure their children's material comfort, their desire to form a community composed of their sacred kin was a strong factor in the communal migration. As Ragsdale puts it, they wanted to "build a community that would foster the temporal and spiritual well-being of their children."[29]

However, although Ragsdale had centered his analysis on the groups' shared religion, he could just as easily have based it on kinship. The shared church denomination was the organizational center of the move and of the resultant new community, but shared kinship was the foundational element in the groups' communal cohesion and was a direct and causative factor in the creation of the clannish congregation. What Ragsdale describes is the prototypical migration pattern of kinship groups, couched as religiously motivated rather than driven by the concerns and priorities of kinship. In this recursive and self-reinforcing process, the sacred family reinforced the secular family while the secular family reinforced the sacred family, making the constituent substances of the group opaque and virtually inseparable. But, whether one regards religion or kinship as the primary motivation, the key here is that group migration with kin, whether fictive or by blood, provided the support and social capital that enabled migrants to survive and to succeed.

In summary, Thomas Keesee Sr., a committed member of the Cumberland Presbyterian Church, had eight children with his first wife. Of those eight (five sons and three daughters), there was one daughter, Jane (Keesee) Jenkins, and one son, Milton Keesee, about whom no information about religious affiliation could be found. Among the other six children, three followed their father's training to remain Cumberland Presbyterians, two became Baptist, and one became a Methodist.

The example above is about average, based on data compiled for the entire Keesee kinship group: children were inclined to follow their parents' lead in their choice of religious denomination, but a strong religious experience could lead an individual to another denomination. Marriage served as the most significant nexus of change of religious affiliation. Although there might be a slight tendency for wives to follow their husbands' lead in religious choices, there were so many factors involved in that decision that a reliable prediction cannot be made. Furthermore, since kin tended to stick with kin, even as members of a particular denomination tended to stick together, in most cases these two tendencies acted together to create a pattern of interconnecting relationships among secular and sacred kin and blur the boundaries between the two.

Another way of examining the contours of connection between the sacred and the secular family in antebellum southern society is to examine the clergy of the various Protestant denominations in the antebellum South. On the one hand, as Christine Leigh Heyrman asserts, the preachers of most denominations "bespoke the evangelical conviction that the obligations to kin must give way before duty to God. No other claim could take precedence over saving oneself and warning others of the wrath to come— to fall under the sway of family attachments was to invite spiritual disaster."[30] Ministers gave their spiritual mission a higher priority than the importance placed on family commitments by most citizens of their society. Instead of plowing a field or harvesting a crop, a preacher was often riding a circuit, studying his Bible in preparation for a sermon, or spending the Sabbath in service to his congregation instead of with his family, playing the traditional role of southern patriarch. An investigation of this disjunction between a man's responsibilities as head of a family and as a clergyman would be another way of opening a window of understanding about kinship and about gender relations in the antebellum South. A minister's wife had to take on many of the roles normally assigned to husbands, while husbands were excused, to some degree, for making service to their God a higher priority than their obligations to their families, at least in theory.

On the other hand, bonds of secular kinship within a religious community often connected preachers to each other. An astonishing degree of intermarriage created a separate layer of kinship among the ministry. In much the same way that children grow up with a predisposition to follow the religion of their parents, ministers' sons were often disposed both by temperament and training to follow in their fathers' footsteps, and, when they married, it was not at all unusual for them to find a wife from among the daughters of other men of the cloth—women already acclimated to the lifestyle of the ministry.

In her study of Baptist and Methodist clergymen over three generations in 1800s Virginia, Beth Barton Schweiger found and documented this tendency of preachers' sons to follow their fathers into the ministry. She writes:

Many [young Virginians] who entered the antebellum ministry did so with the blessing of their fathers, who were preachers themselves. The tendency of

some Virginia clans to become identified with the ministry for several generations increased over the course of the nineteenth century. Where one-third
of the men ordained before 1850 were pastors' sons, half were preachers' sons
by the end of the century. At least twenty-eight father-son pairs appear
among the pastors studied here, in addition to six families in which more than
one brother became a pastor. Joseph E. Potts, ordained in 1853, saw all four
of his sons ordained into the Methodist ministry. His brother, too was a
pastor. . . .

    The sons of pastors grew up in homes ruled by piety and the rhythm of the
church year. Children observed firsthand the trials of the ministry—calls
in the middle of the night, disputes over doctrine and church policy that
dissolved into personal quarrels, the often-demeaning dependence on the
congregation for a salary. Yet they also knew the peculiar rewards—annual
"poundings," when congregations showed their appreciation with barrels of
food and clothing, the esteem in which preachers were often held, the security that grew out of pastors' assurance that their work was significant.
Preachers' sons grew up with fathers who embodied a masculine piety in a society where religious sentiment was often associated with women. Their fathers also knew, often personally, professors and senior pastors who might
smooth the young candidate's path.[31]

Samuel King fits the mold of Schweiger's clergymen. He was born in
North Carolina in 1775, the son of a Revolutionary War veteran, and became one of the men instrumental in the founding of the Cumberland Presbyterian denomination. His parents were Presbyterian, and King was raised
in that faith. He became a Presbyterian minister and was one of the three
ministers who met in Dickson County, Tennessee, on 4 February 1810 to
form a new presbytery breaking away from the mainstream Presbyterian
Church over a disagreement about the educational requirements of ministers and other matters of doctrine. King, along with the Reverend Finis
Ewing, the Reverend Samuel McAdow, and the newly ordained Ephraim
McLean, five licensed preachers, and eight candidates "were the *fathers* of
the Cumberland Presbyterian Church."[32]

    King married Anna Dixon, and they had ten children, five sons and five
daughters. One daughter married the Reverend Daniel Patton, one of the
Cumberland Presbyterian ministers who came together to create Barnett
Presbytery at Lexington, Missouri, in 1828. Patton first met his future father-in-law when he was eleven years old, and he related the story many

years later in his history of the Cumberland Presbyterian Church in Missouri. He wrote that Samuel King "was preaching in my father's house, in Bedford County, Tennessee, to a crowded company, when my father professed faith in the blessed Savior. I saw father passing through the crowd clapping his hands and praising God, and many others doing the same."[33]

King had three sons who became Cumberland Presbyterian ministers like their father. One was the Reverend Finis Ewing King, named after Finis Ewing, another of the "fathers" of the Cumberland Presbyterian Church. Finis E. King came to Texas from Missouri in 1846 and became the minister at Shiloh Cumberland Presbyterian Church in Ellis County, Texas, the same church where Thomas Keesee Sr.'s son Thomas Keesee Jr. and his family were members from the time of their arrival in Ellis County in the 1850s to the present day.[34]

My genealogical research uncovered an interesting sidelight: Thomas Keesee Jr., a member of Shiloh Cumberland Presbyterian Church of Ellis County, was my great-great-great-great-grandfather's brother, while the founders of that church were the Billingsleys, who had lived just north of the Keesees (at that time in Sumner County, Tennessee) in the Cumberland region of Kentucky at the time of the Cane Ridge Revival and of the creation of the Cumberland Presbyterian Church. These Billingsleys who arrived in Ellis County via Missouri along with their kin, the Pattons, were the direct ancestors of James L. Billingsley, whom I married in 1966 in Arkansas. Over 150 years ago, our kin knew each other, went to church together, and were buried together. His direct line moved down into Hamilton County, Texas, while my branch of Keesees never left Arkansas.

The Reverend Samuel King had a nephew named Robert McGee King, born in Sumner County, Tennessee, in 1812, who also became a Cumberland Presbyterian minister. Robert McGee King was the son of Samuel's brother William King and was orphaned as a boy. His father's sister and her husband, John Bell, raised him. Two of John Bell's daughters married Cumberland Presbyterian ministers. Furthermore, two of Samuel King's brothers-in-law, James Farr and William McGee, were also Cumberland Presbyterian ministers. When Robert McGee King's first wife died, he married Sarah H. Braly, the daughter of a Cumberland Presbyterian minister.[35]

The authors of *A People Called Cumberland Presbyterian* describe the problems leading up to the split between the Presbyterian and the Cumberland Presbyterian Churches. In relating this series of precipitating

events, an analysis of the complex kinship ties among the major players in
the religious-political drama is instrumental to a comprehensive understanding of the fissures and alliances. "The Ewings, McLeans, Davidsons,
and Brevards," all actively engaged in Presbyterian Church matters around
1800 in Tennessee and Kentucky, "were related through a series of intermarriages." The complex genealogical chart accompanying the narrative
illustrates the interlocking nature of sacred and secular kinship.[36]

Dudley Hargrove, a member of the Keesee kinship group, was a licensed
local preacher in the Methodist Episcopal Church when he moved with his
family from Georgia to Tuscaloosa County, Alabama, in 1818. One of his
first actions was organizing a local Methodist church at or near his new
homesite. In 1819 the Quarterly Conference of the Tuscaloosa Circuit sub-
mitted his name to the Tennessee Annual Conference

> as a suitable person to be elected and ordained a local deacon. In the order of
> the regular business of that session of the Tennessee Conference that recom-
> mendation from the Tuskaloosa Circuit was presented, and the questions,
> "Shall Dudley Hargrove be elected and ordained a deacon?" . . . [Dudley Har-
> grove] was possessed of an unblemished character so far as his general char-
> acter was concerned, and [he] had endowments and attainments sufficient to
> qualify him for the position he sought, but it was a fact, and the fact was made
> known, that [Hargrove] was a slave-holder. . . . From its organization in the
> latter part of 1812 . . . the Tennessee Conference was pronounced in its posi-
> tion on the subject of slavery as it existed in the United States, and a number
> of its leading members were bitterly opposed to slave-traders and slave-
> owners holding office in the Church, or exercising the prerogatives of the
> ministry. The presentation of [Hargrove and other slaveholding men] for po-
> sition and office in the Methodist ministry made an issue and inaugurated a
> conflict. . . . The Conference decided by a majority of at least three not to elect
> Hargrove to deacon's orders . . . because [he was a] slave-holder.

Sixteen men signed a protest denouncing the decision "as oppressively severe in itself and ruinous in its consequences, and [they] disapprove[d] of
the *principle* as contrary to and in violation of the order and discipline of
[their] church."[37]

When the Hargroves moved into newly created Pickens County, Alabama, in 1820, Dudley and his son Daniel J. "immediately . . . had a
Methodist Society organized," known as Hargrove's Church. Dudley Hargrove died in 1823, never receiving the Tennessee Annual Conference's

confirmation. After his father's death, Daniel Hargrove remained in the area and served the church as class leader, steward, and trustee until his death in 1869, and his son, the Reverend Robert Kennon Hargrove, became a Methodist bishop about 1881. Dudley Hargrove was also a cousin of William McKendree, an early bishop in the Methodist Church.[38] Another of his sons, William Dudley Hargrove, married Charlotte "Lottie" Chappell in Pickens County, Alabama, and he and his family moved to Chappell Hill, Washington County, Texas, where they were staunch supporters of the Methodist Church as related above.

All of these examples make the effects of kinship on religion abundantly clear and complicate any analysis of religious history. Kinship was a causative factor in religious choices, and, in some ways, religious choices effected kinship alliances. Even a cursory examination of the kin relationships among ministers' families makes a clear and convincing argument that the clergy were bound together as much by ties of secular kinship as they were by ties of sacred kinship. Clergymen might have privileged their religious duties above their earthly families, but at the same time they recreated bonds of kinship among families of clergy.

Each of these cases is illustrative of the overlapping bonds between sacred and secular kinship. Just as an individual's default choice of religious denomination was strongly influenced by that of his parents and family, so was a man's choice of the ministry for a profession influenced by his father's example. In the antebellum South, where the marketplace of available professions was limited, the ministry was a popular choice for "young men who intended to make a living with their heads, not their hands," as Schweiger writes.[39]

Kinship was the foundation of virtually every aspect of antebellum southern society, and its entanglement in the Protestant religious denominations that dominated the area was a strong one. Yet the role of kinship is often ignored; it is akin to the oxygen in the air we breathe — essential, always present, but taken for granted and seldom acknowledged or analyzed in discourse. The evidence here amply illuminates the causative role of kinship ties in antebellum southern religious life. Just as kinship groups moved together, they joined churches together, mainly influenced by their families. Moreover, their joint membership in a common denomination reinforced kinship ties, just as kinship ties reinforced joint membership in a common denomination. These connections and insights, however, can be traced and brought to the surface only by understanding the nature of kinship, using the theory of kinship to comprehend how antebellum southerners experienced kinship, and by applying genealogical methodology to reveal the underlying structure of kinship ties. Scholars can add a richer texture to their analyses of southern society if they will only deepen their understanding of religion to include kinship's role.

CHAPTER FOUR

Kinship's Role in Economic and Political Power

No man can know exactly where he is going unless
he knows exactly where he has been and exactly
how he arrived at his present place.
—Maya Angelou

When Robert Calvert was elected county judge in 1846 for the first of two terms, he was forty-four years old, a successful planter, and close to the pinnacle of his economic and political success—a success largely bolstered and facilitated by his extensive family ties. Moving to Saline County, Arkansas, in 1837, soon after the county and state were created, the Keesee kinship group built a moderate political and economic power base at the local level. They used their increasing wealth to further their political power and their political power to increase their wealth largely by using kinship links to their advantage. Although some of these men may have prospered without those kinship links, the synergistic relationship between kinship and political or economic activity is bountifully evident in their lives; moreover, the connection of kinship to political, economic, and social influence is not unique to the men in the Keesee family. (Although I have little doubt that women made contributions to the success of their husbands and to their families, most of their contributions are undocumented, and they had virtually no political or economic power; thus, the discussion here refers exclusively to men.) Any fully realized comprehension of political and economic power in the antebellum South compels us to incorporate the effects of kinship into our analyses of these topics.

This chapter addresses first the development of kinship networks in the American South from the colonial through the antebellum era, with particular emphasis on their role in political and economic spheres. I argue that the scope of that role was undiminished in the South during the antebellum era. A system of plantation agriculture based on slavery in the South encouraged the retention of a rural, agricultural, but market-oriented society in which kinship groups retained their power when other social, political, and economic institutions failed to develop apace. Second, a discussion of the roles and ramifications of marriage vis-à-vis family alliances informs the discussion of kin network development. The focus on the Keesee kinship group then shifts to Robert Calvert, one of Thomas Keesee Sr.'s sons-in-law. I present his experiences as illustrative of the interaction of kinship with politics and economics in the lives of antebellum southerners, particularly among planter families.

Kinship's role in shaping political and economic power has long been recognized in the South, dating to the earliest years of the colonial era. Because kinship's role in gaining and holding political, economic, and social control has long been recognized by historians of the South, the historiography on this topic is particularly rich. However, Bernard Bailyn, in his seminal study *Voyagers to the West,* found that a little less than half of Scottish immigrants and only about 20 percent of English immigrants entered the American colonies as part of any kind of family group. Although Bailyn was using statistics from a specific interval of time, he considered the figures to be fairly representative of the American immigration experience as a whole. Bailyn also points out the gender inequalities in the statistics: "Among the English, nine times as many males as females traveled alone; among the Scots, only twice as many." Also, most of the immigrant family units of any kind were overwhelmingly either nuclear in composition or conjugal (husband and wife) rather than extended family groups. Bailyn summarized by stating that "[t]he emigration was largely a movement of isolated individuals, but it included numerous families," although women and children were most often migrating in family units, and that most of the family units were "small" and "uncomplicated in structure."[1]

His thesis suggesting that kin groups were not a major portion of American immigrants is supported in *Robert Cole's World,* a case study of one English Catholic family that migrated to St. Mary's County in 1652.[2] Using Cole's plantation account and probate record as a foundation, Lois Green Carr, Russell R. Menard, and Lorena S. Walsh illuminate significant aspects of early colonial life and, not surprisingly, find little evidence of kin networks in the nascent colony, although "[t]his is not to say that settlers failed to recognize even quite distant kin links when they were present."

Moreover, despite the apparent absence of local kin, the wealthy "cosmopolitan gentry" of the lower Western Shore of Maryland were nevertheless connected via "ties of trade, kin, and friendship extending beyond the limited, parochial environs of southern Maryland."[3]

Their study also reveals that the *absence* of nearby kin had its own consequences. One result was more sizable property settlements for widows: they "were accorded an influential role in managing the estate [of the deceased husband] and in bringing up the children" given the general lack of nearby male kin to step into the breach. Another consequence was a greater reliance on nonblood relationships. Robert Cole, for example, arranged for two of his close friends and neighbors to see to his children and his plantation after his death, although a cousin in London was directed to see to his affairs there. Carr, Menard, and Walsh point out that Cole was not atypical, given the short life expectancy of early colonials: "In the absence of kin, the burden of supporting, supervising, and educating a good proportion of the first generation of children born in the region fell on friends, neighbors, and local officials."[4]

In other words, during the earliest times of settlement, operational kin networks were present, but they were attenuated and played their part mainly in a transcolonial and transatlantic setting rather than being confined to small neighborhoods. New immigrants to the sparsely populated British colonies were geographically separated from their existing kinship groups and had not yet had enough time to build new interlocking affiliations within their new communities. However, ties of kinship were still present in their lives, although relatives were often either elsewhere in the colonies or still in Great Britain.

But while I agree with Bailyn, Carr, Menard, and Walsh that kinship groups were not nearly as influential or dense as they later became, the fact that Bailyn found that almost half of Scottish immigrants and even as many as 20 percent of English immigrants traveled as part of family groups nevertheless speaks forcefully to the significance of kinship for immigrants. Moreover, a scrutiny of the demographics of his immigrants, using genealogical methodology and with kinship as its focus, would no doubt reveal more kin links than were apparent from the records he used. Bailyn, like many other historians, based his conclusions about family units on the self-reporting of family ties or on the reporting of bureaucrats who had no reason to delve into links beyond the nuclear unit and probably focused on surname matching. Whether or not the wife in one family was a first cousin or sister to the husband in a second family was probably seen as irrelevant. Without employing genealogical methodology, the modern researcher has no real insights into extranuclear family ties among early immigrants to America. However, the fact that so many of the immigrants were single males is also a significant factor in lower rates of kin numbers among those setting out for the Americas, although it is not beyond possibility that at least some of the single men were kinsmen of other immigrating individuals or family groups.

Over the course of time, however, society in the colony of Maryland developed, and the initial generation, with its overwhelming proportion of men and high mortality rates, gave way to a longer-lived native-born population with a much more balanced ratio of males and females. Carr, Menard, and Walsh report that "[a]s children born in the colony came of age and formed families of their own, households were bound together through increasingly dense kinship networks." This finding coincides with assertions in previous chapters: marriage is the nexus of kinship, and since people usually married someone nearby (which ultimately included relatives), most areas eventually became saturated with kin. Carr, Menard, and Walsh further argue that the "developments [of kinship networks] had a profound impact on wealth distribution and inheritance, on group consciousness among the great planters, and on public life in the colony." This greater cohesion and social consciousness of a gentry class "transformed public life as a small group of 'First Families' assumed the responsibility (and captured the benefit) of government at both the local and provincial levels."[5] The creation of kinship connections through marriage was also one of the strategies employed by politically excluded Catholics seeking to strengthen their influence. By the beginning of the 1700s, Maryland, like the rest of colonial America, was a dramatically changed place.[6] The growth of networks of kin played a part in effecting those changes, including the prominence of kinship groups at all levels of economic and political life. This was not a new phenomenon, however, as much as it was a reestablishment of old ways—dense kinship networks had long been a part of the European societies in which the American colonists originated.[7]

During the colonial era, the influence and pervasiveness of kinship networks were not confined to the South. In *The Minutemen and Their World*, Robert A. Gross describes a muster of revolutionary troops in Concord:

> The muster was almost a family reunion. Fathers and sons, uncles and nephews, brothers, cousins, and in-laws often enlisted in the same units. All were

joined together not so much by a chain of command as by a complex network of kinship. When Colonel Barrett issued general orders, they were transmitted through a son and son-in-law, both captains, to a second son and a brother, both ensigns, down to yet another son and nephew, both corporals, and ultimately to several other nephews in the ranks. . . . Indeed, the roster of the Minutemen made an intricate genealogical chart. The two companies embraced ten sets of brothers, ten of first cousins, ten of uncles and nephews, and at least four of brothers-in-law. Filial duty and family loyalty thus reinforced a soldier's obligation to follow orders.[8]

Even in military life, another example of a political power structure, kinship groups were extraordinarily active. These ties of kinship no doubt contributed to a lessening of friction between the various ranks—a soldier would tend to have a higher degree of trust in and loyalty to a superior officer who was also his brother or first cousin. Moreover, family connections also probably enhanced an individual's ability to attain higher rank.

The impact of kinship on political, social, and economic power was strikingly similar throughout the colonies. Gross also found that in Concord, political leadership was often passed down to sons; almost half the selectmen were the sons of selectmen, for example: "Between 1750 and 1780, eight Barretts and in-laws held 35 per cent of the available positions as selectmen and representatives." The age at first election to local office was six years older for men without officeholding fathers than for sons of previous leaders.[9] Daniel Scott Smith asserts the same for Hingham, Massachusetts: "During the second half of [the 1700s] . . . stability in the social structure, especially in the tendency for sons to succeed fathers in economic and political position, showed no signs of weakening; indeed, in the decades before the Revolution, these measures of intergenerational continuity were considerably stronger than they had been in the seventeenth century."[10]

Daniel Blake Smith's research uncovered a similar experience in the Chesapeake by the mid-1700s. By then, he argues, "[a]n elaborate cousinry developed, which offered important marital, economic, and—at least among the elite—political opportunities."[11] This concept is reinforced in Merrill D. Peterson's *Thomas Jefferson and the New Nation*. Even though Peterson's thrust is intellectually rather than socially oriented, passing remarks in his text make the importance of kinship ties and power explicit; for example, "the structure of politics in Virginia consolidated power in a close-knit gentry class. . . . The House of Burgesses [has been described] as one huge cousinship. . . . Jefferson . . . was a member of the club and could

always count half a dozen or more blood relations at the Capitol." Allan
Kulikoff's research confirms this connection between blood and politics
and reveals political generational continuity in Maryland and in Virginia in
the early eighteenth century. In just one of his examples of the significance
of kinship to political power, Kulikoff reports that "[j]ustices, sheriffs, and
assemblymen formed an almost hereditary caste by the mid–eighteenth
century." Moreover, he describes the emergence of gentry and yeoman
classes and the need, "[o]nce gentlemen won political dominance, . . .
[to] secure legitimacy . . . by establishing an intricate web of social and political relations with poorer yeoman planters." In *The Price of Nationhood*,
Jean B. Lee found that "by the third generation, greater longevity and
intermarriage among daughters and sons of elite families had created a self-
perpetuating squirearchy able to pass its political power, in addition to its
status, from one generation to the next." [12]

The foregoing data demonstrate the extent to which historians have long
recognized that kinship played a large role in social, political, and economic
relations during the colonial era. Political dynasties were the norm, and the
web of family relationships assuaged interclass conflict, mitigating tensions
that might have been expected to arise in unequal power relationships
throughout colonial American society. Although one might predict tension
and conflict between typical elite planters and poorer yeoman farmers based
on their disparate status and political philosophies, that perceived potential
for conflict is greatly diminished when one uncovers the family relationships connecting the two groups; instead of conflict, the planter elites were
able to assist their poorer relations in a variety of ways, and the less wealthy
yeomen offered political support to their wealthier relations. The suspi-
cion and mistrust normally existing between the two economic classes was
ameliorated when planter elites were brothers to or first cousins sharing a
common set of grandparents with the yeoman farmers, especially when the
yeoman kinsmen aspired to become elite planters themselves. And, as
noted above, military power tensions for Concord's Revolutionary troops
were at least partially allayed by the family connections up and down the
chain of command. [13]

In the antebellum period, there is some evidence that in the Northeast,
where more urbanization and stronger, more organized institutions outside
the family existed, the power of kinship groups diminished during the nineteenth century. As Daniel Scott Smith explains, "The operative kinship
mentality of eighteenth-century Yankees . . . was intense and focused nearly

exclusively on children. This peculiar, intense, but truncated orientation toward kin before 1800 paved the way for the shift toward individualism during the nineteenth century." But while there was increasing urbanization in the North, the South retained its rural, agricultural nature as well as its dependence on kinship networks as the main organizational institution of life.[14] The bonds of southern families continued to extend well beyond the nuclear family, and their institutions—governmental and economic as well as social—failed to develop at the same pace as did institutions in other regions of the county, leaving kinship groups in firm control of most aspects of society. The question of how big a role the "Puritan mentality" or Max Weber's "Protestant Ethic" and "Spirit of Capitalism" played in differentiating the North from the South is an interesting topic but one deserving a larger forum than can be presented here.

For the slaveholding planters, who used the aggregate power and wealth of kinship groups to advance their own success, living in a slave-based society buttressed that power and wealth through the ownership of human property; the population of southern slaves continued to increase, concomitantly increasing the capital of the planters. Networks of white planter families used their control and ownership of ever-increasing networks of slave families to strengthen their control of southern society. Moreover, these kinship groups, which had been coalescing since the colonial era, burgeoned in a geometric progression as existing networks of kin continued to extend themselves through the intermarriages of their members.

The role of marriage in the creation of kinship groups is one of those concepts, like kinship itself, that seems so self-evident as to be taken for granted, but as scholars of history, we must take care to define and clarify—to deconstruct, if you will—each element in a particular society's development. Throughout this book, marriage is stressed as the central event in creating kinship for the white antebellum southerners under discussion. An examination of their economic and political lives demonstrates the significance of marriage. Not only did it serve as the basis for the creation of kinship networks by linking groups of families through marriages and producing children who enlarged and perpetuated these linkages, it also linked groups of families to other groups of families through marriages between members of two specific families within each group. Within the Keesee kinship group, for example, the marriages of Robert Calvert to Mary Keesee and Mary Calvert to Milton Keesee brought the Keesee family a close association with the Hill family, although the Keesees and the Hills were only linked by their mutual kinship to the Calverts rather than through any intermarriage between them or any mutual grandchildren. As Peter W. Bardaglio has written, "Marriage . . . was less a personal matter involving the private emotions between two individuals than an event that brought together two families and promoted the ties between them."[15]

But the most significant effect of marriage within the context of this chapter is that it also enhanced a man's success in the political and economic arenas by his acquisition of his wife's property, status, and connections. Legally, a marriage for the most part merged the husband and wife into one civil being. Both Blackstone's *Commentaries* (1766) and James Kent's *Commentaries on American Law* (1826–30) make this point: "By marriage, the husband and wife are one person in law"; and "'the legal effects of marriage' were deducible from the common law principle making husband and wife 'one person.'" James Wilson further explained that "a wife's 'legal existence' was 'consolidated' into her husband [and that] almost all other legal consequences of marriage depended on this principle."[16]

How do you define marriage after all? There can be little doubt that marriage for antebellum southerners may very well have been about love, affection, security, protection, or any number of private and emotional issues. Legally, however, marriage was a public matter largely about the protection and transmission of property and was, as Hendrik Hartog writes in his *Man and Wife in America*, "a political institution, signaled by the public power of husbands."[17] Through the creation of a legal infrastructure, antebellum southerners erected social scaffolding influenced by an atmosphere of patriarchy and gender bias in complete accord with the beliefs of the dominant society of that time. The codification of laws about marriage and civil identity had the effect of consolidating and passing on wealth to a set of legal heirs. For the most part, the heirs were the socially and officially sanctioned product of legalized, civil marriages.

As Hartog points out, there was, of course, more to being married than creating heirs and passing on wealth and property. He writes that "we need to remember how important being married was in nineteenth-century America: important in terms of the labor of maintaining a household, important as a public matter of being recognized as a competent (male) adult, important as a defense against the emotional isolation that always threatened in mobile America." But, although he couches these advantages in terms of being married, I would shift his emphasis slightly to assert these as important aspects of *being part of a family*, which is, naturally, the usual result of marriage. And, since this chapter is directed toward demonstrating the effects of kinship on political and economic affairs, I will leave issues about the construction of male (and female) identity to others.[18]

An excellent example of marriage as a successful strategy to accumulate or to augment wealth (as well as the role of an increasing slave population in solidifying the wealth and power of planters) can be found in Lorena Walsh's *From Calabar to Carter's Grove*.[19] In providing background on the slave-owning Burwell family, Walsh exposes kinship as one of the factors that helped propel its members into a level of wealth underlying their vast slaveholdings and their abundant political careers. It was second-generation Lewis Burwell II, Walsh writes, who "established . . . crucial intertwined social and political connections with other leading gentry families," who "forged instrumental alliances with members of the rich and powerful" families of Virginia, and who thereby "established the political and social connections that enabled his offspring to operate comfortably in the highest circles of power in the colony."[20]

Most tellingly, Walsh describes Lewis Burwell II's pattern of wealth consolidation through marriage. His slave property, which was the basis of his financial success, came from four sources, the first of which was a group of twenty inherited from his father. His first wife's father willed his daughter a group of forty slaves, and through Burwell's rights as a husband he gained ownership of this second group of slaves. When his first wife died, he married a widow who brought to the marriage a third group of slaves given to her by her father and a fourth group of eight slaves she inherited from her first husband. When Burwell married her, he gained ownership of both groups of slaves.[21] To Burwell, then, one element of the meaning of kinship was the opportunity for the enhancement of wealth and status through marriage and inheritance.

Although this study is directed at kinship among white antebellum families, Walsh's work provides major insights about the links between free and slave kinship groups. She describes how the Burwell slave community grew into an interconnected slave kinship network over time, and although Walsh does not make this point explicitly, the development of the extended *slave* kinship network that embraced several properties was only possible because of the extended kin network of the *white* families to whom they belonged. Succeeding generations of the Burwell family consistently established plantations in clusters near other family members. Thus, even when slave family members lived on different estates, they still were proximate

Figure 11. Robert Calvert (1802–67)
From John Henry Brown's *Indian Wars and*
Pioneers of Texas (1880).

enough to others to maintain the degree of regular contact Walsh posits.
The impact of kinship in the lives of the white Burwell family manifested
itself in the geographical closeness of their residences, which in turn facilitated the growth of kinship networks in the slave community.

So this, then, was the state of antebellum southern society when the
Keesee kinship group and others like it were migrating to and fro on the
cotton frontier. Political and economic power as well as status were inti-
mately connected to ties of kinship in innumerable ways. The following examination of this one very extended family from the perspective of Robert
Calvert and through the use of genealogical methodology explicates the
pattern of political and economic control by networks of kin in the antebellum South.

Robert Calvert was born on 19 February 1802 near Wartrace (now Bedford County), Tennessee, the son of William and Lucy (Rogers) Calvert.
His paternal grandfather had immigrated to Winchester (now Frederick
County), Virginia, from Ireland and later moved to Tennessee. His
mother's family was English. Robert Calvert and his family were Scotch-
Irish Cumberland Presbyterians.[22] When Calvert was a boy, his parents
moved to the Tuscaloosa and Bibb Counties area in Alabama, probably
drawn by the potential for cotton cultivation in the fertile lands in the Black

Warrior River valley just as his future father-in-law, Thomas Keesee Sr., had been. Cotton prices were high after the War of 1812 and motivated many planters like the Calverts and Keesees into the newly opened territory of Alabama.[23]

In Tuscaloosa County on 28 August 1823, Calvert, age twenty-one, married Mary "Polly" Keesee, age fifteen. In a classic example of sibling exchange, Robert's sister Mary had married Calvert's wife's brother Milton Keesee earlier that same year.[24] From that point on, the Calverts and the Keesees operated as parts of a kinship group that included many other families who intermarried with these two families. As each of the siblings married, kinship ties expanded. Robert Calvert married into a family much like his own—landowning and slaveholding cotton planters. When Calvert's father died in 1823, not only did Calvert inherit his own share of his father's estate, which partially consisted of slaves, but he also gained control of some of his younger siblings' shares of the estate and slaves by serving as their guardian. Although Calvert no doubt saw this as a labor of love on one level, it also provided him with status and profit through his control of a larger pool of economic resources, even if only temporarily. In the same fashion, through marriage to Calvert's sister Mary, Milton Keesee gained control of his wife's inheritance in addition to that of her sister Paulina when he was appointed Paulina's guardian.[25]

As an example of the money and property controlled by guardians, on the 1830 annual guardian's report, Milton Keesee as guardian of Polinia [*sic*] Calvert reported that he was in control of $1,522.52 of her estate from her father during the previous year, including $1,316.43 cash, $105.31 interest on that money, $106.00 for hire of her slave during 1829, and $42.00 for the hire of her "two Small boys" (slaves) during 1829. Robert Calvert reported that same year that he was in possession of $1,613.15 for his ward, his brother William, from a similar list of assets. Since probate records exist for Robert and Mary (Calvert) Keesee's siblings because they were minors, it can be extrapolated from those siblings' inheritances that Robert and Mary probably received a cash settlement and a few slaves as their shares of their father's estate.[26]

On 3 January 1825, a year and a half after his marriage, Robert Calvert first purchased land in Tuscaloosa County. The same day, Lucy Calvert, Robert's mother, purchased land nearby; and between 1825 and 1835 his father-in-law, Thomas Keesee Sr., as well as many of his brothers-in-law bought government land in the same vicinity.[27] During Robert and Mary

Calvert's residence in Alabama, most of their children were born amid a host of kin. About 1826 a son William was born and named for his paternal grandfather. About two years later came a daughter Lucy Ellen, named for her paternal grandmother. Next came a daughter Paulina Jane; a Pauline (Poline) Calvert was married to Samuel M. Qualls in Tuscaloosa County on 26 March 1834, and it seems likely that she and Robert Calvert were related and that this daughter was named for her. The name Pauline is carried down in succeeding generations of the family.[28] About 1834 another daughter Mary M. was born, most likely named for her mother and for her maternal grandmother. The Calverts' last child, Sarah Agnes, was born about 1846 after they moved to Arkansas, but she died at two years of age.[29]

During their residence in Alabama, various members of the Keesee kinship group held minor political offices. Robert Calvert was commissioned as a justice of the peace in Tuscaloosa County, Alabama, in 1825 and 1826, John Hill in 1826, and Milton Keesee and John Hill in 1829; John Hargrove and Jesse Hill were also justices of the peace during the early years of settlement. John and Pharough Hill both held the office of constable from 1823 through 1826. Thomas Keesee Sr. was appointed overseer of the poor in his district in 1824, 1829, and 1831. Others in the kinship group who were also overseers of the poor in their districts include Jesse Hill in 1820 and 1826, Middleton M. and James Hill in 1827, John Hill and John Hartgrove [*sic*] in 1828, Richard Murphy in 1829, Milton Keesee in 1831, and Theophilus Hill in 1832. Thomas Keesee's daughter Jane married Elias Jenkins, who was the Tuscaloosa County sheriff from 1828 until 1831.[30]

The officeholders listed above were all intricately tied together by kinship. Robert Calvert and Milton Keesee were brothers-in-law. John Hill, Jesse Hill, and Pharough Hill were brothers; their brother George was married to Jane Calvert, who was Robert Calvert's sister; their brother James Jones Hill was married to Jane Calvert, who was Robert Calvert's paternal aunt; and James Jones Hill and Jane Calvert had a son Robert who married Nancy Calvert, who was Robert Calvert's sister. John Hargrove was the paternal uncle of Martha Wooding Hargrove, who married Gideon Keesee, who was the brother of Milton Keesee and the brother-in-law of Robert Calvert; John Hargrove was also the paternal uncle of Alfred Battle Hargrove, who married Milton Keesee's daughter Lucy Rogers Keesee. Richard Murphy was the name of George West Murphy's father (although I have no direct evidence that this Richard Murphy is the same man), and George West Murphy married Mary Elizabeth Clardy, who was the daughter of Milton Keesee's sister Agnes. By knowing the kinship connections of these political officeholders, it becomes obvious that during the time of the nascent kinship group's residence in Alabama the members were already developing their small-planter status through political leadership in their local community.

By 1836 the Calverts and the Keesees were ready to move on yet again, no doubt driven by an amalgam of some of the same push-pull factors that had effected their earlier move from Tennessee to Alabama—a desire for soil that had not yet been depleted by cotton in the new state of Arkansas, where land was cheap, as well as the impetus provided by the worsening economy. Although there had been an upsurge in cotton prices in 1825, they began a steady decline to about ten cents a pound, which was the borderline between profitability and unprofitability for planters. Prices remained low for several years, creating a depression in Alabama that became nationwide in scope by 1837; this was no doubt a factor in the families' decision to relocate. However, Edward Eugene Baptist sums up a variety of motivations in a nutshell: "Planter men moved to the plantation frontier to establish and extend the wealth and power of their kinship networks," "[b]ut they did not do so as disembodied, individualistic economic actors. Family and kinship were always at the heart of the decision-making process."[31] Not only was the move to Arkansas designed to provide them with more fertile soil and increased cotton production, but there was also an abundance of cheap land that would provide opportunities for sons and daughters who were reaching adulthood. By migrating together, they maximized those opportunities: they were able to pool their resources and labor, including their slaves, to establish themselves quickly in their new home, clearing land for crops and building new homes. If one man fell ill or was injured and unable to work, his brothers were there to fill in for him until he recovered, and if a woman was unable to care for her children due to illness or even death, there were plenty of other female relatives to take over her daily duties.

The very fact that the Keesee kinship group all migrated west at the same time speaks to the coordinated nature of the decision to move. One can imagine the idea of migration percolating through the community of kinship for years as conditions in Alabama worsened until the proper mixture of push-pull factors instigated action. There must have been a moment when the opinions of family members reached a critical mass, resulting in the decision to migrate to the new state of Arkansas and to abandon what

had been their home for the past sixteen years or so. The decision was un-
doubtedly not without dissension or sadness: Thomas Keesee Sr.'s son
William Keesee realized it was time to move on, but he cast his lot with his
wife's family instead of his own and left for Texas; and Thomas Keesee Sr.'s
daughter Jane remained behind with her husband and his family, later migrating to Mississippi instead of to either Arkansas or Texas, where her
family had settled. Many of the Hill relations chose not to migrate to central Arkansas at that time with the Keesee kinship group but later joined up
with them in southern Arkansas. Most had to have known there would be
loved ones they would never see again, but, on the other hand, no one migrated or remained alone. Kinship groups were constantly in a state of flux,
and at each intersection of change individuals within the group had to make
choices about which branch of the family was most desirable or advanta-
geous for them and for the group. Integration into a kinship group gave
them power and status as well as financial and emotional benefits they
would have lacked as isolated nuclear families.

   The Calverts and Keesees were part of a much larger migration to
Arkansas and westward in general during this time period. In 1836, the year
members of the kinship group began their relocation, public land sales in
Arkansas and in the United States were at their highest point ever, with
1 million and 20 million acres, respectively, moving from the public to the
private domain. Despite this land boom, in 1840 only one third of all tax-
payers in Arkansas owned land—and the Calvert-Keesee kinship group
were members of this minority.[32] As Donald P. McNeilly writes, many of
the immigrants, like the Keesee kinship group, were heeding "the siren call
of the cotton frontier, not the frontier of ordinary men and women who
hoped to stake out a few acres, but the frontier for extraordinary men and
women that would allow those with means and know-how to get the best
land and, with the command of slave labor, enrich and empower themselves
to the top of society."[33]

   Especially in a county and state still in the early stages of formation, opportunities abounded above and beyond land and slaves. Arkansas was developing apace: the total population of Arkansas increased from 30,388 in
1830 to 97,574 in 1840; the white population increased 221 percent in that
ten-year period, and the black population increased over 332 percent. The
Keesee kinship group was part of the spectacular in-migration during this
era.[34] There were county, state, and federal political offices open to enterprising men of the "right sort," especially when they were kin to other

wealthy men of status. These offices provided both political and economic advantages, and members of the Keesee kinship group availed themselves of these advantages.[35]

Calvert and his brother-in-law Milton Keesee arrived in Saline County, Arkansas, in 1836 and began buying land. They were evidently acting as advance scouts or agents for the rest of the family; the bulk of the kinship and community group followed in 1837, with another wave of settlers from Tuscaloosa and Bibb Counties in 1841.[36] A majority of the original Alabama kinship group settled together in Saline County, and that cohesiveness was a factor in their political and economic success. "Family connections were the most common path to the planter class. Many of the pioneering ventures to Arkansas were diversified family business affairs pursued to gain wealth in a variety of ways, the growing of cotton being the most direct and the most prestigious," McNeilly argues.[37] Members of the kinship group utilized the labor of their slaves and quickly began producing cotton in their new home as a first step toward ensuring their success; in December 1839 the *Arkansas Gazette* reported:

> Cotton.—We have neglected to notice for a week or two, the sale of a lot of cotton of 12 bales, which was purchased by Mr. J. De Baun, at 11 cents. It was raised by Mr. Thos. Keesee, jun[ior] of Saline county, and is the largest lot we recollect of seeing in this place. It was an excellent article, and promises well for the farmers of our neighboring county. The crop of Saline will amount this year to some 250 bales, which is much greater than was ever raised in our neighborhood before. The lands of Saline county were overlooked by planters in making locations, till a few enterprising Alabamians [the Keesee kinship group] settled there, who bid fair to produce crops inferior, in quantity and quality, to none in the south, and as soon as the article will bear a[s] good a price, will make it a source of wealth to themselves and the country.[38]

The move from Alabama to Arkansas demonstrates yet again the nature of migration in the antebellum South: it was not the action of individuals but of families and kinship groups. Furthermore, ventures to the cotton frontier were not particularly undertaken by younger sons but, as was the case with the Keesee kinship group, were led or at least participated in by the family patriarchs. Thomas Keesee Sr. was about sixty years of age at the time he arrived in Saline County, Arkansas, with six of his eight adult children along with their spouses and children. In *A Family Venture,* Joan E. Cashin argues that rebellious and domineering sons of planter patriarchs,

Figure 12. Robert Calvert's Family

Children of Robert Calvert and Mary Keesee:
   Lucy Ellen Calvert
       B: ca. 1828, Alabama
       M: George Washington Rutherford, 28 September 1843
       D: 1851, Saline County, Arkansas
   William Calvert
       B: ca. 1830, Alabama
       M: Alabama C. Cottingham, 19 July 1849
       D: 1864, in Sterling/Calvert, Robertson, Texas
   Paulina Jane Calvert
       B: ca. 1832, Tuscaloosa County, Alabama
       M: Joseph Tom Garrett, 4 December 1845
       D: after 1870
   Mary M. Calvert
       B: 4 October 1834, Alabama
       M: (1) Peter H. Smith, 26 December 1848
           (2) William Greene Lee Quaite, 6 June 1864
           (3) T. M. Phaup, 10 March 1880
       D: 28 March 1889, Waxahachie, Ellis County, Texas
   Charles Calvert
       B: ca. 1836
       D: Texas
   Sarah Agnes Calvert
       B: ca. 1846, Saline County, Arkansas
       D: 7 May 1848, Saline County, Arkansas

Robert Calvert, son of William Calvert and Lucy Rogers, was born 9 February 1802 near Wartrace, Bedford County, Tennessee, and died 20 September 1867 in Sterling, Robertson Country, Texas. He married Mary "Polly" Keesee on 28 October 1823 in Tuscaloosa County, Alabama. She was the daughter of Thomas Keesee and Mary McKnight and was born on 11 October 1807 in Sumner County, Tennessee, and died 16 December 1873 in Sterling, Robertson County, Texas.

trying to escape the heavy bonds of kinship and to make their own marks in the world, dragged their wives off to the frontier, where they were left isolated from friends and family. She portrays their settlement of the cotton frontier as the actions of nuclear families, cut off from the old kinship networks.[39] This study contradicts her findings. Fathers often migrated along with their sons and daughters, kinship groups moved together, and, as often as not, individual families migrated with the women's families instead of with the men's families. When Robert Calvert's wife, Mary, arrived in Saline County, Arkansas, for example, she was in the company of her father, four of her five brothers, various sisters-in-law, and one of her two sisters in addition to members of her husband's family.

In 1840 Robert Calvert—one of those "enterprising Alabamians"—was enumerated on the Saline County census, in Saline Township, with his wife, three daughters, a son, and thirty slaves. He was the second largest slave owner in the county after his father-in-law, Thomas Keesee Sr., who owned thirty-one slaves. Many other members of the kinship group were living in the same county and enumerated as heads of household. In fact, of the 397 slaves in Saline County at the time of the 1840 census, members of this kinship group owned 123. Eight men out of a total white population of 2,061 owned over 30 percent of the slave population in the county.[40] This dominance of the slave-owning class gave the kinship group a certain status, particularly at the county level. McNeilly finds that "[t]he man with the most slaves naturally cut the widest swath, and in gaining the most land at the best location . . . such a man naturally assumed leadership of his community. . . . The most important symbol of wealth was slave-ownership, which, more than land or mercantile success, conferred the greatest prestige."[41]

During the Keesee kinship group's residence in Saline County, some family members clearly fit the definition of "planter," but authoritatively categorizing a group of people as planters assumes a static social organization. Were all the members of the Keesee kinship group planters? If we accept the usual dividing line between yeomen and planters to be ownership of twenty or more slaves engaged in market-oriented agriculture, then the answer is both yes and no. In 1840 Thomas Keesee Sr., Thomas Keesee Jr., and Robert Calvert fit the definition of planter, owning thirty-one, twenty-one, and thirty slaves, respectively; but Milton Keesee, Benjamin Clardy, and George Polk Keesee, owners of fifteen, five, and no slaves, respectively, did not fall within the definition of planter—at least not at that particular point in time. So if a man and one or more of his sons or sons-in-law were of the planter class, did that mean his other sons or sons-in-law were *not* members of the planter class? By 1860 Benjamin Clardy (one of Thomas Keesee Sr.'s sons-in-law) had finally acquired a total of twenty-one slaves: does that mean he did not consider himself a member of the planter class until some particular year between 1850 and 1860, when he crossed the magic threshold of owning twenty or more slaves? Although Thomas Keesee Sr. owned no slaves in 1800 when he was a young married man with three children, he was definitely a member of the planter class by 1840, but then by 1858 he only owned nine slaves; how, then, should historians classify his status? Obviously, planter status was fluid—at least as historians define it. (See figure 13 for the changing slave-owning status of selected members of the Keesee kinship group.)

Figure 13. Slave Ownership Numbers, 1840–60

Name	Relationship to Thomas Keesee Sr./ Birth Year	1840 Census	1846 Tax List	1850 Census	1860 Census
Thomas Keesee Sr.	ca. 1778	31	8	40	10
George Polk Keesee	son 1797	0	1	1	8
Thomas Keesee Jr.	son 1804	21	n/a	34	82
Gideon Keesee	son ca.1816	0	n/a	22	28
Robert Calvert	son-in-law 1802	30	18	51	75
Benjamin Clardy	son-in-law ca. 1797	5	n/a	10	21
James A. Hicks	grandson-in-law 1812	0	n/a	3	4
George Washington Rutherford	grandson-in-law ca. 1817	0	6	19	6

Selected members of the Keesee kinship group. Thomas Keesee Sr. did not own any slaves in 1800, according to his census enumeration in Spartanburgh County, South Carolina. Some of the men listed in the chart had already moved away from Saline County, so there is no 1846 tax listing for them. Only slaves who were over eight years of age and under sixty years of age were taxed, so each man owned more slaves than are counted here. For 1840 and 1846: Billingsley, *Early Saline County, Arkansas, Records.* For 1850: 1850 U.S. Census, Slave Schedules, Union County, Arkansas; Saline County, Arkansas; Hot Springs County, Arkansas; and Ouachita County, Arkansas. For 1860: 1860 U.S. Census, Slave Schedules, Ashley County, Arkansas; Union County, Arkansas; Robertson County, Texas; Falls County, Texas; Hot Springs County, Arkansas; Saline County, Arkansas; and Columbia County, Arkansas. Note that "Will of Thomas Keesee" (written 1858) lists nine slaves to be distributed to his heirs. Since George W. Rutherford died in October 1858, there is no 1860 Slave Schedule listing for him, but his probate papers listed six slaves as part of his estate; "Estate of G. W. Rutherford, dec^d," Loose Probate Files, Robertson County Courthouse, Franklin, Texas.

Another aspect of the slipperiness of classifying antebellum southerners by class arises from the natural ebb and flow of a man's fortunes, status, and situation over the span of his life. Young men were naturally not as rich or prominent in the normal course of affairs as they would be later in life as mature men. Furthermore, a part of the natural cycle of life was the divestiture of a man's wealth and possessions as he aged or upon his death; children matured, married, and had children of their own, inclining fathers to begin the distribution of at least part of their estates that was completed upon their deaths. Like Thomas Keesee Sr., this natural progression would have the effect of moving the father out of the planter class over time and his sons into it. Over the course of his lifetime, as shown in figure 13, Thomas Keesee Sr. went from being a nonslaveholder to planter status and then in his old age no longer owned sufficient numbers of slaves to qualify for planter status. Nevertheless, the entire narrative of his life places him squarely in the planter class.

The evidence presented in this study indicates that members of a kinship group seemed most likely to derive their status and their class identity from the range of their effective kin as a whole, whether or not a particular individual met the standards for membership in the planter class as modern-day historians have constructed it. At any one given point in time, one or more individuals may not meet the explicit definition of "planter," but they were still members of the planter class by virtue of their affiliation with family members who did meet such a definition.

Saline County was created in November 1835, and Arkansas Territory became a state in June 1836; the Keesee kinship group began their transferal to Arkansas immediately upon the heels of statehood. They quickly established their status as men of substance in this newly organized region, acquiring a great deal of federal land, supplemented by private purchases of land, and then putting in cotton crops. But they also took advantage of county, state, and federal officeholding to enhance both their prestige and their wealth.

In 1837 Calvert's brother-in-law Benjamin Clardy, who had married Thomas Keesee's daughter Agnes in Alabama, was captain of the township slave patrol, an organization of men appointed by the county court to keep the slave population under control. The patrol that year also included Clardy's son-in-law James Moore (who was also Robert Calvert's stepfather at one time), and Moore was also a Saline County commissioner.[42] On 9 April 1840 Robert Calvert and brothers-in-law Benjamin Clardy and Thomas Keesee Jr. were appointed to the slave patrol for Saline Township. Less than a year later, Calvert was appointed overseer of the third division of the Military Road by the court, and on 22 January 1841 he was reappointed to the Saline Township company of patrols, along with nephews George West Murphy and James Moore (also his one-time stepfather). It certainly made sense for members of this kinship group to serve as patrollers, since they constituted the largest group of slaveholders in the area; they earned money from the county while protecting their own property and interests.[43] Next, Calvert was elected Saline County representative to the Arkansas legislature in 1842, serving two years, and in 1846 and 1848 was elected and served as Saline County judge until shortly before he left the county.[44] These and other examples of public service helped establish the family as members of the elite class (by Saline County and early Arkansas standards), which furthered their political careers. Those political careers provided them with fees and salaries that supplemented their cotton profits and also kept their fingers on the pulse of local events, which, in turn, brought other financial opportunities to their attention. It was a self-perpetuating loop, enhanced by felicitous marriages and, at the same time, enhancing their chances to make felicitous marriages.

George Washington Rutherford's marriage to Robert Calvert's oldest daughter, Lucy Ellen, in 1843 demonstrates the synergistic effects of the alliances created by marriages because of the tendency of the wealthier, politically involved families of status to marry into similar families. Rutherford's brothers included Samuel Morton Rutherford and Archibald Hamilton Rutherford. Samuel M. Rutherford was elected sheriff of Pulaski County for the years 1825 through 1830 (three terms of office), was a member of the Seventh and Eighth Arkansas Territorial House of Representatives from Pulaski County (the parent county of Saline) from 1831 through at least 1833, was the territorial treasurer of Arkansas from 1833 through 1836, and was an agent to the Indians. In 1840 he served on a Democratic Party committee with Thomas Keesee Sr.[45] Archibald H. Rutherford was a merchant, lawyer, and newspaper editor who was also extremely active in local, state, and federal (including Confederate) politics.[46] The three Rutherford brothers were the sons of Archibald Hamilton Rutherford (Sr.) and Margaret Massie Parrish, who were first cousins. The Rutherfords' migration pattern was similar to that of the Keesees: Virginia, to Tennessee, to Arkansas. Interestingly, when Thomas Keesee Jr. and other members of the Keesee kinship group settled in Ellis County, Texas, in the late 1860s and 1870s, they were preceded to that county by another Rutherford brother, William Booker Rutherford, who had migrated there during the Civil War. It seems unlikely this was a coincidence, but there is no proof of communication between the two families, who were connected by the marriage of kin.

Given the prominence of his older brothers, it is not surprising that George W. Rutherford was able to secure an appointment as deputy marshal of Saline County, District of Arkansas, to take the census in 1840, was elected to a two-year term as Saline County sheriff from 1842 to 1844, held an appointment as a major in the Eighteenth Regiment (Saline County) of the Arkansas State Militia in 1843, and was appointed colonel commandant of that same unit in 1846.[47] Both his status and his political career were no doubt only enhanced by his marriage to the oldest daughter of Judge Robert Calvert, and Calvert's sphere of influence was also improved by his connection to a prominent family group such as the Rutherfords.

Although no explicit evidence exists to indicate that Rutherford's or Calvert's political career was directly assisted by kinship ties, there have been several studies demonstrating the importance of family networks in similar circumstances. In the antebellum South, where public institutions and organizations were relatively weak or lacking, family often served as an economic and political power base. As Baptist has so aptly demonstrated in his study of a planter kinship group on Florida's cotton frontier, "kinship enabled these migrant planters to obtain and then control access to scarce political, economic, and cultural resources: kinship was power." The members of the Calvert-Keesee kinship group, like Baptist's Florida planters, were able to use their unity to create a faction more powerful than any one of them would have been alone. "They knew," Baptist argues, "that power came from the collective strength of families, bound together in a web of assistance and kinship."[48]

In 1850 Calvert was again enumerated in Saline County. The value of his real estate was listed on that census as $7,200. He owned thirty-six slaves in the county, and fifteen more were on loan to his son in Union County; two other slaves he owned had died within the past year. He owned five hundred acres of improved land and nineteen hundred acres of unimproved land. He produced seventy-four bales of cotton; that year, only one other man in the county produced as much. He raised twenty-five bushels of wheat, fifteen bushels of rye, four thousand bushels of corn, and one hundred bushels of oats in addition to hay, peas and beans, potatoes, sweet potatoes, and barley. His plantation also produced wool, butter, and honey, and he had horses, mules, oxen, cattle, sheep, and swine valued at $1,315.[49] Obviously, Calvert was one of the county's wealthiest and most respected planters, and he had ascended to the upper rung of the region's planter class.

Robert and Mary Calvert's four surviving children married during their years in Arkansas. First, Lucy married George Washington Rutherford on 28 September 1843. Next, her sister Paulina married Joseph Tom Garrett on 4 December 1845. Mary and Dr. Peter H. Smith married on 26 December 1848. Each of the daughters married in Saline County, but William, the only son, married Alabama C. Cottingham, the daughter of a prosperous cotton planter, on 19 July 1849 in Union County, Arkansas, where they resided at the time of the 1850 census.[50] Of Robert and Mary Calvert's four children who survived to adulthood, one daughter married a young man who later became an affluent planter, one married a doctor, one married a politically well-connected man ensconced in a kinship network of his own, and their only son married the daughter of another slave-owning planter. Consciously or unconsciously (or a bit of both), the kinship network incorporated other families that increased the overall wealth and status of the group as a whole.

The Calvert children continued the tradition of naming patterns when their children were born. William and Alabama Calvert named their oldest son for William's father (Robert), the oldest daughter for William's mother (Mary), and their second son for Alabama's father (Charles). George and Lucy Rutherford named children for Lucy's father (Robert Calvert Rutherford), for Lucy's paternal grandfather (William), for Lucy's mother (Mary), and for Lucy's sister (Pauline J.). Joseph T. and Pauline Garrett named children John T. (namesake not known), Mary (for Pauline's mother), and Lucy (for Pauline's sister and paternal grandmother). Dr. Peter and Mary Smith named children Margaret (namesake unknown), Peter P. (for father), Sarah F. (namesake unknown), and Robert Calvert Smith (for Mary's father). These naming patterns are quite similar to those in other branches of the kinship group.

Marriage alliances and kinship also aided the kinship group by diversifying their wealth-producing activities in a way that supported the kinship group's political and economic goals. Robert Calvert, for example, not only bought and sold town lots (apparently a speculative activity) but helped his son William establish some type of entrepreneurial enterprise (Smith and Calvert) in Saline County. Then he sent his own slaves with William to Union County to help William establish himself as a planter there. One of Robert Calvert's daughters married a physician, and another married a politician. McNeilly aptly summarized this point: "Family networks of brothers, cousins, and uncles would pool resources—slaves, land, and capital—and pursue a variety of vocations—planting law, medicine, merchandizing—to seek wealth."[51]

One of the ways kinship ties and politics went hand in hand is the advantage kinsmen had when one of their relatives served as sheriff or county commissioner. Men in these types of offices were often the first to know of prime land or property that would soon be sold. A sheriff, for example, served warrants on debtors and handled sales of the properties of men with judgments against them, and a commissioner might be appointed to sell the property of someone who had died; thus, they had the inside track on knowledge about the sale property. In a typical case from the Saline County deed records, James Moore, who was Robert Calvert's stepfather and nephew, as a Saline county commissioner appointed by the circuit court "to sell the real estate of Joshua W. Smith Dec^d," along with William Calvert, Smith's former partner in the firm of Smith and Calvert, "did on the 16th day of June 1838 sell at public auction lots No. One and two in Block or Square Number ten in the town of Benton for twelve hundred dollars and Robert Calvert became the purchaser."[52] This is not to say that this or other records point to any type of illegal or underhanded tactics between family members (in fact, the auctions where these sales took place were public), but having a relative who was a county commissioner or sheriff would, no doubt, have alerted family members to sales well in advance of other citizens. In this particular case, it appears that Robert Calvert was either helping out his son William, who may not have been able to buy out his deceased partner's share of their jointly held land, or that Robert Calvert was increasing his investment in town lots through this opportunity, or both. The next year, James Moore was one of three petitioners making a formal application to incorporate the town of Benton (the county seat), which would have the ultimate effect of increasing the value of town lots, many of which were owned by members of the Keesee kinship group.[53]

Once various men of the kinship group achieved a toehold in county politics, it became a self-reinforcing loop; public service begat more public service and greater responsibility. The results were increased stature in the community as well as the potential for profits for kin. For example, when twenty-seven-year-old James A. Hicks, who was married to Thomas Keesee Sr.'s granddaughter and who was a nephew of Robert Calvert and Milton Keesee, did some blacksmithing for the county and was paid four dollars by the county court in 1839 or when he made some repairs on the county jail and was paid forty-seven dollars that same year, he probably owed those small commissions as much to the influence of his kin as to his own public service as a road viewer, justice of the peace, and associate justice for a term of the county court.[54] Although he was a young man, owning no slaves at all and not wealthy in 1840, he was connected by a myriad of links to the biggest slave-owning planter kinship group in the county. His kinship to such prominent people certainly did him no harm when local governmental officials, operating out of the same courthouse where Hicks's kin worked, were distributing paying jobs.

The late 1840s and early 1850s were a time of transition for most of the kinship group. Milton Keesee, along with many other family and community members, left Saline County sometime in the early 1840s and relocated approximately one hundred miles south in Union County, Arkansas. Keesee wasted no time becoming involved in political life: in 1848 he was elected and served one term in the Arkansas House of Representatives.[55] The lands in the Ouachita River bottoms of Union County had been noted as rich and suitable for cotton cultivation a decade previously when the Calverts, Keesees, and others had migrated from Alabama to Saline County, Arkansas.[56] The planters may also have been influenced by the effect of the panic of 1837, which only began to affect Arkansas by 1845. Even though the average Arkansas taxpayer's aggregate property (total acres of land, number of slaves, and head of livestock) increased between 1840 and 1845, the value of that property declined.[57] Sometime between 1846 and 1850, Milton's father, Thomas Keesee Sr., also left Saline County for Union County. Other families who relocated to Union County in this same time period include those of two daughters of Benjamin and Agnes (Keesee) Clardy, Robert Calvert's son William and daughter Lucy (Calvert) Rutherford, Robert Calvert's brothers-in-law Gideon Keesee and Thomas Keesee Jr., Thomas Keesee Jr.'s daughter and son-in-law Ann and E. H. Hammond and most of his other grown and minor children, Thomas D. Keesee, William Calvert, and others too numerous to mention.[58]

Shortly after the 1850 census was taken, Robert Calvert, along with his extended family and slaves, relocated to the rich Brazos River bottoms of Robertson County, Texas, following his brother-in-law Milton Keesee, who had once again blazed the trail into new territory for the family after remaining in Union County, Arkansas, for only a few years. Calvert's new plantation was also just up the Brazos River from his brother-in-law William Keesee's residence in Washington County, Texas. William Keesee, who had moved to Washington County about 1837 with a group of his wife's kin, was prospering and may have influenced his brother Milton, his brother-in-law Robert Calvert, and others of the kinship group to come to this area of Texas. When he arrived in the county, Calvert bought 653 acres in 1851 and, in 1852, another parcel of 1,307 acres of land for $3,900.[59]

According to J. W. Baker's *History of Robertson County, Texas,* Calvert's "was the first great plantation in the county and it was the best equipped in

all of Texas."⁶⁰ In 1853 he assessed 2,111 acres of first-class land on the Brazos River valued at over $6,000, 38 slaves valued at $19,000, 18 horses, 54
head of cattle, and miscellaneous property valued at $525 for a total taxable
value of $27,618. Seven years later, in 1860, he assessed 3,827 acres valued at
$38,270, 74 slaves valued at $44,400, 36 horses, 202 head of cattle, and other
property for a total taxable value of $88,800 — an increase in wealth of well
over 300 percent in just seven years.⁶¹

The town of Sterling grew up in the area around Calvert's plantation in
Robertson County. It was founded about the same time the Calverts arrived. In addition to all of Calvert's children along with their spouses and
children, other members of the kinship group who relocated to Robertson
County included Milton Keesee, Thomas Keesee Jr., Edward Calvert,
James Calvert, and Alexander Calvert. Even Calvert's minister from his
time in Arkansas, William Wharton, along with his family, came with him
to Robertson County, Texas.⁶² Many other members of the kinship group
came to Texas and settled in counties nearby; some came with Calvert directly from Saline County, Arkansas, and some made an intermediate stop
in Union County, Arkansas, before following Calvert to Texas.

In the decade before the Civil War, Calvert and his kin prospered and
were active on many fronts. According to the 1860 slave schedule, Calvert
owned seventy-five slaves who lived in twenty-five slave houses on the
plantation. Along with supervising his vast cotton plantation, he bought
and sold land and town lots, and, although his daughter Lucy had died in
Arkansas, he financed her widower, his son-in-law George W. Rutherford,
in a mercantile business in Sterling. Calvert was elected to and served one
term in the Texas legislature in 1853. He was also a champion of the benefits of the railroad; along with two other Robertson County men, he con-
tracted with the Houston and Texas Central Railroad to build the grade
and cut ties for the railroad in their area.⁶³ Calvert was a ruling elder in the
Cumberland Presbyterian Church for thirty years and was a Knight Tem-
plar in the Masonic order. He was a member of Pierce Masonic Lodge
No. 144, AF&AM, in the town of Sterling along with other members of the
kinship group, including Calvert's kinsmen H. D. Bennett, J. T. Garrett,
and William Calvert.⁶⁴

Milton Keesee (Robert Calvert's double brother-in-law, so to speak) died
in Washington County, Texas, on 10 March 1860. Although Milton had a
wife, a family, and a fairly large estate, Robert Calvert, in applying for letters of administration on Milton's estate, wrote that "Milton Kessee, at the

time of his decease, had no fixed domicile or place of residence: but that he died in Washington County, having no property of any importance there; and, being at the time, a non-resident, so far as petitioner is advised, of any county in the state."[65] No explicit evidence has been found to clarify this puzzling statement. It is probable, however, that since Milton's estate consisted mainly of horses and mules and because he left outstanding notes from a variety of locations in Texas and Louisiana, that he may have been a horse trader who kept on the move, leaving his wife and son to manage slaves and cotton.[66] Since he had no set residence, Robert Calvert no doubt found it more convenient to probate the estate in his own home county, although the claim about Keesee's residence may have been merely a subterfuge on Calvert's part for the sake of expedience. Calvert's sons-in-law J. T. Garrett and P. H. Smith posted a forty-thousand-dollar bond as securities for Calvert as administrator of Keesee's estate.[67] Keesee's probate files make it clear that his business dealings often involved kin. For example, at the time of Milton Keesee's death he owed over $300 to James Moore, presumably the husband of Milton's sister Agnes's daughter Sarah Ann Clardy. He had also borrowed money and bought a slave on credit from his son William Calvert Keesee in 1859 or 1860; the debt was outstanding at the time of Milton's death. At the time of the 1860 census, Milton's wife, Mary (Calvert) Keesee, was residing in Falls County, Texas, with her son William Calvert Keesee (who died the following year) and his family, along with her unmarried daughter Nannie C. Keesee. Mary had considerable property, indicating perhaps that she rather than her husband was the owner of record of the slaves and land.[68]

Milton Keesee's probate file represents an illustrative portrait of his financial modus vivendi: instead of obtaining money at a bank, antebellum southerners like Keesee acquired needed funds from an informal network of friends, neighbors, kin, and business acquaintances. In exchange for loans of cash, Keesee left notes promising payments all across Texas and Louisiana, and, when his estate was probated, these notes were presented for payment to the administrator of his estate, Robert Calvert. A typical voucher filed with the estate papers includes a promissory note (which looks much like a modern bank check, complete with an engraving of a Native American man as decoration), signed by Milton Keesee, for $100. The note promises to pay John J. Cain of Harris County, Texas, "At Sight," is dated 15 October 1859, and was executed in Houston. Another note submitted for payment to the estate is for a cash advance "on wool" (presumably cotton) in the amount of $200, paid to Milton Keesee in 1859 by the firm of E. B. Nichols and Company of Galveston, Texas. In a notarized document executed in Liberty County, Texas, in 1861, Milton Keesee's kinsman by marriage, James Moore, swears that Keesee's estate owes him $330.75 for money Moore paid in Keesee's name in Union Parish, Louisiana, in 1859. The payment was for an amount "paid Jno. L. Barrett as att[orne]y for Jno [John] Hill [another kinsman by marriage], being amt of Judgment & cost in the case of Jno Hill *vs.* James Moore et al, which amt I [James Moore] paid as Security for Milton Keesee," and for the cost of "atty fee for defending same." In another notarized statement executed in Nueces County, Texas, Thomas M. Gay stated that "on the 10th of October A.D. 1859, the late col. Kazee [*sic*] borrowed the said sum of Fifty Dollars from me in cash [at his special instance and request], and that it is still due and unpaid to me. So Help me God!" All these claims (and many others) were approved as valid and paid from the estate by Calvert.[69]

Even while traveling and in the absence of a banking system, southerners like Keesee could access cash, borrow money, or pay for services or property merely by writing out and signing an IOU. Many of these transactions were between kinsmen and are hidden unless the researcher employs genealogical methodology to ferret out the entire range of kinship for an individual. These financial transactions demonstrate but one of the many ways that kin provided a wealth of social capital to members of a kinship group: an individual could usually count on a relative to advance him money even when he was traveling or short of cash.

Shortly after Keesee died, the Civil War began, and Robert Calvert carried on with the administration of Keesee's estate amid the turmoil of the war. Calvert was a strong supporter of secession, giving "the cause of the Confederacy very substantial aid, fitting the wagon-trains and supplying the soldiers with horses and equipments." One of his grandsons (probably Robert Calvert Rutherford), age eighteen, enlisted in the Confederate Army and died in service. Calvert's fortunes were badly damaged by the war: not only did he lose about half his financial capital when his slaves were emancipated, but he spent heavily supporting the Confederacy while holding much of his cash in Confederate money, which was worthless after the war. Before he could attempt a complete recovery, he died from yellow fever on 20 September 1867 in Robertson County upon his return from a business trip to Houston.[70] Despite his financial setbacks resulting from the war, his probate record reveals that he owned real estate in Robertson, Falls, and Brazos Counties as well as in Houston appraised at over $30,000, and the list of claims due the estate totaled over $82,000.[71]

The railroad Calvert had promoted finally came through the area after his death, and the new town that arose at the local railroad station on land he donated was named in his honor. But as Calvert arose, the town of Sterling died, and Sterling Cemetery, where Robert Calvert and many of his kin were buried, became a muddy pasture where cattle now graze; of all the tombstones that once stood there, only tombstones for Robert Calvert, Mary Calvert, and a granddaughter remain alongside a historic marker in honor of the Sterling Cemetery.[72] By 1871 the town of Calvert had the largest cotton gin in the world. Today the town of Calvert is a National Historic District with a treasure trove of late-nineteenth-century architecture but a population of only about fifteen hundred.[73]

After Robert Calvert's death, his extensive estate was divided among his wife, his surviving children, and his grandchildren. In a variety of ways, the records of Calvert's estate reveal the intricate nature of family ties. For example, although Calvert named only his spouse, children, and grandchildren as heirs, he had property (mostly mules and horses) in the possession of his brother-in-law Thomas Keesee in Ellis County at the time of his death, and he held the mortgage on property owned by Francis Asbury Thompson (Milton Keesee's son-in-law) in Brazos County. But the most striking evidence lies in one of the plats that indicate how Calvert's land was to be partitioned. This plat illustrates, through a graphical representation of the landscape, how a great many people with varying surnames are all closely related to one man from whom they inherited property (see figure 14). Without using genealogical methodology, a researcher would see little connection between the people owning adjoining plots of land when they had varied surnames such as Garrett, Calvert, Quaite, Fort, and Rutherford.[74]

The end of the Civil War definitively demarcates the end of an era in the lives of the Keesee-Calvert kinship group. Before the war, the best strategy for planters seeking political and economic success on the cotton frontier was to act in concert with a large group of kin, pooling resources and skills and enhancing social status through membership in the group. But above all, their financial and economic success as well as status were founded on the twin pillars of slavery and cotton: not only did slaves constitute the majority of the planters' financial capital, that same slave property also provided the labor to produce the cotton. After emancipation, the capital previously lodged in the bodies of slaves was lost to the planters; concomitantly, the planters had to buy the labor of their ex-slaves. The central paradigm of antebellum southern society shifted, eliminating slavery in a

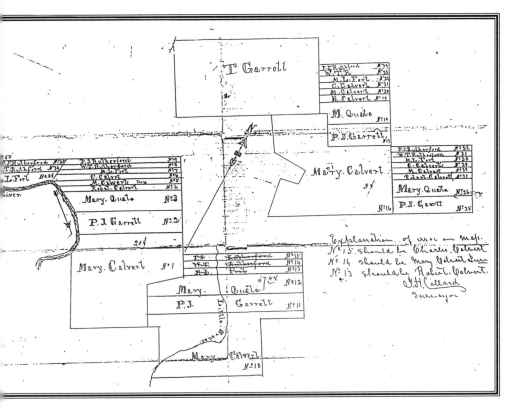

Figure 14. Partition of Lands—Estate of Robert Calvert
Land on the Brazos River in Robertson County, Texas. After Calvert's death,
his land had to be divided among his surviving heirs: his widow Mary Calvert,
his Rutherford grandchildren (including Mary Fort), his Calvert grandchildren,
and his daughters Mary Quaite and Paulina J. Garrett. From "Estate of
Robert Calvert," Loose Probate Packet, Robertson County, Texas.

single stroke, decreasing the wealth of the planters, and gradually bringing
forth greater institutional complexity, all of which ushered in a decrease in
the authority of planters and marked the beginning of a decline in the
power of kinship groups.

Robert Calvert and the many family members composing the web of kinship that enfolded him are excellent examples of antebellum southern lives
rich with close interactions with family, kinfolk, and community. In
Calvert's world people needed the security of a network of relationships—
relationships as necessary to their well-being as they were comforting. And

the social capital Calvert and other antebellum southerners derived from their membership in a kinship group was just as instrumental to their political and their financial success as was their financial capital. If they had migrated to the cotton frontier in nuclear family units without a supporting network of kin, their chances of successfully achieving status, wealth, and political power would have been greatly decreased. Women needed their sisters, cousins, and granddaughters to provide emotional support in a harsh environment and to assist them with childbirth, child rearing, and sickness; they also needed their fathers, brothers, and sons to assure their safety, material comforts, and financial security. Men needed their male relatives to loan them money, to share labor (their own and that of their slaves), and to give them a helping hand in political and economic arenas. Although the bonds between fathers and daughter, husbands and wives, mothers and sons are difficult to quantify, they surely played a major role as well in the emotional and social health of family members. United, the kinship group was stronger and more adaptable than individual families acting alone would have been.

Kinship played a significant role in the lives of antebellum southerners, and the extent of kinship ties was much broader than that usually recognized in the present-day United States. In history, as in life, no person exists in a vacuum. Every life is like a tapestry woven of the warp and woof of relationships and events. To trace any of the threads in Robert Calvert's life tapestry would lead into a complex interplay with the threads of the lives of others and, foremost, with the lives of a community of family. There were many influences—economic, political, religious, and social—shuttling in and out, weaving the structure of Calvert's life and directing his economic decisions, but none were as embedded in his concerns as the attachments of kinship.

Over his lifetime and through at least three migrations to the cotton frontier, Robert Calvert leveraged his family connections and utilized his network of kin to achieve the planter ideal. Planter Stephen Duncan of Natchez, Mississippi, whom Martha Jane Brazy writes about in "An American Planter," operated in exactly the same fashion although on a far larger scale:

> [T]he economic, social, and familial networks that comprised the Natchez elite [contributed to Duncan's power base]. The overlapping networks were deeply intertwined with one another, and cemented by marriage among the elite. As the nascent networks developed over time, an inner-circle emerged.

This privileged group shared membership in all the networks. Through a variety of social and economic connections as well as marriage into prominent Natchez families, Stephen Duncan first positioned and then anchored himself at the center of this inner-circle. The connections Duncan made early in his career helped propel him into the planter elite; later, such connections helped maintain his power. The bonds Duncan fostered and maintained were clearly vital to his success.[75]

Robert Calvert began life as the son of a man who raised cotton with a few slaves, increased his status and wealth through inheritance and through his marriage to the daughter of a planter, then used his own talents to bootstrap himself into the planter class by supplementing plantation agriculture with political officeholding and a bit of land speculation and entrepreneurship. The marriages of his children to those with political and/or economic clout of their own expanded his influence and status, as did the expanding political, social, and economic successes of his extranuclear kin. In turn, he aided his kin in achieving their own political and financial success. Politics and economic diversity were essential components of his success, but their influences were founded on his position within a kinship group and cannot be thoroughly understood outside of the context of kinship.

The antebellum South had a long history of kinship's commingling in the arenas of politics and economics, and although historians of the South have long recognized kinship's role, it has yet to be fully explored or pushed far enough. Many historians have incorporated some kinship data into their works, but few if any have distinguished kinship as a separate and distinct category of analysis, nor have they analyzed the meanings and ramifications of kinship in the lives of antebellum southerners. Explicitly exploring and defining theories of kinship and using the methodologies of genealogical research—that is, using more sources normally viewed as genealogical in nature, prioritizing kinship links as a research goal, and going beyond surname matching—aid in painting the complete canvas depicting political and economic aspects of southern society and will no doubt prove to be a large factor in proving that kinship was at the heart of most elements of southern society during the antebellum period.

CHAPTER FIVE

The Kinship Group
in the Postbellum Era

To be ignorant of what occurred before you were born
is to remain always a child. For what is the worth
of human life, unless it is woven into the life
of our ancestors by the records of history?
—Marcus Tullius Cicero

Although this is a book about antebellum southerners, many of the principals in the narrative played out their lives in the postbellum South. A brief
explication of the Keesee kinship group during the last decades of the nineteenth century hints at the gradually descending arc of kinship's importance
as the major organizational element in southerners' lives through the rest of
the century and beyond and at the concomitant transitional impact of kinship on social, political, religious, and economic concerns. Individuals are
born and they die, but the kinship group lives on.

It is imperative to remember that there was no stark defining line between kinship's overriding importance in the antebellum period and its de-
clining significance after the war. The waning of the family's position in the
lives of white southerners was a gradual process that was still taking place
well into the twentieth century and, some might well argue, through the
present day. Moreover, the family has never ceased to be a compelling element in people's lives—it simply lost much of its power as the primary organizational factor of those same lives.

Drew Gilpin Faust states: "As the major agency of socialization, the family was perhaps the most important institution in the creation of a southern
mentalité [during the antebellum era]."[1] If, then, the institution of the family changed after the Civil War, changes in southern attitudes and culture surely followed. A brief examination of the postbellum Keesee kinship

group clearly illustrates how they experienced the changes affecting the South in this era and can serve to illuminate many of the issues raised by historians, if only in a tantalizing way.

When Thomas Keesee Sr., the patriarch of the primary Keesee kinship group studied in this work, wrote his will in 1858, he was a fairly wealthy man for that time and place. But by the time he died in 1861, much of that wealth was destined to dissipate as a result of the war. He left the bulk of his estate to his second wife, Malinda, and their two children: Malinda, about forty-one years of age, was to receive a slave woman, a carriage and bay horses, all household and kitchen furniture, and $3,000 in cash; daughter Virginia (Keesee) Thornton, a married woman of about twenty years of age, was to receive six slaves and $3,000 in her own right; and son Benton Keesee, age nineteen, was to inherit his father's 636-acre farm in Ashley County, four slaves, and $6,000. To his other children, all middle-aged adults by this time, Thomas Keesee Sr. left less: sons George, Milton, Thomas, and William were to receive $3,000 each; daughter Mary (Keesee) Calvert was to inherit $1,000; and to his children Gideon Keesee, Agnes (Keesee) Clardy, and Jane (Keesee) Jenkins he gave "nothing[,] believing [he had] made ample provisions for them heretofore."[2]

But it is likely that few of Thomas Keesee Sr.'s descendants benefited from their inheritances. His youngest son, Benton Keesee, survived his father by only a few months. He joined the Confederate army and died in 1862 at Antietam, leaving no known issue.[3] Thomas and Malinda Keesee's daughter Virginia had married in 1855, at the age of fourteen, David L. Thornton, who was ten years her senior.[4] Family stories state that the Thorntons, their children, and Virginia's widowed mother moved to Texas after Thomas Keesee's death, but no further record of them has come to light. Other Keesee family members migrated to Texas about this same time in an effort to protect their slave property from the exigencies of war, and perhaps the Thorntons fled Arkansas for the same reason. It is doubtful they retained significant wealth after the war, especially if they had converted their cash inheritance to Confederate money. Their main source of wealth was the slaves they owned, but these slaves passed from their control at the end of the war.

Thomas Keesee Sr.'s older children show much the same pattern—most of their wealth had been invested in slaves, who were freed, and in land that could only be highly profitable with slave labor to produce large amounts of cotton. Thomas Keesee Sr.'s oldest son, George Polk Keesee, born in South

Carolina in 1797 and himself a veteran of four moves across the South with family members, decided to remain in Saline County, Arkansas, when most of the family moved on into southern Arkansas, northern Louisiana, and Texas about 1850. George seems to have dropped out of the race for wealth on the borders of the cotton frontier. He was prosperous but never wealthy. He owned but one slave in 1850 and eight slaves in 1860, although he owned a great deal of land, some of which he bought from the federal government but most of which he bought or acquired from his father and other relatives when they left the county. The census of 1860 listed him with $9,000 in real estate and a personal estate valued at $700.[5] When George died in August 1864, he was about sixty-seven years of age. His estate, probated in the years after the war, was valued between only $4,000 and $5,500, most of it land. Since it took over a decade to settle George's estate, it is impossible to tell if George's slaves were included in the early valuations of his estate, but the loss of his slaves probably explains the drop in value of his worth from almost $10,000 in 1860 to about half that by the time his estate entered probate in 1865. However, it appears he still owned several slaves as late as September 1863; on 29 September 1868, the estate paid Dr. A. F. Mitchell's itemized claim for medical bills incurred by George Keesee from July 1862 through September 1863, which included charges for treating members of George's immediate family but also for Ned, Dan, Aaron, and unnamed "Negroes." Since Ned, Dan, and Aaron cannot be identified as members of George's white family and because Aaron Keesee is found listed on the 1880 census as "black," it appears they were slaves in George's household as late as 1863.[6]

Neither George P. Keesee's children nor his grandchildren held any real wealth in the postbellum era, although they were landowners for the most part—a legacy of George P. Keesee's estate. Even before the war, the members of this family were no more than fairly prosperous farmers. In 1860, for example, George's eldest son, Isaac Newton Keesee, reported only $630 in real estate value and $2,000 in personal property to the census enumerator; most of the worth of his personal property was contained in the one slave he owned and whose value was lost to Isaac after Emancipation.[7]

George P. Keesee's son-in-law (and brother-in-law) Daniel Leech was even less financially stable than other family members in the postwar era. Leech was married to George Polk Keesee's daughter Emelia Miranda "Millie Manda," who died in June 1860, at the age of thirty-six, after giving birth to nine children in twenty years of marriage; the timing of her death suggests she may have died giving birth to her tenth child, since she had had a baby every two years and her death occurred two years after the birth of her ninth child. Moreover, Leech's sister Unity was George P. Keesee's second wife. George had sold his Leech son-/brother-in-law 275 acres of land in Saline County in 1857, in return for which Leech gave George Keesee a note for $727.50, due on 1 January 1859. When George P. Keesee's estate was probated, his administrator filed an application to compromise debt in 1867, in which Leech agreed to return the land to the estate in exchange for forgiveness of his debt. In the application Isaac N. Keesee (as administrator) wrote that "he is informed and believes and so states that said Daniel Leech has but a trifle of property in amount outside of said lands in comparison to the amount of said note . . . if indeed he has any such property at all; that petitioner is perfectly satisfied from information and belief and so states that said note can never be realized in money or if so it would be at a remote period."[8] Leech obviously possessed little wealth.

In 1862 Daniel Leech enlisted as a private in Company B, Thirtieth Arkansas Infantry, C.S.A., at Little Rock along with other friends and relatives from Saline County. After the war, the widowed Leech moved to Columbia County, Arkansas, with his children, living in the same township as his deceased wife's sister Elizabeth (Keesee) Hicks and her family. In 1869 he married for the second time a widow with two children, and they had five more children together. Leech died in 1895 at the home of one of his sons in Stephens County, Texas; he was seventy-five.[9]

A list of George P. Keesee's heirs at law, taken from the papers filed with the court during the probate of his estate, provides an excellent snapshot of the state of the central Arkansas portion of the kinship group during the decade after the war. In addition to Isaac Newton Keesee and Millie Manda (Keesee) Leech (mentioned above), George P. Keesee's other heirs were the four surviving children of his daughter Dorothy (Keesee) Russell, who died just before her father; his eldest daughter, Elizabeth (Keesee) Hicks, who lived in Columbia County, Arkansas, near her brother-in-law Daniel Leech; grandson George W. Keesee, the one surviving child of George P. Keesee's son Thomas J. Keesee, who had died, as did his wife and other son, before George P. Keesee; the one surviving child of George P. Keesee's son, George W. Keesee, who died before the completion of the probate of his father's estate; grandson Robert Jolly (who died before the completion of probate), an orphan whose mother was George P. Keesee's daughter, Martha Mary Jane Jolly; and George P. Keesee's three children by his second marriage, Milton McKnight Keesee, Priscilla Keesee, and James K. Polk Keesee, all minors at the time of his death. George P. Keesee's son William J. Keesee was a private in Company H, First (Monroe's) Arkansas Cavalry, C.S.A., and died of acute diarrhea in prison camp, leaving no wife or children. Since he died before his father, he is not mentioned in the probate file as an heir at law.

By his first marriage, George P. Keesee had ten children, seven of whom predeceased him or died during the first decade after the Civil War—an unusually high mortality rate that hints at the hardships endured by white southerners living in a war zone. Federal troops occupied Saline County, Arkansas, during most of the war, and many local skirmishes took place between Confederate soldiers and irregulars and the occupying Union army. Nevertheless, at the close of Reconstruction and on through the nineteenth and twentieth centuries, there was still a significant core of George Polk Keesee's descendants in Saline and Grant Counties. They were overwhelmingly farmers who owned some land, trying to make a living raising an increasingly unprofitable cotton crop. Many are still in the area today, although most eventually migrated from farming to jobs in the local lumber and bauxite industries, to supplemental occupations such as carpentry, and to other employment in the growing urban areas around Little Rock. Over 160 years after George P. Keesee came to Saline County, descendants are still being buried in the cemetery of the Philadelphia Baptist Church, where their ancestor George Keesee worshiped. It appears that the members of this Keesee kinship group lost any claim to elite status or political prominence during the postbellum era and that the war years exacted a heavy toll on these families.

Thomas Keesee Sr.'s second son (and George Polk Keesee's brother) was Milton Keesee, born in South Carolina in 1799. During the kinship group's antebellum heyday, Milton was somewhat economically and politically prominent. He acquired a great deal of land in each place he lived as an adult—Tuscaloosa County, Alabama; Saline and Union Counties, Arkansas; and Robertson, Milam, and Washington Counties, Texas. Over the years, he held positions as a county road overseer and viewer, an overseer of the poor, a justice of the peace, a trustee of school lands, an appointed member of the local patrol, a representative in the Arkansas legislature, and a member of the board of trustees for the Texas Orphan Asylum.

Like many other slaveholders, Milton Keesee moved his immediate family to Texas along with others of the kinship group shortly after 1850.

Figure 15. William Jefferson Keesee Family
Left to right: Lucinda Evalina (Jolly) Keesee (1824–95), widow of Isaac Newton
Keesee; son William Jefferson Keesee (1846–1913); Sarah Jane Elizabeth Keesee
(standing), WJK's daughter by second wife; Mary Lucinda Keesee (b. 1888), WJK's
daughter by third wife; Hettie Ann (Dugan) Keesee (m. 1887), WJK's third wife.
Photograph taken ca. 1893–95 at William Jefferson Keesee home, Poyen, Grant
County, Arkansas. From Carolyn Earle Billingsley Photograph Collection.

After the family initially settled in Robertson County, the county lines changed, and he resided in Falls County. No diary or letter clarifies his and other family members' decision to move to Texas, but the following excerpt from an account of the history of the area likely provides at least a partial explanation:

> The first years of the 1850s witnessed a new influx of settlers to Falls County [formed from Robertson and Milam Counties in 1850] of a different type from those who had previously come. There were a large number of landed and wealthy slave holders. Among them may be mentioned . . . Colonel [Milton] Kezee, [*sic*] on the river, and the Billingsleys. A good many of these cotton planters brought their slaves to Falls County on account of the current agitation of the slave question. They thought that if slavery was abolished in the Old South, perhaps it would not be done away with in Texas or that probably they could move on to Mexico.[10]

The probate of Milton Keesee's estate suggests that he became a traveling horse or livestock trader at some point during his residence in Texas, that is, between the early 1850s and his death in 1860. When he died, his entire estate consisted of about forty head of horses, jacks, and jennets, along with "500 Acres of Land on the West Bank of Brazos River in Milam County."[11] Meanwhile, his wife and children used slave labor to raise cotton in Falls County, Texas; his wife, Mary, no doubt held slaves and other property in her own right originating from the estate of her father, William Calvert. Milton died at or near his brother William Keesee's home in Washington County, Texas, in 1860, and his brother-in-law Robert Calvert asserted in a claim to probate Milton's estate in Robertson County, Texas, that Milton "had no fixed domicil[e] or place of residence" and was, at the time of his death, "a non-resident . . . of any county in the state."[12] Unfortunately, there is nothing to enlighten the researcher about whether this meant Milton and his wife were estranged or if he simply traveled most of the time.

The value of Milton Keesee's estate was relatively small ($6,441.00), and he had debts totaling $4,603.53 for notes he had signed all across Texas and Louisiana.[13] In 1863 Milton's heirs—his widow and three daughters—received a final settlement of $1,698.64 to be divided among them.[14] By the time the war was over just a few years after his death, his wife and remaining children had lost their slave property and moved to the town of Calvert in Robertson County. At the time of the 1870 census, Mary Keesee claimed only $3,000 in real estate value and no personal estate.[15] Mary (Calvert) Keesee died of yellow fever in 1873.[16]

As far as can be ascertained, none of Milton's immediate family held any wealth or prominence during the postbellum era. It is not known if their inheritance from their grandfather Thomas Keesee Sr. had any effect on their status. Milton died before his father, and his share of his father's estate—$3,000—would have been divided among Milton's three daughters who survived into the postwar era; it is entirely probable that the inheritance had been converted into Confederate currency and rendered worthless before the division of the estate was complete.

Although Milton and Mary "Polly" (Calvert) Keesee had ten known children, only three lived until the close of the war. Their oldest child, Thomas D. Keesee, died from a fall from a horse in 1859 at the age of thirty-four, leaving a wife and two young sons. Milton and Polly's son William Calvert Keesee was also only thirty-four when he died in 1861.[17] He left a wife, who lived but six years after his death, and four small children. Five of Milton and Mary Keesee's children died as infants or when very young, predeceasing their father; only daughters Lucy Rogers Keesee, Mary McKnight Keesee, and Nancy "Nannie" Caroline Keesee lived into the postbellum era.[18] Obviously, conditions were difficult for these pioneers on the cotton frontier even before the war.

Thomas Keesee Sr.'s third child (and sister of George P. and Milton Keesee) was Agnes Keesee, born about 1800 in South Carolina. She married Benjamin Clardy III in Alabama in 1822 and had at least ten children. She died in Hot Spring County, Arkansas (a contiguous county to Saline), in 1853 at the age of fifty-three. Although her husband was a small slave owner, he, like his brother-in-law George Polk Keesee, settled down in Arkansas, abandoning the continual migration to the cotton frontier in which most of the family engaged.

Some of the Clardy children, however, could not resist the siren call of the cotton frontier; they followed other members of the kinship group into Union County, Arkansas, and eventually settled in Union Parish, Louisiana. Benjamin and Agnes's daughter Mary Elizabeth Clardy married George West Murphy in Saline County in 1840, and she and her husband were enumerated in Union County, Arkansas, in 1860, listing eight slaves on the slave schedule for that year.[19] Over his lifetime, Murphy also patented a great deal of federal land in Saline and Union Counties, Arkansas, and Union Parish, Louisiana, following the general planter pattern of mixing land speculation with plantation agriculture.[20]

To create yet another tangle of family relationships, Benjamin and Agnes (Keesee) Clardy's daughter (and Thomas Keesee Sr.'s granddaughter) Saryan (Sarah Ann) Clardy married James Moore in 1841 in Saline County, Arkansas. Moore's previous wife was Lucy (Rogers) Calvert, the widow of William Calvert, who was the father of Robert Calvert, husband of Thomas Keesee Sr.'s daughter Mary.[21] Moore owned sixteen slaves in 1840, and he migrated to Union County, Arkansas, and Union Parish, Louisiana, with his brother-in-law, George West Murphy.[22] Both Moore and Murphy increased their wealth through cotton and slaves during the antebellum era. In 1850 Moore and Murphy were neighbors in Union Parish; according to the census data, Murphy had no real estate (probably because his purchase of federal lands was not yet complete), while Moore's real estate was valued at $1,000.[23] By 1860, still in Union Parish, Murphy's personal estate was valued at $13,500, while he had eight slaves in Union County, Arkansas, that same year; Moore's census enumeration attributes to him $3,240 in real estate and $2,720 in personal estate values.[24]

However, James Moore died between the censuses of 1860 and 1870, and when his widow and children were enumerated in Union Parish in 1870, Sarah A. Moore had only $100 in personal property and no real property. Her four sons were all farm laborers.[25] Apparently, the war and the emancipation of their slaves had a devastating effect on this family's wealth. The Murphy family seems to have weathered the war years in better financial shape than the Moores. George West Murphy reported $700 in real property and a personal estate value of $3,000 in 1870.[26] About 1891 his son, Civil War veteran Robert Calvert Murphy, purchased Cherokee Plantation, Cane River, Natchitoches, Louisiana, which has been on the National Register of Historic Places since 1973 and is still owned by Murphy family descendants.[27] Given the purchase of this distinctive plantation, it is doubtful the Murphy family was reduced to poverty after the war. Robert Calvert Murphy's grandson Charles Haywood Murphy Jr., born into a prominent family in 1920 in Union County, Arkansas, founded Murphy Oil, "ranked by Fortune and Forbes magazines . . . as from the 312th to the 370th largest industrial concerns in the United States." Charles H. Murphy Jr. was also prominent in the banking and timber industries as well as in philanthropy and education. These details about the postbellum and twentieth-century

Figure 16. Children of George West Murphy and Mary Elizabeth Clardy

Front row, left to right: Agnes Murphy Ingram, b. 1844; Annie Murphy Harrison, b. 1849;
Henrietta (Etta) Murphy Gulley, b. 1854; Lou C. Murphy Slade (holding a picture of brother George);
Alice Murphy, b. 1865. Back row, left to right: Robert Calvert Murphy, b. 1842;
Dr. William (Billy) C. Murphy, b. 1845; Fannie Murphy Samples, b. 1863; John M. Murphy,
b. 1857; James Murphy, b. 1847. This picture was taken at the Cherokee Plantation (owned by
Robert Calvert Murphy) in Natchitoches Parish, Louisiana, sometime before 14 October 1906
(the date William Murphy died), probably at the funeral of brother George Murphy. Used
with permission from Ann Finkenstaedt, the great-granddaughter of Lou C. Murphy, daughter of
George West Murphy and Mary Elizabeth Clardy.

lives of the Murphy family indicate a continuation of elite status, at least in
some branches.[28] Further research on the families of James Moore and
George W. Murphy into the post–Civil War period should contribute to
our knowledge about the contrast in the status of small planters before and
after the war.

Thomas Keesee Sr.'s fourth child was Thomas Keesee Jr., born in 1804 in
Sumner County, Tennessee. Thomas Keesee Jr. accumulated a great deal of
wealth during the antebellum era. He married Jane Caroline Green in 1826

in Tuscaloosa County, Alabama, and by 1830 owned seven slaves. About 1838 he followed his family to Saline County, Arkansas; in 1840 Thomas Keesee Jr. owned twenty-one slaves; in 1850, now a resident of Union County, Arkansas, he owned thirty-four slaves; and in 1860 he owned eighty-two slaves (forty-seven male, thirty-five female).[29] On 18 July 1861, when he was fifty-seven years of age, he became a member of the Johnson Township Home Guard (Confederate) in Union County, Arkansas.[30] A sketch of one of Thomas's sons from an 1892 history of Ellis County, Texas, includes some details, probably exaggerated, regarding Thomas Keesee Jr.: "During his residence in Union county he was the largest taxpayer in that county, owning 150 negroes and 100 field hands."[31]

A couple of years after the war began, Thomas Keesee Jr. deemed it prudent to follow his brothers and brother-in-law to Texas, probably to protect his slaves from Union troops and, according to family stories, to save his strapping fifteen- or sixteen-year-old son, John Hill Keesee, from conscription into the Confederate army. It is said that John spent a great deal of the trip to Texas hiding in the wagon under a big wash pot to avoid detection. The family first joined Thomas's sister Mary and her husband, Robert Calvert, in Robertson County, Texas, sometime in 1863. The year after the war ended, Thomas Keesee Jr.'s family moved northward into Ellis County, Texas.

This last move, however, was different from the previous moves: the family had no slaves and was moving from a heavily black area into a relatively white area of Texas to become farmers instead of planters. Reputedly, Thomas Keesee Jr. "was nearly broken up by the late war, and for some time afterward he had to labor very hard in order to maintain a livelihood. Besides his Negroes, he lost $100,000 in Confederate money, which he could have invested in the finest lands in Texas; but, being a true southerner, he could not think of parting with his money, which depended for its value upon the success of the Southern cause, of which he had no doubt."[32]

Thomas Keesee Jr. and his wife, Jane Caroline Green, had thirteen known children, eight of whom lived into the postbellum period. One daughter, Mary Jane Keesee, married Gus Franklin and lived in Ellis County, Texas, where she died in 1896. She is buried in the Shiloh Cumberland Presbyterian Church Cemetery. Another daughter, Emeline Keesee, married Sidney T. Wheelis, and, rather than follow her parents to Texas, she and her family lived out their lives amid kin in Union Parish, Louisiana. Daughter Eleanor Keesee married B. H. Tucker in Union

County, Arkansas; the only thing known thus far about her is that she died before 1892.[33]

Thomas Keesee Jr. and his wife, Jane, also had sons Milton S. and Thomas J. Keesee, who both served in Company G, First Arkansas Mounted Rifles, C.S.A., before moving to Texas with their parents. Both then lived out the remainder of their lives in Ellis County, Texas, raising large families. Thomas J. Keesee applied for a Confederate pension in 1907. In his application affidavit, when asked what real and personal property he owned now and the value of it, he wrote, "54 ¹/₂ acres of the value of $20.00 per acre, or about $1100.00. I have no other property of any kind." He also stated that he had not sold or conveyed any property within the prior two years and that he had no income. He stated: "I am in indigent circumstances, I have the above property as stated but the income does not support me and am forced to rely on others for help." The claim was denied, as the value of the land prevented him from being classified as "indigent."[34] Thomas J. Keesee died in 1909 in Ellis County, Texas; both he and his brother Milton are buried in the Shiloh Cumberland Presbyterian Church Cemetery.

Another son, William Fortenberry Keesee, also lived in Ellis County, Texas, but was in Dallas County by 1880, and in Austin, Texas, by 1892. He died in Canyon Diablo, Arizona, in 1923. His brother John Hill Keesee married Evalina "Lina" Dorman. They had six children and died in 1926 and 1930, respectively; both are buried in Shiloh Cemetery in Ellis County, Texas. Thomas Keesee Jr.'s youngest child, George S. Keesee, married Ida La Clair "Clara" Jenks and had six children. George and Ida lived out their lives in the Ellis County, Texas, area, dying in 1931 and 1956, respectively, and were also buried at Shiloh.

Thomas Keesee Jr. also applied for a Confederate pension based on his service in the Home Guard in Union County, Arkansas. His claim was denied—like his son, he owned land, and that was enough to prevent his being classified as indigent. He died at his residence in Ovilla, Ellis County, Texas. His wife, Jane, died in 1897, and both are buried at Shiloh with so many others of their kin.

Even this brief study of Thomas Keesee Jr. and his immediate family shows how devastating the Civil War and Emancipation were to their status and wealth. Thomas went from being a very large slave owner and wealthy man to the ignominy of applying for the pittance he might have received from a Confederate pension, had it been approved. Like many other members of the kinship group and southerners in general during this time period, he was "land poor."

The fifth child of Thomas Keesee Sr. was Mary "Polly" Keesee, born in 1807 in Sumner County, Tennessee. She married Robert Calvert, the son of another prosperous planter family, in Tuscaloosa County, Alabama, in 1823. By 1840 they were living alongside most of the rest of the kinship group in Saline County, Arkansas, where Robert Calvert had accumulated thirty slaves, making him the second largest slave owner in the county after his father-in-law, Thomas Keesee Sr. By 1850 he owned thirty-six slaves (two others having died that same year); and by 1860 the Calverts were established in the Brazos River bottoms in Robertson County, Texas, with seventy-five slaves, twenty-five slave houses, real estate valued at $43,000, and a personal estate of $75,500.[35] Robert and Mary Calvert were the wealthiest of Thomas Keesee Sr.'s offspring.

The Calverts had six children, but both of their sons and two daughters died before the Civil War ended, leaving only daughters Paulina (Calvert) Garrett and Mary M. (Calvert) Smith Quaite Phaup. Robert Calvert and his wife, Mary, lived into the postbellum era but were financially and emotionally devastated: one of their grandsons died in service to the Confederacy, and, having heavily supported the Confederacy, they lost a great deal of their wealth. Calvert died in 1867 and his wife, Mary, in 1873, both of yellow fever.[36]

Despite the loss of their slaves and a great deal of capital, Robert and Mary still had substantial estates to leave to their two daughters and their grandchildren. The tracts of land they owned, located in one of the best cotton-producing areas in Texas, were still valuable, and there was even some capital left in the estate. Their daughter Mary was married to Dr. Peter H. Smith and gave birth to six children. Smith died in November 1861; there is no indication whether he died while serving the Confederacy or through illness or accident. His widow, Mary, then married the Reverend W. G. L. Quaite in Robertson County, Texas, in 1864 and, after the death of her father, moved to Ellis County, Texas, where her maternal aunt, uncle, and other kin were living. In 1874, when Mary M. filed for divorce from Quaite, testimony was introduced to demonstrate her ability to support their child and her other children. Mary testified that she had "separate property of her own adequate to maintain herself, & to maintain & educate her said child," even though Quaite had already taken possession of $28,800 of her estate during the less than ten years they had been married. Testifying in her behalf, J. M. Strong said Mrs. Quaite had "large and ample means."[37] This and other testimony establishes that, despite the setbacks of the Civil War, the Calvert heirs retained vestiges of their former wealth.

The sixth child of Thomas Keesee Sr. and his first wife, Mary, was William Keesee Sr., born in 1809 in Sumner County, Tennessee. William married Mary Jane Chappell in 1828 in Tuscaloosa County, Alabama, and migrated to Washington County, Texas, with her family in 1837. There he prospered as a landed slave owner raising cotton. In 1830 he owned but three slaves, but by 1860 he owned twenty-one slaves with three slave houses, held $26,000 in real estate value, and had a personal estate of $16,400.[38] After giving birth to twelve children, Mary Jane died in 1850, and William remarried. He died in Chappell Hill, Washington County, Texas, in November 1864, and by the time the Civil War ended, the family's prosperity was largely dissipated. Moreover, Reconstruction hit the county hard; many of William's children left Washington County, where freedmen had gained a good bit of political power and occupation forces held sway.[39]

Thomas Keesee Sr.'s seventh child by his first marriage was daughter Jane. She was born in Tennessee about 1813, and in 1831 she married Elias Jenkins in Tuscaloosa County. About the same time the Keesees migrated to Arkansas and Texas, Elias and Jane Jenkins moved to Mississippi, where they were among the small-planter class; Elias owned thirty-three slaves when the 1840 census was taken.[40] Jane (Keesee) Jenkins died about 1851 in Choctaw County, Mississippi, at the approximate age of thirty-eight. She had at least five children, but nothing more is known of the family during the postbellum era.[41]

Thomas Keesee Sr.'s eighth and youngest child from his first marriage was Gideon Keesee, born about 1816 in Franklin County, Tennessee. Sometime before 1840, Gideon married Martha Wooding Hargrove. They followed Gideon's family to Arkansas and were also small slaveholders — Gideon owned twenty-two slaves in Union County, Arkansas, in 1850, according to the 1850 census slave schedule; in 1860 he reported a real estate value of $15,000 and a personal estate of $30,000.[42] Martha died in Ashley County, Arkansas, in 1859, leaving nine known children.

At some point after 1860, Gideon Keesee moved his family to Washington County, Texas, to which Martha's family had immigrated about 1837. In 1874 Gideon was convicted of murder and sentenced to five years in prison; he was pardoned on 5 May 1875. He probably died shortly after his release from prison. This information leaves little doubt that Gideon was no longer of elite status after the war.

This brief review of the postbellum Keesee kinship group indicates that small planters apparently were unable to weather the financial crises brought on by the defeat of the Confederacy unless they were wealthy enough—in more than land and slaves—to be able to make a fresh start after the war. If they had invested all their profits into buying new land and more slaves, they lacked the ready capital to recover during the postbellum era. With that loss of wealth came loss of status; very few if any of the Keesee kinship group members held political or economic power after the war or retained any type of elite status. For the most part, they became landowning farmers with good educations.

A couple of caveats are in order, however. The evidence limned here from the expansive Keesee kinship group applies to the western part of the South—the cotton frontier—and may or may not be as apt a characterization of the older, more established eastern seaboard society, although there too kinship studies have the potential to answer many of the same questions.[43] Nor does this study address the impact of kinship ties on African Americans, although there is no doubt that family ties were integrally bound to African American issues in the ante- and postbellum South as much as race, class, or gender.

Overall, this appraisal of the Keesee family foregrounds three elements that stand out as powerful dynamics effecting changes in the lives of the kinship group and other small-planter kinship groups during the post-bellum era: the end of slavery, the strengthening of institutional organizations in the South over the course of the late 1800s, and the deaths of so many key family members during the war. Each of these contributed to the gradual loosening of tight interpersonal, social, political, and economic relationships based on kinship ties.

The end of slavery had the most impact on the entwined lives of ante-bellum kinship groups. During the antebellum period the goal of small-planter and yeoman-farmer families like the Keesees was to acquire and amass wealth through land, slaves, cotton, and frequent migration to the cotton frontiers. In one way or another, the whole of southern society was built on slavery, which produced profit through the production of cotton and the increase in slaves held as property. After the war southern society was redefined. The bulk of slave owners' capital had been invested and held in land and in their slave property. Slavery was the lynchpin of much of southern wealth, and it gave way in one fell swoop. Slave owners' sense of self, their status, their class identity, and their society had been based on the plantation system, as much a social system as an economic one, which was radically altered after Emancipation.

The old South was devastated. In *Ordeal by Fire*, James M. McPherson writes: "The South in 1865 presented a bleak landscape of destruction and desolation. Burned-out plantations, fields growing up in weeds, and railroads without tracks, bridges, or rolling stock marked the trail of the conquering Union armies. The collapse of Confederate authority left large areas without law and order. Roaming bands of guerillas and deserters plundered defenseless homes. Hundreds of thousands of black freedmen and white refugees suffered from disease, exposure, and hunger." [44]

A new society was cobbled together from the remnants of the old, still heavily based on cotton but with freedmen and freedwomen instead of slaves and with far less wealth in the hands of former elites. Furthermore, the process of acquiring cheap government land in new areas was almost at an end for cotton planters, as the westernmost area viable for raising cotton without irrigation had been reached about the time of the war. The Keesees and other kinship groups like them had been planters on the make; postbellum realities left them without fresh cotton lands or slaves to acquire and thus with fewer paths to wealth. Moreover, with the South shattered, a Reconstruction government in control, and their kinship networks in disarray, the old elites lost much of their political power, at least temporarily. [45]

Moreover, the loss of slavery had an enormous impact on the day-to-day lives of the women of the Keesee kinship group. Scholars of southern white women have made us aware of many of the changes in women's lives postbellum: they had greater educational and occupational opportunities as well as improved property rights, for example, that accompanied the changes in everyday life brought about by Emancipation and a general loss of wealth in many families. [46] If women's lives changed, then so too did the lives of their integrally interwoven families.

One of the biggest changes in the lives of the Keesee kinship group would have been the absence of slave labor for the first time in their lives and the loss of social status. The experiences of the Keesees were probably quite similar to those of Harriet Bailey (Bullock) Daniel; born in 1849, she wrote her memoirs of life on an Arkansas plantation, and she spoke of the experiences of her family during and after the Civil War. She recalls that her father was prescient about what the ultimate effect of the war would be, and, knowing that slavery would end, he preemptively sent all the housemaids but one back to the fields and "encouraged [his daughters and family] to learn to wait on ourselves and to carry on the housework." Before his action "each of [the family] had had a Negro girl at [their] beck and call." After the war, when her father's prediction became reality, Harriet returned from a stint at boarding school and shared with her sisters the burden of running a home without slaves, who "were sorely missed." She recalls: "Being unaccustomed to hard work, we did not know how to go about it. This made us irritable and fussy. . . . Neither did things on the plantation go on so smoothly." The Bullocks, Harriet recalled, had difficulty getting the freed slaves to work and could not get their cached cotton to market. Her father lost a court case on charges brought by a freedman whom Bullock had assaulted after the "hand spoke impertinently to [him]," which is an indication of the adjustments men had to make in facing their loss of mastery.[47]

Although the modern reader may have little sympathy for these women who spent most of their lives being waited on by their human property, there can be little doubt that the postwar changes were traumatic and stressful. Changes in the status of women contributed to changes in the family and in southern society. These adjustments affecting southern society and southern families come into sharper focus through the lens of the Keesee kinship group study and thus add complexity to our understanding of the South as a whole and of other families like the Keesees.

The void of institutional strength that had placed southern kinship groups in the catbird seat during the antebellum era began to fill over the course of the decades after the war, simultaneously lessening the hold of family power over southern society. Cotton buyers, for example, began to infiltrate the countryside, railroads proliferated, and communication improved, negating the need for the local planter to assist the small farmer in transporting and marketing his cotton. Even the small farmer raising cotton had access to markets and to information about those markets. Banks and credit eventually began to be more accessible.

Moreover, the hand of government became heavier, particularly during Reconstruction, and more laws were passed superseding (at least technically) local laws or custom. Foremost were the amendments to the U.S. Constitution granting citizenship and rights to African Americans, but lien laws and other significant laws pertaining to the business world also had an effect. Furthermore, much of the South was occupied by U.S. troops during Reconstruction. These troops, the Freedman's Bureau, and the disfranchisement of ex-Confederates weakened the political control of prewar family dynasties, at least during Occupation.

Another institution—public schools, which were practically nonexistent in the prewar South—became a good deal more common during the late nineteenth century. The forces of Reconstruction pushed for education, and state legislatures made provision for universal public education, for both white and black students, for the first time. Public institutions replaced yet another important function of the family—the education of children.[48]

Urbanization and industrialization played their parts as well. A good portion of the Keesee kinship group was living in towns and cities by the close of the nineteenth century, in stark contrast to the virtually exclusive rural settlement patterns of the antebellum era. Factories and mills began to vie with agriculture as economic forces in the South. Although kinship still mattered, its relevance to matters outside the family was reduced.

When Thomas Keesee Jr. and his son Thomas J. Keesee applied for Confederate pensions, claiming indigence, they were not the only members of the Keesee kinship group to do so. Scott Field, the husband of one of Robert Calvert's granddaughters, was a successful attorney during his working years but applied for and received a Confederate pension in 1931. In 1923 Isaac Newton Keesee's daughter-in-law filed for and received a Confederate pension based on the service of her deceased husband, John Jolly Keesee; Cary P. Keesee, widow of Gideon Keesee (the son of William Keesee Sr. of Washington County, Texas), also claimed indigence in her 1906 application for a Confederate pension based on her husband's service; and Gideon's brother Walstein H. Keesee received a Confederate pension in 1909. There are many more examples from the family that amply demonstrate how Keesee descendants depended on what amounted to government welfare—a distinct difference from the members of the antebellum kinship group, who relied on their own wealth and the wealth of their families. This reliance on the government demonstrates yet another instance of increasing institutional organizations replacing functions formerly handled within the family.

Perhaps most damaging to southern society were the immense numbers of southerners who were dead or disabled due to the war. McPherson estimates that over a quarter million Confederate soldiers lost their lives during the war. Many thousands more were wounded or lost limbs.[49] Adding to the toll were the huge numbers of civilian casualties from hunger and disease as well as from other stressors resulting from living in a war zone and during a time of deprivation. For a society challenged with rebuilding, the South faced an uphill battle with so many of the youngest and the best no longer available to help raise the South from the ashes of war and to cope with the winds of change. The Keesee family kinship study demonstrates the loss of key family members and the impact of those losses on the family and the larger society.

Scholars are still engaged in many debates about the nature of southern society during the postbellum era. One of the questions most often pondered and debated is, Did the antebellum elites retain or regain control of power after the war, or was political and economic control taken over by "new men"? Taking a broader perspective, Which best characterizes late-nineteenth-century southern society: change or continuity? Kinship studies provide another way of approaching such questions. A complete analysis of the postbellum South is beyond the scope of this study, but a glimpse into the lives of the Keesee kinship group—a group characterized here mainly as belonging to the small-planter class—provides tantalizing clues to how kinship studies using genealogical methodology could address such historiographical issues. And, as such a study has done for providing an increased depth of understanding of the nature of the antebellum South, a similar study of southern society after the Civil War promises to reveal new insights.[50]

The study of kinship and the employment of genealogical methodology are excellent tools for dissecting antebellum southern society. These same methods, employed during the postbellum era, should also reveal the shifting South from yet another angle. The Keesee kinship group was changing and evolving before the antebellum period covered here, and it continues to change and evolve into the twenty-first century. There are a myriad of other family groups—some similar and some quite different—that have stories to tell and insights to offer the scholar if only we will examine and interpret their actions rather than dismissing them because they failed to leave written expressions of their life experiences.

The Prospects for Kinship Studies

The family is one of nature's masterpieces.
— George Santayana, *The Life of Reason*

This study of the Keesee kinship group demonstrates a method and a theoretical framework capable of circumventing many of the difficulties involved in pinning down what antebellum southerners thought, intended, or felt when we have little explicit evidence of their interior motivations. It would be much simpler if Thomas Keesee Sr. had left a diary detailing why he moved so many times, what his aspirations were, exactly how he interacted with his extended family on a daily basis, how significant they were in his life, and what kind of impact they had on his actions. Since he was not so thoughtful as to do so (or perhaps because someone tossed some "worthless old papers" in a burn pile while cleaning out an attic or old trunk), we can only glean and assemble evidence from every possible source to build a plausible record of the many facets of his life and the lives of his kin. Using that evidence and assembling it with kinship links in mind, using genealogical methodology to move beyond superficial surname matching, we can evaluate it through the interpretive framework of kinship theory. And from that we can make educated guesses about motivations and feelings based on the actions of antebellum southerners whose lives were permeated and framed by kinship. By decoding their behavior, we can bring the hidden contours of their lived experiences into focus by examining the evidentiary minutiae of their lives, elevating kinship to a category of analysis, and using genealogical methodology in concert with anthropological kinship theory to understand their lives as they understood them.

Employing this technique has shown that the received wisdom of antebellum southerners migrating ever westward as rugged individuals or in nuclear families units is patently false—the overwhelming majority migrated as family groups and formed settlements of kin. In a society with weakly organized or nonexistent institutions, families remained the main organizing principle in the everyday lives of antebellum southerners. Kinship groups also provided the social capital necessary for success, from shared emotional and physical burdens to financial capital or aid and even to survival at times. Without the united strength of related groups of families, successful migration and settlement would have been extremely problematic.

Moreover, in contrast to most modern American families, kinship groups acknowledged and honored a much wider range of kin—cousins to almost any degree, for example, were recognized in a meaningful way. After all, since kinship groups were the means of success and survival, the larger the group committed to each other, the more powerful they all were. Sibling exchanges and cousin marriages tightened the interlocking grid of kinship, creating families of children whose relationship to each other was closer than that of cousins and who had grandparents doubly bound to their grandchildren. Even two families who were merely connections, who had no blood ties to each other but who had mutual blood ties to other families, were considered within the effective range of kinship. Genealogical methodology allows one to see networks of kin far more complex than simply the people who share the same last name. Many historical studies have failed to go beyond mere surname matching, which not only misses the complexity of kinship but also is gender-biased, since women change surnames over their lifetimes.

Southerners' affiliation with their kinship group had a strong tendency to manifest itself in their religious preferences. More often than not, individuals followed in the steps of their families when they chose a church to attend. When they changed religious affiliation, it was often at the time of their marriage; their culture deemed it wisest for couples to attend the same church for the sake of the children; to accomplish that, sometimes one or both opted to switch denominations. Since children followed their parents' religious affiliations, church and family groups were all but merged, especially given that church services offered social contacts that often resulted in the marriages of members to one another. Churches also presented opportunities for contacts and communication over wide areas as ministers and elders went to local, state, and regional denominational meetings. They brought information from their travels and contacts back to the community and many times were able to report on lands to which the kinship group soon migrated. The high levels of kinship among ministers and ministers' families also contributed to the transmission of specific information from and about other regions. Clergymen were highly mobile and tied into kinship networks, both of which enhanced their role as conduits of information.

But perhaps the most important role of kinship groups in the antebellum South, at least among planter families like the Keesees, was their enormous impact on political and economic activity. In a self-perpetuating loop, slave ownership increased wealth and status, while wealth and status facilitated political power, which, in turn, produced financial success and status, especially when a kinship group moved into a virtual power vacuum in a newly created political jurisdiction, as Saline County, Arkansas, was in the late 1830s. Moreover, through marriage alliances with families originally outside the group, the kinship group continually incorporated new members with other skills, occupations, and connections that enhanced the overall strength of the group through diversity. This tendency, however, highlights one of the perils of trying to study the antebellum South—the difficulty of pinning down the intrinsically fluid nature of that society and of the people who inhabited it. The Keesee kinship group members were essentially planters, even though not all individuals achieved the planter class as defined by historians and even though some who did failed to maintain that status. Virtually all, however, identified with the planter status of the group as a whole: they became slave owners themselves, they benefited from the status of their planter kinsmen, and they continued to migrate to the cotton frontier seeking wealth through slavery and cotton. If we were to look at the members of the kinship group individually or at any one frozen moment in time, we would be forced to divide them into groups labeled "planters" and "yeoman farmers," and, although that would be technically accurate, it would be an artificial construct.

George W. Rutherford is a good example of an individual whom we would be forced to label as something other than a planter, and yet, when we view his life over time and space and in the context of his family relationships, his status becomes more complicated. He came from a politically well connected family of slave owners and married into a similar family group, the Calverts and Keesees, who were planters. Rutherford served as an assistant U.S. marshal, then served as the Saline County, Arkansas, sheriff as a young man, married Robert Calvert's daughter, acquired a few slaves, served in the state militia, then moved to the cotton frontier of Union County, Arkansas, with other members of the kinship group and became a slave owner with nineteen slaves by 1850. Shortly afterward, even though his wife died, he followed his former father-in-law to the fertile lands of the Brazos River valley in Texas, where Calvert financed Rutherford in a mercantile business. Rutherford died in 1858, owning six slaves at the time of his death. Thus he was never a member of the planter class, since he apparently never achieved ownership of twenty or more slaves. And yet his class identity was clearly grounded in the planter class, and he derived that class identity from his membership in his kinship group. That can only be intuited, however, by looking at his life in the context of that kinship group. In isolation, Rutherford was a politician, a military man, a yeoman farmer with a few slaves, and a merchant. Integrating kinship into the other categories of analysis in our repertoire enhances our understanding of the lives of antebellum southerners like Rutherford and the society in which they lived and offers fresh insights into issues of class.

Classifying antebellum southerners as planters or yeoman farmers is also problematic because of the ebb and flow of their financial status and amount of slaveholding over the course of their lifetimes. A man might be technically a yeoman farmer at one stage in his life, rise to the planter class, then return to yeoman status later in life. Neither were kinship groups static entities: they shifted and changed, formed and re-formed, gained and lost members as circumstances dictated. When people or a group are examined in place in one community or one state or are only investigated through a snapshot of one slice of their lives, the very process of trying to freeze and examine them in situ skews the image of antebellum southerners. By examining an entire kinship group over both time and space, as I have done in this study, a broader, more complex picture of southern society emerges. By focusing on kinship ties and on the various branches of the kinship group over a span of time, including the families who migrated and the ones who stayed put, the essence of the totality of the lives of antebellum southerners comes into sharper focus. Individual identities were not totally subsumed by the kinship group but were greatly incorporated into it— antebellum southerners made decisions about migration, settlement, and religion as well as political and economic matters as part of the kinship group, seeking to maximize their own success. When studied as an organic whole and followed through various migrations and permutations, a kinship group comes closer to revealing the essential nature of the antebellum South because kinship and group affiliation ultimately shaped individuals' religious, political, economic, and class identities.[1]

In addition to matters of religion, politics, economics, and class, kinship studies also have the power to illuminate issues of gender. Sally G. McMillen's *Motherhood in the Old South*, for example, speaks to the issue of women and family. McMillen describes the experiences of elite southern mothers in great detail and argues that their roles and situations were in many ways distinctively different from maternal experiences elsewhere in the United States. Southern mothers "perceived [motherhood] as their sacred and singular occupation. For most women, bearing and rearing children brought tangible rewards in a society that offered few alternatives. Despite the risks and demands, mothers took their duty seriously and rarely faltered. They must have found satisfaction in the role. Out of deep affection and the acceptance of their maternal duties, southern mothers devoted their health, energy, and even their lives to bearing and rearing children. The South glorified this occupation, and southern mothers apparently responded."[2]

McMillen makes it clear how fully southern women played out their social role as mothers and that motherhood virtually subsumed their identities as individuals. She presents persuasive evidence that the family was without a doubt the most important institution in these women's lives. If motherhood and other kin relationships were totally instinctual in nature rather than socially constructed, we should see no difference in the roles of mothers in varied regions. Southern society, via its cultural exaltation of women and mothers, shaped the way women experienced their gender and their family connections. Southern women experienced the meaning of kinship in ways demonstrably different from northern women. Thus, using the methodology and theoretical framework embodied in this work, kinship studies have the potential to open up discussions about gender relationships in the Old South.

Finally, the use of kinship as a category of analysis can expand our understanding of race, while, concomitantly, race as a category of analysis promises to enhance our understanding of kinship. For example, the strongest evidence that kinship is concerned more with social relations than "blood" can be found in the mulatto slave population of the antebellum South. In *New People*, Joel Williamson describes the effects of miscegenation between white men and slave women, that is, a large population of mulattos, both free and slave. Although Williamson refers to "[t]he deep confusion of kinship across the race line," in fact, although some men perceived a tie of kinship with mulatto children they fathered, many more did not.[3] Clearly, social recognition of kinship was determined by factors other than biology.

Legally, morally, and socially, in the Old South interracial family ties usually were not recognized. A mulatto child born to a slave woman had no legally recognized father; the child derived status from his mother. Even if one tries to make the argument that white fathers would have freed their slave children more often if it had not been legally difficult begs the question—the very fact that laws were enacted erecting barriers to the emancipation of slaves and ascribing mothers' status to their children speaks to the fact that, as a whole, society did not acknowledge kinship across race lines even in the face of blood ties. Mulatto slaves of white slave owners experienced the concept of kinship in a radically different way from their white "relatives."

Williamson also discusses the recurring question of whether or not Thomas Jefferson fathered children by his slave Sally Hemmings.[4] The question of interest for this study is not the possibility of a sexual relationship between Jefferson and Hemmings. Rather, given that there seems to be little doubt in either Jefferson's contemporaries' minds or present-day minds that Hemmings was Jefferson's wife's half-sister, why wasn't she treated as kin? In a society almost obsessed with family relationships, why was Hemmings kept in bondage and even assigned to serve her half-niece as a maidservant? Why did Sally carry the surname of her mother instead of that of her acknowledged (white) father? The answer is, once again, that kinship was and is a social relationship constructed by the culture in which it resides—in Hemmings's case, racial slavery was the operative social relation that trumped kinship.

That Sally and her siblings shared blood ties to Jefferson's beloved wife, Martha Wayles, apparently did not make them accepted kin to Jefferson or their white relatives, even though, to all accounts, Sally was "mighty near white" in appearance. Some might argue that "Jefferson seems to have put all of [Sally Hemmings's] children into training for some trade or service," which was an indication of his concern for them, or that Jefferson might have been constrained from freeing Sally by legal restrictions or financial circumstances, or that Jefferson's daughter finally freed Sally after her father's death—but none of these potentially mitigating circumstances overshadows the bald fact that the Wayles and Jefferson families held people who were biologically related to them in bondage.[5] Nor were they by a long shot the only southerners to do so.

Historians routinely clash over race, class, and gender, but kinship can often transcend and subsume all three of these categories of analysis. In the end, family, in the broadest sense, may prove to have as much explanatory power in the narrative of history as the other categories. Kinship shaped virtually every aspect of antebellum southerners' lives and had an impact on how they experienced and made decisions about everyday life, migration, settlement, religion, politics, status, and economic success. This study explores the meaning of kinship on a number of levels—by borrowing from the discipline of anthropology to probe at the symbolic definition of kinship as a socially constructed reality, by applying that symbolism to the world of southerners through the study of a large kinship group, and by exploring the pivotal role of the family in southern life using genealogical methodology to focus on kinship links. By adding another tool of investigation to the repertoire of historical scholarship (a more complete reconstruction of the way southerners themselves experienced some aspects of their culture), historians of the antebellum South can develop an even more nuanced and complex representation of the past.

APPENDIX

A Neighborhood Study of Kin in Union County, Arkansas

The following families were enumerated in Union County, Arkansas, in 1850 and are listings from one section of that census. Each listing states the name and age of each person in the household, the birth states of the first two individuals listed, the dwelling number, and the name of the township where the family resided. In general, dwelling numbers that are consecutive or close together indicate that the families lived near one another. The total white population of Union County in 1850 was 5,526, with 5 free blacks and 4,767 slaves. Following each entry are my comments about the individual's relationship to the Keesee kinship group. Note that there were other families from this census, not listed here, who were neighbors of the Keesees and/or Calverts in Alabama and in Saline County, Arkansas, but for whom I could not state a family relationship with any authority.[1]

Quarles, Peter L., 24, Mary A., 18, Saml. F., 2, **Neale**, Jack, 26, Ala./Ala., Dwelling 143, El Dorado Township. Probably related to Samuel Washington Quarles, who was married to Paulina Calvert, the sister of Robert Calvert, and also to Lucy Elberta Quarles, the daughter of Samuel Washington and Paulina (Calvert) Quarles, who married James Montgomery Hill, son of James and Nancy (McMath) Hill and grandson of James Jones and Jane (Calvert) Hill; this Jane (Calvert) Hill was Robert Calvert's paternal aunt.

Hill, Wm. W., 25, Sarah A., 25, Mary, 3, Margaret, 1, La./Ala., Dwelling 146, El Dorado Township. Cannot identify, but probably related to other Hills.

Hill, Abel, 36, Martha, 17, Jno., 11, La./Tenn., Dwelling 147, El Dorado Township. Cannot identify, but probably related to other Hills.

Kesee, Gideon, 34, Martha W., 27, Mary C., 10, Wm. H., 9, Permelia A., 7, Pauline J., 6, George R., 4, Robert H., 2, **Smith**, George, 22, **Bryant**, Wm., 25, Tenn./Ala., Dwelling 173, El Dorado Township. Son of Thomas Keesee Sr.

Hill, Jesse, 31, Cynthia, 31, Rachel, 20, Jno. W., 2, Ala./Ala., Dwelling 204, Cornie Township. Jesse Hill was the son of Jesse and Nancy (Barnett) Hill and the grandson of John and Elizabeth (Kyle) Hill; his aunt Jane (Calvert) Hill was Robert Calvert's sister; his other aunt Jane (Calvert) Hill was Robert Calvert's paternal aunt.

Fortenberry, A., 42, Mary, 31, Henry C., 16, Elisha C., 13, Catherine, 11, Mary, 9, Wm. H., 6, D. C. R., 7 months, Mo./Ill., Dwelling 327, Van Buren Township. Absolom Fortenberry was a Cumberland Presbyterian minister at churches attended by Keesees and Calverts. He moved here from Saline County at the same time.

Hill, Jno., 40, Sarah A., 27, Alex, 20, William, 17, Jessee, 11, Jno., 2, Tenn./Miss., Dwelling 404, Johnson Township. Cannot identify, but probably related to Ira and John W. Hill, below.

Quarles, H. G., 25, Eliza, 20, Whitt, 3, Cora, 11 months, **Miller**, James, 30, Ala./Ala., Dwelling 411, Johnson Township. Probably related to Samuel Washington Quarles, who was married to Paulina Calvert, the sister of Robert Calvert, and also to Lucy Elberta Quarles, the daughter of Samuel Washington and Paulina (Calvert) Quarles, who married James Montgomery Hill, son of James and Nancy (McMath) Hill and grandson of James Jones and Jane (Calvert) Hill; this Jane (Calvert) Hill was Robert Calvert's paternal aunt.

Quarles, W. W., 20, **Cook**, Ephraim, 28, Tharmintha, 22, Isbella, 4, Susan, 2, Clarissa, 1, Ala./Ala., Dwelling 415, Johnson Township. Probably related to H. G. Quarles, above.

Hill, Ira, 31, Mary F., 27, Sarah A., 8, John E., 5, Wm. C., 3, Columbus, 1, Ala./S.C., Dwelling 416, Johnson Township. Cannot identify, but probably related to John W. Hill, who lived "next door" (below).

Hill, John W., 32, Martha, 32, Eliza J., 12, Jessee W., 10, William, 8, Mary E., 5, Buenavista, 3, Josephine, 1, Ala./S.C., Dwelling 417, Johnson Township. John W. Hill is the son of Jesse and Nancy (Barnett) Hill and the grandson of John and Elizabeth (Kyle) Hill; his aunt Jane (Calvert) Hill was Robert Calvert's sister; his other aunt Jane (Calvert) Hill was Robert Calvert's paternal aunt.

Calvert, William, 24, Alabama C., 17, Ala./Ala., Dwelling 419, Johnson Township. William is the son of Robert and Mary (Keesee) Calvert and the grandson of Thomas Keesee Sr. He and Alabama were married on 19 July 1849; she is the daughter of Charles Cottingham.

Rutherford, George, 31, Lucy E., 22, Robert C., 6, William T., 4, Mary, 2, **Calvert**, William Sr., 32, **Firth**, Saml., 26, **Ellis**, John, 22, Tenn./Ala., Dwelling 425, Johnson Township. Lucy Ellen Rutherford is the daughter of Robert and Mary (Keesee) Calvert and the granddaughter of Thomas Keesee Sr.

Hill, Alex, 26, Malinda, 22, Virginia, 4, Alabama, 2, Ala./Ala., Dwelling 429, Johnson Township. Alexander Hill was the above Jesse Hill's half-brother, the son of Jesse and Malinda Hill, and the grandson of John and Elizabeth (Kyle) Hill; his aunt Jane (Calvert) Hill was Robert Calvert's sister; his other aunt Jane (Calvert) Hill was Robert Calvert's paternal aunt. He and Malinda (Greenwood) were married on 27 March 1845 in Talladega County, Ala.

Hill, Jno., 46, Rachel, 45, Tenn./Ga., Dwelling 495, Johnson Township. John Hill was probably the John who was a son of John and Margaret (Stover) Hill and a grandson of John and Elizabeth (Kyle) Hill; his aunt Jane (Calvert) Hill was Robert Calvert's sister; his other aunt Jane (Calvert) Hill was Robert Calvert's paternal aunt.

Keesee, Thos., 44, Jane, 43, Milton, 13, Thos., 11, Louisa, 9, Elenor, 7, Wm., 5, Jno., 2, Patience, 9 months, **Morrison**, Wm., 28, **Walker**, Joseph, 35, Tenn./S.C., Dwelling 496, Johnson Township. Thomas was a son of Thomas Keesee Sr. He and Jane Caroline (Green) were married in 1826 in Tuscaloosa County, Ala.

Kinard, Martin L., 31, Sylba, 29, William D., 8, Rebecca A., 6, Lorina A., 4, George, 3, Charles, 2, **Lightsey**, Adam, 25, Jno., 23, S.C./S.C., Dwelling 499, Johnson Township. Probably related to C[harles] W. Kinard below; Martin Kinard, like the Keesees and Calverts, was from the Tuscaloosa/Bibb County, Alabama, area previous to his residence here.

Hammons, E. A., 28, Ann S., 18, T. F., 21, Tenn./Ala., Dwelling 500, Johnson Township. Annastasia S. (Keesee) Hammond was the daughter of Thomas Keesee Jr. and the granddaughter of Thomas Keesee Sr.

Kinard, C. W., 33, Elizabeth P., 26, Sarah F., 7, George W., 5, Jno. M., 2, Mary E., 7 months, Ga./Ala., Dwelling 505, Johnson Township. Elizabeth P. (Hill) Kinard was the daughter of John and Margaret (Stover) Hill and the granddaughter of John and Elizabeth (Kyle) Hill; her aunt Jane (Calvert) Hill was Robert Calvert's sister; her other aunt Jane (Calvert) Hill was Robert Calvert's paternal aunt.

Keesee, Thos. D., 23, Martha, 20, Wm. G., 2, Ala./Ala., Dwelling 550, Lapile Township. Son of Milton Keesee, grandson of Thomas Keesee Sr.

Bennet, Henry L., 43, Jane M., 43, Albert L., 15, Tenn./Ky., Dwelling 555, Lapile Township. Henry L. Bennett and Jane M. (Logan) were the parents of Mary E., who married William Calvert Keesee ca. 1848. William Calvert Keesee was the son of Milton Keesee and the grandson of Thomas Keesee Sr.

Quarles, Mary, 49, Carl M., 6, Nancy, 81, Ga./Ga., Dwelling 579, Harrison Township. Probably related to the Quarleses above.

Keesee, Thos., 72, Malinda, 30, Va. [*sic*, Virginia], 9, Benton, 8, **Bond**, George A., 21, Va./Ark., Dwelling 596, Harrison Township. Thomas Keesee Sr. with second wife, son Benton, and brother-in-law George Bond.

Green, George S., 37, Mary, 25, Francis P., 9, Jno. E., 7, Elias D., 5, Benj. C., 3, George W., 2, **Allen**, Jno., 18, S.C./Ala., Dwelling 598, Harrison Township. Mary Green is the daughter of Benjamin and Agnes (Keesee) Clardy and the granddaughter of Thomas Keesee Sr.

Hammon, Richard, 64, Sarah, 60, Woodson N., 21, Va./N.C., Dwelling 686, Wilmington Township. Richard and Sarah Hammon are the parents of E. H. Hammond (above), the husband of Anastasia Keesee.

Hammon, James M., 35, Caroline, 24, Alemeda J., 3, Benj. F., 1, Tenn./Miss., Dwelling 688, Wilmington Township. Probably related to Richard and Sarah Hammond, above, and to E. H. Hammond, above, the husband of Anastasia Keesee.

Cottingham, Charles, 50, Elmira, 30, Alfred, 21, Elvira, 17, Walter, 12, Elizabeth, 10, William, 1, Tenn./Ala., Dwelling 691, Wilmington Township. Father of Alabama (Cottingham) Calvert, who is the wife of William Calvert.

Pumphrey, J[ohn] R., 46, Martha (Dorrough), 45, Jno., 16, Mary A., 13, Louis, 11, Dennis, 7, Ga./Ky., Dwelling 840, Franklin Township. John Pumphrey is the son of Jesse Pumphrey. He is distantly related to the Keesees by marriage; they were neighbors in Alabama and in Saline County, Ark. There were also other related Pumphreys, not listed here, in this county.

NOTES

Introduction: A New Category of Analysis

1. Thanks to Elizabeth Shown Mills for bringing this to my attention.

2. See, for example, Bob Tedeschi, "Genealogy's Lucrative Online Niche," *New York Times,* 23 September 2002, <http://www.nytimes.com>, which describes genealogy as "a consumer category that has truly flourished in the digital era."

3. Ulrich, *A Midwife's Tale;* Stevenson, *Life in Black and White;* Burton, *In My Father's House Are Many Mansions;* and Carr, Menard, and Walsh, *Robert Cole's World.*

4. Rutman and Rutman, *A Place in Time: Middlesex County,* 99–100 (first quotation). In *A Place in Time: Explicatus,* chapter 8, "Social Networks," the Rutmans chart the rising percentages of kinship links and the unchanging percentages of friendship links in the years 1687, 1704, and 1724. See also Vos Savant, "Ask Marilyn" (second quotation).

5. Cash, *The Mind of the South,* 26.

6. Ibid., 85.

7. Kenzer, *Kinship and Neighborhood,* 6 (first quotation), 2–3, 27–28 (second quotation), 29 (ties between kinship and class/economics), 62 (kinship and politics).

8. Cashin, "The Structure of Antebellum Planter Families," 56, 60, 70.

9. Ibid., 67. There is no known relationship between J. W. Calvert and the Calvert family in this book.

10. Ibid., 70.

11. Rundell, "Southern History from Local Sources"; and Campbell, "Family History from Local Records," 13–26, 13 (quotation).

Chapter One. Theory, Methodology, and Evidence

1. Billingsley, *Early Saline County, Arkansas, Records,* 9–18.

2. For a discussion of anthropology's relationship to the study of kinship, see, for example, the introduction to Holy, *Anthropological Perspectives.*

3. For South American societies with a belief in "'partible paternity'—the conviction that it is possible, even necessary, for a child to have more than one biological father," see "Anthropology, Paternity Test," *Economist,* 30 January 1999: 74; and "Biology: A Case of Twins with Different Fathers," *Washington Post,* 16 June 1997, both accessed online via Lexis®-Nexis® Academic Database, 30 October 1999.

4. Smith, "Daddy No More," 85 (quotation). See also "Ex-Husband Seeks Visitation for Child He Helped Raise," *Indianapolis Star,* 29 July 1999; "U.S. Supreme Court Upholds California Law on Paternity," *Los Angeles Times,* 16 June 1989: Metro, pt. 2; and Daniel B. Wood, "Is Love or Biology the Tie That Binds a Dad to Kids?" *Christian Science Monitor* (United States), 12 June 1997.

5. Texas Family Code §151.002 (1999) (first quotation). See also, for example, Arkansas Statute Annotated §28-9-209 (1997) and Code of Alabama §26-17-5 (1999). Some of the articles discussing the percentage of children who were not fathered by the man who thinks himself the father are "The Seeds of Infidelity," *Washington Post,* 9 December 1996; "Mother's Dilemma: Whose Son Is He?" *Times* (London), 22 November 1997; and Martin Cohen, "Kid Looks like the Mailman?" *U.S. News and World Report,* 27 January 1997: 62, all accessed online via Lexis®-Nexis® Academic Database, 30 October 1999. See Wright, "Sin in the Global Village" (second quotation); and Allen, "Mama's Baby, Daddy's Maybe."

6. Wagner, "Incest and Identity," as quoted in Holy, *Anthropological Perspectives,* 15 (quotation).

7. Radcliffe-Brown and Forde, eds., *African Systems,* 4 (quotation). Although the subject matter of the book is African kinship systems, the introduction is an excellent overview of theories of kinship (see 1–85).

8. Schneider, *American Kinship,* 23 (second quotation), 37–40 (for the meaning of coitus as the central symbol of the American cultural system), 114 (first quotation). Note that in modern American culture, sexual intercourse is not always equated with marriage, but, although that is not the norm, it is still the cultural ideal.

9. Anderson, *Imagined Communities.*

10. See, for example, Holy, *Anthropological Perspectives,* 13.

11. Schneider, *American Kinship,* 50 (second quotation), 51–54 (for discussion of diffuse, enduring solidarity).

12. Holy, *Anthropological Perspectives,* 1 (both quoted phrases).

13. Quoted definition from Busch, *Family Systems,* 89.

14. Ottenheimer, *Forbidden Relatives.* For modern scientific research on the subject, see Denise Grady, "Few Risks Seen to the Children of 1st Cousins," *New York Times,* 4 April 2002, <http://www.nytimes.com>; Corliss, "Cousins"; and Bennett et al., "Genetic Counseling." See also *Cousin Couples: Support for Kissing Cousins* (website), <http://www.cousincouples.com> (quotation).

15. For families that expressed preference for first-cousin marriages, see Ball, *Slaves in the Family;* and Rosengarten, *Tombee,* 94. For discussions of cousin marriages in the antebellum South, see Kulikoff, *Tobacco and Slaves,* 252–55; Censer, *North Carolina Planters,* xxii, 75, 84–88; Bardaglio, *Reconstructing the Household,* 41 (first quotation), and, for a discussion of laws regarding marriage between cousins, 40–44, 202–3. See also Glover, *All Our Relations,* x, 9–10 (for her statement that the English elites did not approve of cousin marriages), 48–49 (second quotation), 96–97, 175

n. 74. For an anthropological view of exogamy (marriage outside the group) versus endogamy (marriage within the group), see, for example, James Casey, "The Arranged Marriage," in Casey, *The History of the Family.*

16. Holy, *Anthropological Perspectives,* 2 (quotation). The first quotation is cited from M. Fortes, *The Web of Kinship among the Tallensi* (1949), 340, and the second quote is attributed to Collier and Yanagisako, eds., *Gender and Kinship,* 3.

17. The phrasing of the first part of this sentence is adapted from a statement by James Faubion, professor of anthropology, Rice University, in discussions with this author at various times in 1999.

18. Carp, *Family Matters,* 5 (quotation), citing as a source on 240 n. 8, Cremin, *American Education,* 113.

19. Woodman, *King Cotton and His Retainers* (see esp. chap. 9, "Bankers and Planters"); and Cashin, *A Family Venture,* 6–7.

20. Kurtz, *Kinship and Politics,* 7 (first quotation); and Baptist, "The Migration of Planters," 553 (second quotation). See also Mann, "Mountains, Land, and Kin Networks"; and Billingsley, "Antebellum Planters."

21. Moneyhon, *Arkansas and the New South,* 5, 9 (quotation).

22. Ibid., 46 (first quotation), 47 (second quotation), 48–50. While Moneyhon makes good use of family analysis in furthering his thesis, he fails to accord it the weight even he seems to think it should have. Although he places it "clearly" above race and class in importance as a social organization, he devotes more space to addressing issues of race and class. According to a survey of the index, there are five pages about family, seven pages referring to class, and twelve pages referring to race relations. Nor does Moneyhon attempt to address any of the issues of black families but instead leaves his discussion of family undifferentiated by race in any way.

23. Pasternak, Ember, and Ember, *Sex, Gender, and Kinship,* 262–63.

24. Cashin, *A Family Venture,* 146 n. 5 (quotation and also a brief discussion of some issues of modernity).

25. Fields, "Ideology and Race," 144.

26. For a fuller discussion of descent groups, see chapter 12, "Descent Groups: Kinship beyond the Family," in Pasternak, Ember, and Ember, *Sex, Gender, and Kinship,* 255–77, 255 (quotation).

27. Casey, *The History of the Family,* 17 (first quotation), within a discussion of the theories of Emile Durkheim's 1893 work, *The Division of Labor in Society,* and 10 (second quotation). Note that the surname Keesee is spelled many ways in various records (e.g., Kazee, Kizzee, Keessee, Keezee, Kissee, Kesee, Kozee) and is generally pronounced kuh-ZEE. For the purposes of this study, however, the spelling is standardized as per the modern spelling in my branch of the family, while references to specific records reflect the spelling contained in that record. Before the twentieth century, spelling was a creative art form, particularly in the South—there was virtually no "right" way to spell a name, and, even if the individual himself had a particu-

lar way of spelling his name, there was no guarantee that county clerks, tax assessors, and census enumerators would style the name thus. A phonetic rendering of names (and other words) was the standard.

28. Maynes et al., eds., *Gender, Kinship, Power,* 14 (quotation). For the significance of naming patterns, see Smith, "Child-Naming Practices," 541–66; and Gross, *The Minutemen and Their World,* 139. For "aspects of kinship relations and family structure in a non-English [Dutch] subculture of early America," see Tebbenhoff, "Tacit Rules and Hidden Family Structures," 567–85.

29. Censer, *North Carolina Planters,* 32–34, 33 (quotations).

30. Glover, *All Our Relations,* 29 (first quotation), 30.

31. Finis Ewing was one of the founders of the Cumberland Presbyterian Church, Francis Asbury was a prominent Methodist, and Martin Luther is significant to Protestants in general.

32. Rutman and Rutman, *A Place in Time: Explicatus,* 83 (first quotation), 88 (table 16), 89 (second, third, and fourth quotations), 90, 93–97. The Rutmans also discuss Smith's "Child-Naming Practices" and note the intriguing contrasts in naming patterns between the regions studied by each. They found almost 6 percent of all sons and daughters were named for kin other than parents, grandparents, aunts, or uncles; 14 percent of sons and 22 percent of daughters were named for "no one" that could be ascertained to be a family member. These data from table 16 cover the years 1650 to 1750 and show a pattern: first sons named for paternal grandfathers, second sons named for fathers, and a similar pattern for daughters, grandmothers, and mothers.

33. Rutman and Rutman, *A Place in Time: Explicatus,* 93–95; Smith, "Child-Naming Practices," 541–54; and Smith, "All in Some," 53–54, 73.

34. Rutman and Rutman, *A Place in Time: Explicatus,* 93–95 (quotation); and for a comparison of New England and English patterns, see also Smith, "Child-Naming Practices," 541–54; and Smith, "All in Some Degree," 53–54, 73.

35. A link to my curriculum vitae, listing genealogical as well as academic activities, is online at <http://home.earthlink.net/~cebillingsley/>.

36. Although they are used interchangeably, "family history" rather than "genealogy" has gradually become the more preferred term in genealogical circles. Many leaders in the genealogical field recognize the stigma attached to the word "genealogy"; for some it carries the taint of a type of elitism and pride of family during an era when family historians are increasingly taught to look beyond the litany of names, dates, and honors to learn the full context of their ancestors' lives. However, in academic circles, family history has another connotation: the term is used for the study of the history of "the family." See, for example, Censer, "What Ever Happened to Family History?" for an overview of the ways in which family history is generally studied. For this reason, I will use "genealogy" rather than "family history" when I refer to detailed research into the relationships between families.

37. See Rundell, "Southern History from Local Sources," 217–18 (quotations). My thanks to colleague Bethany Leigh Johnson, Rice University, 2001, for bringing this article to my attention.

38. The website at <http://www.geocities.com/Heartland/Pointe/3043/blkshp .html> is one example of an individual proudly acknowledging the flawed "black sheep" in his family tree. For the International Black Sheep Society of Genealogists (IBSSG), see <http://blacksheep.rootsweb.com>, accessed 15 September 2003. For the trend toward acknowledging the imperfections of ancestors, see Stone, *Black Sheep and Kissing Cousins;* and "The Latest Tips," July 31, 2000, <http://www.genealogy .com>, accessed 6 October 2000: "As your research progresses, you will encounter a family scandal, or at least a story you are not particularly proud of. If learning these things about your ancestors will upset you, then consider another hobby. In one hundred years, our descendants may learn unpleasant things about us. It's important to remember that virtually all families have these stories and your ancestors' actions can have no direct bearing on your behavior."

39. See, for example, Hatcher, *Producing a Quality Family History.* In enumerating the eight major elements that make "a quality family history," Hatcher includes going "beyond records, placing people in context" (3), and she devotes an entire chapter to "Turning Paper into People." In Allen and Billingsley, *Beginner's Guide to Family History Research,* readers are exhorted to add "an historical touch to your research, an understanding of the times in which your ancestors lived" (3) and "[t]o get the full picture [by framing] your family within historical context" (62). See also Sturdevant, *Bringing Your Family History to Life.* Bookstores catering to genealogists often stock a wide variety of historical works from university presses. See, for example, Frontier Press Bookstore, Karen Mauer Green, Proprietor, <http://www.frontierpress.com/ frontier.cgi>, accessed 9 October 2002. Note also the considerable numbers of genealogists who attend historical conferences and lectures, obviously in search of context rather than particular names and dates.

40. For instance, if a genealogical narrative includes the name and marriage date for a particular woman, a combined citation to a family Bible and to a county marriage record placed at the end of a paragraph would be unacceptable, because it is crucial to distinguish which source provided the name of the wife and which source provided the date of the marriage. In this case, the reader needs specific information about which source provided which fact in order to assess the information properly— we would give greater credence to the spelling of a daughter's name as recorded by her mother in the family Bible than we would to its spelling in a public record written by a clerk, but we would expect that the clerk's recording of the actual date of the marriage might tend to be more accurate than a date recorded in a Bible by someone other than the principals involved and, perhaps, at a date long after the event. The standard reference work for genealogical documentation is Mills, *Evidence!* esp. 24–27, for the advantages of footnotes versus endnotes and for specific source cita-

tions of individual statements of fact. For the Genealogical Proof Standard, see Rose, *Genealogical Proof Standard;* and Mills, "Working with Historical Evidence." Note that Mills has played a huge role in shaping the precepts of genealogy and raising the standards over the past two decades. Her call for academia to dispense with its discrimination against genealogists can be found in her editorial "Academic Discrimination." For genealogical computer programs, see, for example, Family Tree Maker and the Master Genealogist, two of the most popular genealogy computer programs.

41. Excellent examples of books that enrich our knowledge of history by focusing on moderately ordinary people include Carr, Menard, and Walsh, *Robert Cole's World;* Leslie, *Woman of Color, Daughter of Privilege;* and Rosengarten, *Tombee.* Among the best examples of works based on more prominent people are Woodward, ed., *Mary Chesnut's Civil War;* and Faust, *John Henry Hammond and the Old South.*

42. The first incarnation of this study was as an undergraduate honors program senior project for the Donaghey Scholars Program, University of Arkansas at Little Rock, 1994.

43. I still vividly recall the research I did for one client who mailed me the names of her four grandparents and hired me to find an ancestor, *any* ancestor, who would qualify her to join her friends in the Colonial Dames in Virginia. Many, many hours and dollars later, after wandering around the extensive landscape of the past and of the entire country, I found such an ancestor, but he was very nearly the last hope. Yet she was extraordinarily lucky: one rarely knows where an explication of the average American's family might lead after countless hours of research.

44. That is, intermarried groups of African Americans, whites, and Native Americans, the members of which, because of their ill-defined and contested racial identities, often seem to be invisible on the southern landscape. Members of such groups generally married within the group or within similar groups. One of the best-known triracial isolate groups is the Melungeons.

45. At one time, genealogical research for a client was considered to be a "work for hire" and was therefore the property of the client. Often, however, it was my practice to include a clause in the contract granting permission for me to make use of any information resulting from my work for the client. When there was no contract, I often sought usage permission in a letter if the material looked promising for further development. In more than one case I used the results of research done for a client in a research paper or a published article. Virtually overwhelmingly, family genealogists are more than happy to have their family histories publicized.

46. Although genealogical standards stress broad horizontal (collateral) as well as vertical (lineal) ascent of the family tree, the majority of hobby genealogists confine their investigations to direct ancestors and their siblings, only rarely following all lines of descent from a common ancestor. Indeed, this would be a daunting task: there is more than one lifetime's work to be done merely learning about the

lives of two parents, four grandparents, eight great-grandparents, sixteen great-great-grandparents, thirty-two great-great-great-grandparents, and so forth in a geometrical progression.

47. Among the things I have uncovered during genealogical research, in my own and in others' families, are illegitimate births, forgery in a family Bible, children born previous to or too early after a marriage, bootleggers sentenced to prison, horse thievery, and (gasp) a presumably respected southern grandfather who served in the Union Army during the Civil War. In some of these cases (and before the advent of "black sheep" genealogy), descendants were occasionally ashamed of the behavior of ancestors and often preferred keeping it hidden. Any "taint" of an interracial relationship, whether Indian or African American, is widely disavowed by many in the older generation and occasionally by those of a younger generation. And those fondly regarded family links to famous personages embedded in family tradition are not given up without a struggle, even in the face of overwhelming evidence.

48. The data were entered into Family Tree Maker (FTM) 10.0 by Broederbund, a widely used genealogical record-keeping program that allows the user to create and link family groups, to make source citations for each fact, and to sort and compile the data in a variety of formats. Moreover, the database can be converted into a GEDCOM file ("GEnealogical Data COMmunication, created by the Church of Jesus Christ of Latter-day Saints [Mormons]," quotation from *Rootsweb Review: Rootsweb's Genealogy News* 3, no. 3, 19 January 2000, <rootsweb-review@rootsweb.com>). GEDCOM is the genealogical standard, creating a text file that can be exchanged with others on disk or via e-mail attachment. The recipients of GEDCOM files can open or merge them with their own data in most other genealogy software programs. All data merged into an existing database in FTM automatically cite the received file as the source of each piece of acquired information.

49. For the immigrant ancestor, see Keesee, "Origins of the Keesee Family in Virginia," chap. 1 in *A History of the Keesee Family*, 1–8.

50. The first generation is the man and wife; the second generation consists of their 4 children grown to adulthood; the third generation—each of the 4 adults in the second generation having had 4 children—numbers 16; fourth generation equals 64; fifth generation equals 256; sixth generation equals 1,024; seventh generation equals 4,096; eighth generation equals 16,384; ninth generation equals 65,536; tenth generation equals 262,144; eleventh generation equals 1,048,576; twelfth generation equals 4,194,304. When the numbers from each of the twelve generations are added together, the total number of descendants (not all alive at one time, of course) is 5,592,404.

51. My thanks to Robert J. Earle, Medina, Washington, October 2002, for his help in working out the mathematical logic involved in this computational statement.

52. Bob Niesse <JagXKE69@aol.com> to Family Tree Maker Discussion List

<ftmtech-l@lyris.genealogy.com>, 28 November 2000, Subject: New to List— Kinship Report Errors; and subsequent replies on list on that and following dates.

53. "Last Will and Testament of Thomas Keesee Sr.," written 16 December 1858, proved 1861, Will Record 1, 157–59, Abstract Office Volume, Ashley County, Arkansas.

Chapter Two. Kinship, Migration, and Settlement Patterns

1. Ellison, *Bibb County, Alabama,* 13–14; and, for Thomas Keesee's 1812 service, see the biography of grandson T. J. Keesee in *A Memorial and Biographical History of Ellis County, Texas,* 476. No official record of Keesee's service has been located, however.

2. Royce, *Indian Land Cessions,* 678–79, 684–85, pl. CVIII ("Map of Alabama Showing Indian Cessions"); and *The Handy Book for Genealogists,* s.v. "Alabama."

3. Abernethy, *The Formative Period,* 26–28, 40–42, 88.

4. For the effects of African American culture on the South, see Vlach, "African Influence," in Wilson and Ferris, eds., *Encyclopedia of Southern Culture,* 1:230–31 (page references are to the reprint edition); and "Black Life," in Wilson and Ferris, eds., *Encyclopedia of Southern Culture,* 1:221–395. For the development and influence of black cultural life, see Boles, *Black Southerners,* chap. 6 and 232–33. For the blending of ethnic cultural influences, including African American, Native American, and "Celtic," see Pozzetta's introduction to "Ethnic Life," in Wilson and Ferris, eds., *Encyclopedia of Southern Culture,* 2:3–10.

5. For migration issues in American history, one of the earliest and most significant works is Turner, *The Frontier in American History.* For migration as an issue for scholars of the South, see, for example, Otto, "The Migration of the Southern Plain Folk"; Censer, *North Carolina Planters,* 127–34; Cashin, *A Family Venture;* Owsley, *Plain Folk,* 23–77; and Walz, "Migration into Arkansas," 309–24.

6. Radcliffe-Brown and Forde, eds., *African Systems,* 3. The introduction (1–85) is a general overview of the study of kinship.

7. See, for example, Cashin, *A Family Venture,* 7.

8. Phillips, *American Negro Slavery,* 169–86. For a discussion of migration and the motives behind migration, see Barnhart, "Sources of Southern Migration," 49–62.

9. Walz, "Migration into Arkansas," 1.

10. Oakes, *The Ruling Race,* 76, as quoted in Jones, "Seeding Chicot," 149.

11. Hughes, "The Real Australia," 104 (first quotation); Billington, *America's Frontier Heritage,* 28 (second quotation).

12. Pasternak, Ember, and Ember, *Sex, Gender, and Kinship,* 262–63.

13. George Keesee, 1790 U.S. Census, Greenville District, South Carolina, 69; Thomas Kizzee, 1800 U.S. Census, Spartanburgh District, South Carolina, 179; Government Land Office Records, U.S. Department of the Interior, Bureau of Land

Management, <http://www.glorecords.blm.gov/>, accessed 16 September 2000; will of George F. Keesee, Sumner County, Tennessee, Archives, Will Book 2, 36–37; and, for Thomas Keesee's slave numbers, see Billingsley, *Early Saline County, Arkansas, Records*, 6, 15.

14. Thomas Kissee, Tennessee General Land Grant 3154, Bedford County, G District, Book I, 499, listed in Sistler, Sistler, and Sistler, *Tennessee Land Grants: Surnames I–K*, 52. Although this grant was recorded as being in Bedford County, Franklin and Bedford Counties were both created in 1807 and were adjacent until 1871; my surmise is that when boundary lines between them shifted during the early years, the land fell into Franklin County. When Thomas Keesee sold the land in 1821, it was in Franklin County. For the evolution of counties, see *The Handy Book for Genealogists*.

15. Kenzer, *Kinship and Neighborhood*, 163, table 1 ("Distance between Household of Bride and Groom, 1850–80").

16. Ellison, *Bibb County, Alabama*, 3, 20–21. Emphasis has been added to denote the Keesees' kinship connections.

17. For the marriage data listed below, see Murray, *Tuscaloosa County, Alabama Marriages*, 12, 46, 47; and J[ohn] A[lexander] Hargrove, "Autobiography," Rockdale, Texas, 1903, manuscript and typescript copies on file at Chappel Hill Historical Society Museum, Chappell Hill, Texas. Martha Hargrove and Gideon Keesee and Agnes Keesee and Benjamin Clardy probably married in Pickens County, Alabama, adjoining Tuscaloosa County, but the early marriages for this county are not extant.

18. Robert Wooding Chappell patented land in Section 28, Township 21 South, Range 14 West in 1823. See Government Land Office Records, U.S. Department of the Interior, Bureau of Land Management, <http://www.glorecords.blm.gov/>, accessed 16 September 2000.

19. Radcliffe-Brown and Forde, eds., *African Systems*, 6.

20. *State of Alabama v. Harris Mitchell and George Hill Jr.* and *State of Alabama v. Harris Mitchell and Milton Keesee*, 398–401, 8 January 1825, in Minutes of the Circuit Court, Tuscaloosa County, Alabama, unlabeled ledger, Tuscaloosa County Courthouse, Tuscaloosa, Alabama.

21. Tuscaloosa County, Alabama, Deed Record Book E, 241–46, and Book F, 205–8; see also *Harris v. Purdy*, in George N. Stewart, reporter, *Cases Determined in the Supreme Court of Alabama, Embracing the Years 1827 and 1828* (Atlanta: Constitution Job Office, 1891), 1:210–13, located in the Law Library, University of Alabama, Tuscaloosa.

22. The executor was the man named by the person who died testate (with a will) to oversee the execution of the directions in his or her will. The person who oversaw the distribution of the estate of a deceased person who died intestate (without a will) was an administrator and was appointed by the court. A female can be the executrix or administratrix, but women seldom fulfilled these roles during this era. Although

the court appointed the administrator, the appointee was clearly the person favored by the surviving family members. See Moore, *Black's Law Dictionary*, s.v. "Administrator," "Administratrix," "Executor," "Executrix," "Guardian," "Intestate," "Testate." Although a guardian is technically charged with the "general care and control" of his ward, minor heirs usually continued to live with their surviving parent or were at school.

23. All of the guardianship information for this and the following paragraphs is taken from Orphans Court Records, Tuscaloosa County Courthouse, Tuscaloosa, Alabama, 39, 46–47, 56, 59, 63–64, 215, 220, 300, 392–93, 445, 447, 453, 521; "Report, Milton Kesee, Guardian of Polinia Calvert," 5 April 1830, 4–5, "Final Settlement of Robert Calvert, Guardian of William Calvert," 6 September 1830, 11, and "Citation to Robert Calvert, Guardian of the Minor Heirs of William Calvert, Decd.," 10 August 1846, 372, all in vol. 3, Minutes, Orphans Court Records, Tuscaloosa County Courthouse, Tuscaloosa, Alabama.

24. For women's legal status and rights, see Salmon, *Women and the Law of Property*.

25. See, for example, Morris, *Becoming Southern*, 91–92.

26. Payne, "Independent Minds and Shared Community," 35–41.

27. "Walter Scott's Personality Parade," 2.

28. Billingsley, "Settlement Patterns."

29. For date and place of death and for probate, see Milton Keesee Probate, Robertson County, Texas, Loose Probate Files, Robertson County Courthouse, Franklin, Texas, which gives the date of death as 10 March 1860 and states that Milton had no fixed domicile or residence; for alternate date of death, see the family Bible of Mary Keesee Sims: "Milton Keesee departed this life 12 March 1860" (transcribed by Lucy Foster Miller, copies in possession of Carolyn Earle Billingsley); and 1860 U.S. Census, Population Schedule, Falls County, Texas, Dwelling 202.

Probate files are composed of the collection of all the original loose papers stemming from the probate of an estate, including but not limited to the original will, letters of administration, vouchers for payments to creditors, vouchers for disbursements to heirs, inventories of estates, sale bills, and petitions to the probate court. Once the probate of the deceased was completed, the papers were gathered into a packet and marked on the outside with the name of the deceased whose estate was being probated and, often, with an identifying number. In most cases, courthouses have thrown out these old papers and have retained only the official books that record the significant filings regarding estates. When extant, however, these loose probate packets are an invaluable window into the family and finances of those who died with enough property to constitute an estate.

30. Texas State Police Files and Texas Penitentiary Files, both in Texas State Archives, Austin, Texas.

31. Billingsley, *Early Saline County, Arkansas, Records*, 10, 12–15; "Saline County Commissioned Officers [Arkansas State Militia]," *Saline* 6, no. 3 (September 1991): 113–16, 114.

32. Thomas S. Hickman, transcriber, "Minutes of the Mound Prairie Presbytery of the Cumberland Presbyterian Church 1842–1910," microfilm, Historical Foundation of the Cumberland Presbyterian Church, Memphis, Tennessee, 26 (February 1844), 34–35 (February 1846).

33. Thomas S. Hickman, transcriber, "Minutes of the Arkansas Presbytery of the Cumberland Presbyterian Church 1823–1876," Historical Foundation of the Cumberland Presbyterian Church, Memphis, Tennessee (from original records, 1842–1903, at Presbyterian and Reformed Foundation, Montreat, North Carolina, and 1906–10 at Department of History, Philadelphia), 42. Another source says Wharton appeared in 1839; see Hickman, "Minutes of the Mound Prairie Presbytery of the Cumberland Presbyterian Church, 1842–1910," 18.

34. Hickman, "Minutes of the Mound Prairie Presbytery of the Cumberland Presbyterian Church, 1842–1910," 19, 21, 23, 27, 36, 38, 39, 41, 42, 45.

35. McLane and Allen, *1850 Census of Southern Arkansas*, 100–101. For example, in Johnson Township, Union County, there were Hills enumerated in Dwellings 404, 416, 417, 429, and 495; Keesees and kin were enumerated in Dwellings 419, 425, 496, and 500. 1860 U.S. Census, Population Schedule, Ashley County, Arkansas, 149 (John Hill, John L. Hill, James Hill), 152 (Gideon Keesee, John Hill), 155 (Thomas Keesee), 156 (Ira Hill).

36. "Union County Probate Records (1845–1855), Officers Bonds and Wills, Book A," *Tracks and Traces* 9, no. 2 (November 1987): 67, recorded 27 October 1850 in Will Book A, 198. This was probably Thomas Keesee Jr. and John Hill Jr., since Thomas Keesee Sr. generally appended the "Sr." to his name.

37. The part of Saline County where George Polk Keesee lived became part of the new county of Grant in 1869.

38. "Thomas Keesee Sr. to George Keesee Deed" (acknowledged in Union County, Arkansas, 6 November 1854), Saline County, Arkansas, Deed Book D, 421–22, Office of the Saline County Clerk, Benton, Arkansas, transcribed by Pauline Brown, Benton, Arkansas.

39. *Biographical and Historical Memoirs of Southern Arkansas*, 825.

40. After Robert Calvert died, the railroad came through Robertson County but passed a few miles from the town of Sterling, where Calvert's lands and the church were located. Sterling was abandoned in favor of the new town on the railroad (named "Calvert" in honor of Robert Calvert), and the Cumberland Presbyterian church was deeded to church trustees and physically moved to Calvert, where it remains today. See Texas Official Historical Medallion on church, photograph in possession of the author; *Calvert Grave Site*, <http://www.rtis.com/reg/calvert/

cagrave.htm>; and "Heirs of Robert Calvert to Cumberland Presbyterian Church," Robertson County, Texas, Deed Book O, 498–99, dated 31 January 1868, Robertson County Courthouse, Franklin, Texas.

41. Barbara Scott Wyche of Richmond, Texas, telephone interview, 1 November 2000; Armour, "From Union County, Arkansas Court Record Book E, 1853–1866"; and Confederate pension application of Thomas J. Keesee (Texas 2915), Texas Confederate Pension Application Files, Texas State Archives, Austin, Texas.

42. See *Shiloh Cumberland Presbyterian Church, Navarro and Dallas County, Texas, 1847–1872: Ovilla Community, Midlothian, Texas, Ellis County,* transcribed Shiloh Cumberland Presbyterian Church minutes, 2nd Sabbath [14] July 1867, 42, Lawrenceburg, Tennessee, Buffalo River Chapter, National Society Daughters of the American Revolution, 1978–79, Historical Foundation of the Cumberland Presbyterian Church, Memphis, Tennessee.

43. Letter dated 29 August 1871 to Texas State Police officer, Lt. Clayburn Johnson, Texas State Police Papers, and Giddeon [*sic*] Keesee, Texas Penitentiary Files, both in Texas State Archives, Austin, Texas.

44. Censer, "Southwestern Migration," 418.

45. Ibid., 410.

46. Cashin, *A Family Venture,* jacket blurb by Catherine Clinton (first quotation), 32 (second, third, and fourth quotations), 79 (fifth and sixth quotations), 80 (seventh quotation).

47. Ibid., 34 (first quotation), 4 (second quotation).

48. Ball, *Slaves in the Family.* Although I have little doubt that there is at least the possibility that some members of the Keesee kinship group were little different from members of other planter groups (like the Balls) in siring children with slaves, I have not been able to uncover any explicit evidence pointing to a mingling of the black and white families.

49. Lévi-Strauss, *The Elementary Structures of Kinship,* chap. 5, "The Principle of Reciprocity." Note that antebellum southerners did not "exchange" women in ritualized ceremonies fraught with social implications in quite the same manner as did, for example, the Nambikware Indians of western Brazil described by Lévi-Strauss.

50. Faragher, *Daniel Boone,* 71, 90–91 (migration with family), 341 (first quotation), 73 (second quotation). In the service of full disclosure, Daniel Boone is my first cousin, six times removed; that is, his father and my great-great-great-great-great-grandfather were brothers. My ancestor, however, did not go to Kentucky with Boone.

Chapter Three. Kinship and Religion

1. Boles, *The Great Revival,* 183 (quotation); Hill, *Encyclopedia of Religion in the South,* 311–13. For the development and influence of religion in the South, see also

Heyrman, *Southern Cross;* Raboteau, *Slave Religion;* Loveland, *Southern Evangelicals;* Gewehr, *The Great Awakening;* Mathews, *Religion in the Old South;* Isaac, *The Transformation of Virginia;* Ownby, *Subduing Satan;* and studies of the developments of various denominations in specific states such as Flynt, *Alabama Baptists.*

2. As argued in greater depth elsewhere, most of the elements of everyday life fell under the dominion of the family amid the paucity of other strong southern economic, political, and social institutions.

3. See also Shoumatoff, *The Mountain of Names,* 84–85, for the "cultural inheritance" of religious values.

4. MacKethan, ed., *Recollections of a Southern Daughter,* xxxii, 60 (quotation), 115–16.

5. Phelan, *A History of Early Methodism,* 127ff., emphasis added.

6. Bolsterli, ed., *A Remembrance of Eden,* 11–12 (for information about the Bullocks), 37 (quotations). See 27–28 for Charles L. Bullock's religious upbringing.

7. West, *A History of Methodism,* 319–22.

8. Note that Martha's name came from her maternal great-grandmother Martha Wooding, who married James Chappell. For Martha's dates of birth and death, see *Tombstone Inscriptions of Ashley County, Arkansas,* Colonel Francis Vivian Brooking Chapter, National Society Daughters of the American Revolution, 1968, 1:142. She is buried at Mt. Zion Cemetery. For family information, see J[ohn] A[lexander] Hargrove, "Autobiography," Rockdale, Texas, 1903, manuscript and typescript copies on file at Chappel Hill Historical Society Museum, Chappell Hill, Texas. J. A. Hargrove was Martha's brother. See also Judy Winfield and Nath Winfield, comps., loose-leaf notebook, Chappel Hill Historical Museum, Washington County, Texas, citation to records of final settlement, Washington County, Texas, Book F, 490; Chappell, *A Genealogical History,* 235; and "Obituary," *True Democrat* (Little Rock), 7 December 1859: 3 (quotation).

9. *Biographical and Historical Memoirs of Pulaski . . . Counties, Arkansas,* hereafter cited as *Biographical and Historical Memoirs of Central Arkansas,* 240. Although this source names Harland as pastor, I believe this to be an error, as there is no trace of anyone with this name. William Wharton, on the other hand, is known to have been a Presbyterian minister in this community and is mentioned often in the records between 1839 and 1850. See, for example, the marriages Wharton performed in Akins and Moore, transcribers, *Saline County, Arkansas, Marriage Records,* 1–11, 13–14. For more information about early Saline County churches, see Cloud, "Early Devotion in Saline County," 9.

10. "Last Will and Testament of William Wharton," W. H. Warton [*sic*] Probate, Robertson County, Texas, Loose Probate Files, Robertson County Courthouse, Franklin, Texas.

11. *Biographical and Historical Memoirs of Southern Arkansas,* 825.

12. Glover, Polk, and Baker, "Report of the History Committee of the Pine Bluff

Baptist Association, 1974," in *Pine Bluff Missionary Baptist Association, 1974 Minutes and Yearbook,* 20–25; and Cloud, "Early Devotion in Saline County."

13. For Clardy family presence in South Carolina, see Pendleton County, South Carolina, Deed Book B, 178–80, 269–70, in Hendrix, comp., *Pendleton County, S.C., Deed Books A & B.* For the evolution of counties in South Carolina, see Thorndale and Dollarhide, *Map Guide,* 297–305.

14. "History of Francois Missionary Baptist Church," 77. William G. Frost was or became a Baptist minister. See McLane, *Hot Spring County, Arkansas, 1860 United States Census,* 54, which lists Frost's occupation as Baptist clergyman, born about 1795 in South Carolina, living in Dwelling 357, Ouachita Township, Hot Spring County.

15. West, *A History of Methodism,* 154–58.

16. The early marriage records for Pickens County, Alabama, are not extant. For county formation and availability of county records, see *The Handy Book for Genealogists,* 9. For the marriage date in Pickens County, see Winfield and Winfield, comps., loose-leaf notebook, citation to Mrs. Irma Haynie Haynes, Beaumont, Texas.

17. Phelan, *A History of Early Methodism,* 15, and passim for background on the restrictions on religion in Texas during Mexican rule and the development of the Methodist denomination in Texas during the republic and early statehood eras.

18. For proof of the various kinsmen's early presence in Texas, see the following records: William Keesee bought 1,034 acres (part of the Lawrence League) for $2,058 from David Gilleland on 25 December 1837, and one of the witnesses was Keesee's brother-in-law James Chappell (Deed Book B, 15); William Keesee bought 300 acres (partly in Austin County and on Caney Creek) for $900 from James Stephens, also on 25 December 1837 and also witnessed by his brother-in-law (Deed Book B, 275); Robert Chappell was the witness to his son James's purchase of 200 acres (part of Miller's League) for $600 on 9 February 1838 (Deed Book D, 166); and Robert Chappell bought 100 acres (part of the Kuykendall League) for $400 on 13 February 1840 (Deed Book D, 208)—all in Murray, comp., *Washington County, Texas, Deed Abstracts,* 39, 58, 103, 105.

19. For Keesee's land, see Murray, comp., *Austin County, Texas, Deed Abstracts,* 25, certificate 124, for 320 acres, entered 5 December 1838 at the Land Office in Austin, Texas. See also Texas General Land Office Records, Austin, Texas, File Houston-2-55, certificate 68, copies in possession of the author. For more information (although not reliably accurate), see Ray, *Austin Colony Pioneers,* 43–45 (Chappell Hill), 77 (Robert W. Chappell), 43, 137 (Keesee), 114, 118 (Hargrove).

20. See Cashin, *A Family Venture,* 4–5 (quotations on 5), and for the Chappell family migration, see Chappell, *A Genealogical History,* 235–36.

21. Abstract of Deed Book B, 23–25, in Murray, comp., *Austin County, Texas, Deed Abstracts,* 31, emphasis added.

22. Phelan, *A History of Early Methodism,* 37–48 (for Methodist activity in Washington County), 215–16 (for the camp meeting; quotation on 216, emphasis added).

23. Ibid., 296, 296 n. 1; and Winfield and Winfield, *All Our Yesterdays*, 10.

24. Winfield and Winfield, *All Our Yesterdays*, 10.

25. Phelan, *A History of Early Methodism*, 352.

26. Winfield and Winfield, *All Our Yesterdays*, 14–17. The Winfields cite Washington County, Texas, Deed Record K, 288–89, Washington County Courthouse, Brenham, Texas; H. P. N. Gammel, *The Laws of Texas, 1822–1897*, 10 vols. (Austin, 1898), 3:1128–29, 4:134, 732–33; and Phelan, *A History of Methodism*, 358.

27. Phelan, *A History of Methodism*, 359–61 (quotations on 361).

28. Winfield and Winfield, *All Our Yesterdays*, 13, 36.

29. Ragsdale, *They Sought a Land*, 1 (first three quotations), 108 (fourth quotation). For more information on the Associate Reformed Presbyterian Church, see Hill, ed., *Encyclopedia of Religion*, 76. The distinguishing factor in the sect's dissent was "its recognition of the biblical Psalms as the only suitable hymns."

30. Heyrman, *Southern Cross*, 134.

31. Schweiger, *The Gospel Working Up*, 20. See also the tables in the appendix for Schweiger's compiled statistics on topics such as "Father's Profession" (197–208). Thanks to colleague Charles A. Israel, Rice University, 2001, for bringing this work to my attention.

32. For biographical information about King, see the Cumberland Presbyterian Church Historical Society, <http://www.cumberland.org/hfcp/minister/Kings .htm>, accessed 2 December 1999; and for the formation of the Cumberland Presbyterian Church, see Crisman, *Origin and Doctrines*, esp. 43–44 (quotation on 44, emphasis in original); McDonnold, *History of the Cumberland Presbyterian Church;* and Hill, ed., *Encyclopedia of Religion*, 188–89.

33. McDonnold, *History of the Cumberland Presbyterian Church*, 185–86.

34. Campbell, *History of the Cumberland Presbyterian Church*, 69–74.

35. Crisman, *Biographical Sketches*, 54–56.

36. Burrus, Baughn, and Campbell, *A People Called Cumberland Presbyterians*, 83–104, 99 (quotation), 100–101, "A Genealogical Chart Showing the Intermarriage of the Ewing, McLean, Davidson, and Brevard Families."

37. West, *A History of Methodism*, 154–58 (quotations on 155–57); and Hargrove, "Autobiography."

38. West, *A History of Methodism*, 158, 552.

39. Schweiger, *The Gospel Working Up*, 21 (quotation).

Chapter Four. Kinship's Role in Economic and Political Power

1. Bailyn and DeWolfe, *Voyagers to the West*, 137, 141–42 (first quotation), 145 (second, third, and fourth quotations).

2. Carr, Menard, and Walsh, *Robert Cole's World*.

3. Ibid., 145 (first quotation), 21 (second quotation).

4. Ibid., 146 (first quotation), 147, 150 (third quotation).

5. Ibid., 158–59 (first quotation), 164–65 (second quotation). The authors point out that in the 1650s almost 70 percent of the (white) population were adult males, but males only constituted 28 percent of the total by 1712; the proportion of children in the population increased over the same period from about 25 percent to about 50 percent (158).

6. Daniel Scott Smith employs the "natural history" model of population development, which is one way of explaining the burgeoning of kinship networks. Borrowed from biologists but adopted by historians, it describes a three-part process in the evolution of rural communities: settlement, the growth of population and a progression to maximization of agricultural lands, and finally population stabilization, accompanied by out-migration and lower natural population growth. "Thus kinship density increases," Smith notes, "as communities pass from the first to the final stage of settlement" ("All in Some Degree," 58). Smith describes this "natural history model" of local population development as one "that lays out a sequence of regular stages that depend on the evolving relationship between numbers of inhabitants and the resources available in the economic environment" (ibid., 45). He cites as examples of this model's use in early American studies Lockridge, "Land, Population, and the Evolution of New England Society," 62–80; Rutman, "Assessing the Little Communities," 172–78; and others. Smith also notes that the model factors significantly in Kulikoff, *Tobacco and Slaves* (ibid., 58 n. 28). This model provides a commonsensical framework for explaining the transition from mostly male and significantly nonfamily immigration to the "dense kinship networks" that Carr, Menard, and Walsh report. Rutman and Rutman describe a similar process of increasing kin density over time in *A Place in Time: Middlesex County,* 99–100. Stated simply, the three stages of the natural history model of population density applied to one county in Virginia comprise the narrative of the book—with the addition of the massive effects of large-scale Negro slavery. In *A Place in Time: Explicatus,* chapter 8, "Social Networks," the Rutmans chart the rising percentages of kinship links in the years 1687, 1704, and 1724. Marilyn Vos Savant summed up this phenomenon in a nutshell: responding to an inquiry about why it seems one has to buy more and more gifts every year, Vos Savant answered, "It's this way for everyone who has relatives. The problem with relatives—unlike friends—is that, even without the slightest effort on our part, they still multiply with time" ("Ask Marilyn").

7. Gies and Gies, *Marriage and the Family,* esp. 4: "Relationships of consanguinity played an important part in the society of the past"; Stone, *The Family, Sex and Marriage in England;* Goody, *The Development of the Family and Marriage;* and Rosenthal, *Patriarchy and Families of Privilege.*

8. Gross, *The Minutemen and Their World,* 71.

9. Ibid., 13, 212 n. 29 (quotation). For intergenerational economic mobility, see

234–35 n. 21. For evidence that ties of blood were not always determining factors in political struggles, see 26.

    10. Smith, "Child-Naming Practices," 559.

    11. Smith, *Inside the Great House,* 177 (quotation). See especially 177 n. 5: Smith cites Snydor, *Gentlemen Freeholders,* and Green, "Foundations of Political Power," "[f]or the growing intermarriage of planters in local and provincial politics in the eighteenth-century Chesapeake."

    12. Peterson, *Thomas Jefferson and the New Nation,* passim and 37 (first quotation); Kulikoff, *Tobacco and Slaves,* 9, 10 (third quotation), 270–75 (second quotation, 275). Like Gross, Kulikoff found a correlation between age at first political office and degree of kinship with related leaders (ibid., 275). See also Lee, *The Price of Nationhood,* 19 (fourth quotation), 20, 23, 38, 56, 71, 73; for kinship ties among slaves, see 69–73.

    13. Gross, *The Minutemen and Their World,* 71.

    14. See, for example, Ogburn, "The Family and Its Functions," in which Ogburn discusses the diminishment over time of the status derived from membership in particular families: "Property holdings in land are very likely to help fix family status, especially in small communities where everybody knows everybody else. . . . The growth of large cities, in which the effectiveness of gossip and other forms of non-legal social control is diminished, tends also to diminish family prestige. With few exceptions the personality of the individual family is lost in the crowd" (288). See also Smith, "All in Some Degree," 73 (quotation): Smith's argument is often obfuscated by his demographic theorizing, confusingly complex statistics, and murky writing, and yet it has much merit as a mechanism of explanation and offers a contrast of the "truncated orientation toward kin" in the Northeast with the extended and denser kinship ties of the South.

    15. The relationship between the Keesees, the Calverts, and the Hills is discussed fully in chapter 2. See Bardaglio, *Reconstructing the Household,* 42 (quotation).

    16. Hartog, *Man and Wife in America,* 106 (all quotations). The Wilson quotation comes from his *Commentaries on American Law* (1827), 2:109. For a full discussion of this topic, see Salmon, *Women and the Law of Property.*

    17. Hartog writes: "A marriage was both legally constituted and private. Law was not everything in a marriage. Love, lust, hatred, duty, friendship, respect, affection, abandonment, commitment, greed, and self-sacrifice, all the feelings and practices that made up a nineteenth-century marriage, were not primarily legal. But law was always there as well" (*Man and Wife in America,* 24). He also touches on women's rights advocates' view of marriage as being similar to slavery.

    18. Ibid., 22 (quotation).

    19. Walsh, *From Calabar to Carter's Grove.* Walsh focuses on seventeenth- and eighteenth-century Burwell family slave communities in Virginia.

    20. Ibid., 22 (first quotation), 23 (second quotation), 24 (third quotation). See also

Brazy, "An American Planter," for a study of Natchez planter Stephen Duncan and the "[v]ital connections" of marriage and kinship that propelled his "ascendancy to planter status" (514 [quotations]).

21. Walsh, *From Calabar to Carter's Grove,* 26–27.

22. Brown, *Indian Wars and Pioneers of Texas,* 638–39. Other undocumented sources says Robert Calvert was a descendant of Lord Baltimore, although that seems unlikely given presently available evidence; see, for example, *Texas State Travel Guide,* 95. The tombstone is inscribed: "Hon. Robert Calvert was born in the State of Tenn. Feb. 19, 1802" (Sterling Cemetery, Robertson County, Texas, site visit by author, 6 March 1997). The Cumberland Presbyterians broke off from the Presbyterian Church in 1810; previous to this time, the Calverts were Presbyterian. For a cogent explication of the roots of the Cumberland Presbyterians, see Gore, *A History of the Cumberland Presbyterian Church,* esp. 1–33.

23. Abernethy, *The Formative Period,* 26–28, 40–42, 88. See also Boucher, "Factors in the History of Tuscaloosa, Alabama," 78–80, for the importance of the Black Warrior River as a transportation mode for cotton to Mobile as well as merchandise to Tuscaloosa from Mobile. Boucher notes, "As early as 1832 there were at least two cotton storage houses having a capacity of 2,000 bales each" in Tuscaloosa (ibid., 82). Boucher's history of the town of Tuscaloosa is perforce a narrative overview of the development of the county and the region as well. For an interesting if quaint overview of early Tuscaloosa society, see Brown, "A Social History of Tuscaloosa."

24. Murray, *Tuscaloosa County, Alabama Marriages,* 47 (both marriages); and Brown, *Indian Wars and Pioneers of Texas,* 638.

25. Guardian Record Book, 1830–1842, Orphans Court, Tuscaloosa County, Alabama, 4, 6, 11, 24, 28, 44, 54–55, 74–75.

26. Ibid., 4, 11.

27. Barefield, *Old Tuscaloosa Land Office Records,* 12, 20–22, 44, 68, 69, 86; and cash entry index cards, surname Keesee, supplied by the National Archives. It is likely that the family had been living on these parcels of land for years before they officially filed to purchase it from the federal government.

28. Murray, *Tuscaloosa County, Alabama Marriages.*

29. Parker, *Historical Recollections,* 137–38, 150; and Billingsley, *1840 Saline County, Arkansas, Census,* 12, original census 212, Saline Township; age and gender groupings are fairly consistent with the children as given in text. See also "Obituary of Sarah Agnes Calvert," *Saline* 6, no. 4 (December 1991): 195: "Departed this life in Saline county, on the 7th inst.—after a few days' severe illness, Sarah Agnes, infant daughter of Hon. R. Calvert & Lady. She has left Parents, relations, and friends to mourn her irreparable loss. Although a child of only 2 years old she was a universal favorite of all who knew her, very sprightly, beautiful, and prepossessing, in all her manners, a fond father's delight, a tender Mother's joy."

30. Lambert, *History of Tuscaloosa County, Alabama,* 23–24, 47; and Reese, transcriber, *Overseers of the Poor,* 1, 8, 11, 14, 17, 19, 21, 24, 28–29.

31. Abernethy, *The Formative Period,* 83–85. The panic of 1837 didn't affect Arkansas until about 1845; see Bolton, *Territorial Ambition,* 54; and Baptist, "Creating an Old South," 56 (first quotation), 55 (second quotation). Baptist also presents an excellent overview of the decision-making process involved in migration to the plantation frontier (39–66).

32. Bolton, *Territorial Ambition,* 73–74. See also Walz, "Migration into Arkansas," for an exhaustive analysis of black and white immigrants into Arkansas—their states of origin, migration patterns, reasons for coming to Arkansas, and settlement patterns within the state.

33. McNeilly, *The Old South Frontier,* 55 (quotation).

34. DeBow, *The Seventh Census,* 548.

35. McNeilly, *The Old South Frontier.* McNeilly's study is an excellent overview of the development of the planter class in Arkansas with great applicability to the Keesee kinship group. Bolton's *Territorial Ambition* also argues that the wide-open setting of territorial and early-statehood politics and Arkansas's natural resources were magnets for ambitious families.

36. Allen and McLane, *Arkansas Land Patents,* 84 (Calvert), 5 (Benjamin Clardy, who was married to Mary [Keesee] Calvert's sister Agnes), 101–2 (Keesees); Jackson, *Arkansas Tax Lists,* 380; Suddath, *Tuscaloosa County, Alabama Records,* 4–6; Baker, "A List of the Taxable Property"; and *Biographical and Historical Memoirs of Central Arkansas,* which states that ninety families from Tuscaloosa and Bibb Counties, Alabama, "took up their abode" in Saline County in the summer of 1837 and that among the "leaders of this colony were Thomas Keesee, Robert Calvert," and others (234). Note that Thomas Keesee Jr.'s biography in *A Memorial and Biographical History of Ellis County, Texas* states that he moved to Saline County, Arkansas, in 1838 (476).

37. McNeilly, *The Old South Frontier,* 68.

38. *Arkansas Gazette* (Little Rock), 4 December 1839. My deepest appreciation to Tom W. Dillard, curator, Butler Center for Arkansas Studies, Central Arkansas Library System, 100 Rock Street, Little Rock, Arkansas 72201, for sending me this article.

39. Cashin, *A Family Venture.*

40. 1840 U.S. Census, Saline County, Arkansas, 208, 210, 212, 213; see also Billingsley, *1840 Saline County, Arkansas, Census,* 3, for a list of slave owners.

41. McNeilly, *The Old South Frontier,* 78.

42. James Moore is a very common name, but I am reasonably certain that the James Moore who married Robert Calvert's widowed mother, Lucy (Rogers) Calvert, in 1825 in Tuscaloosa County, Alabama (ceremony performed by kinsman Jesse Hill), and the James Moore who married Benjamin Clardy's daughter Saryan in 1841 in

Saline County were the same man, even though he was much younger than Lucy and much older than Saryan. James Moore and his wife, Lucy, sold land in Saline County in 1839, and Lucy is probably the oldest female enumerated in Moore's household in 1840. Lucy probably died shortly after the census, and Moore, age forty-one, then married Saryan Clardy, who was not quite sixteen. For the Moore-Calvert marriage, see Gantrud, *Alabama Records,* 47; for Lucy and James Moore as husband and wife in Saline County, see Saline County, Arkansas, Deed Book A, 457–60, Office of the Saline County Clerk, Benton, Arkansas; and for the Moore-Clardy marriage, see Saline County, Arkansas, Marriage Book A, 35, Marriage Records, Office of the Saline County Clerk, Benton, Arkansas.

43. Crawford, *Saline County, Arkansas, County Court Record Book Vol. 1,* 18; Crawford, *Saline County, Arkansas, County Court Record Book Vol. 2,* 12, 30, 35 (original record book 105, 127, 133). See, for example, *Laws of Arkansas Territory* (Little Rock, Ark. Terr.: J. Steele, Esq., 1835), 520–32 (slaves), 530–32 (patrols). Patrols were appointed by the circuit court in each township as required, "consisting of one discreet person to be called the captain of the patrol, and as many others under his direction as the court may deem necessary, not exceeding four . . . and the said company . . . shall patrol as many hours in each month as the court appointing the same may direct, not to be less than twelve hours in each month within their respective townships, and visit negro quarters, and other suspected places of unlawful assemblies of slaves." The captain and the members of the patrol were to be paid "one dollar for every twelve hours" of patrolling and, unless the patrollers served without compensation, a tax on all slaves over the age of sixteen in that township was to be assessed to pay the costs of the patrol. For the activities of slave patrols in South Carolina, see Rosengarten, *Tombee,* 118–20. For James Moore as Saline County commissioner, see, for example, Saline County, Arkansas, Deed Book A, 295, 299, 302, Office of the Saline County Clerk, Benton, Arkansas.

44. *Central Arkansas,* 235; and Harper, ed., *Historical Report,* 254, 624.

45. Harper, ed., *Historical Report,* 202 (for territorial treasurer service), 248–49 (for legislature service), 615 (for terms as sheriff). The journals for the Ninth Territorial General Assembly of 1835 are not extant, and Rutherford was not reported as a member of the First General Assembly after statehood (1836–37). See also "Abstract of Payments to Members of the Legislative Assembly [Held 1833]," in Clarence Edwin Carter, ed., *The Territorial Papers of the United States* (Washington, D.C.: Government Printing Office, 1954), 20:942–43; Samuel M. Rutherford was paid for thirty days at the rate of three dollars per day and received no payment for mileage (indicating he probably lived at that time within the city of Little Rock, where the session was held) for a total of ninety dollars; and *A Memorial and Biographical History of Ellis County, Texas:* "[A]fter the admission of the State into the Union he was agent for the Choctaws, and then for the Seminoles, after which he was elected county Judge;

he was sent to Florida as an agent for the Seminole Indians, and after one year he was successful in making a treaty with them" (285). For service on the Democratic Nominating Committee, see Allen, *Arkansas Imprints*, 24–25. Since no state convention was held, the Democratic Party formed the committee on which S. M. Rutherford and "Thos. Kesee, Sen." served "to prepare an address to the people of Arkansas on the subject of the presidential election."

46. See *Biographical and Historical Memoirs of Southern Arkansas*, 164, for an extensive biography of Archibald Hamilton Rutherford. See also Harper, ed., *Historical Report*, 202, for service as treasurer of Arkansas from 1855 to 1857; and Mrs. E. E. [Rutherford] Wall, "Archibald H. Rutherford: An Arkansas Pioneer," *Arkansas Historical Quarterly* 5, no. 4 (1946): 338–401.

47. *A Memorial and Biographical History of Ellis County, Texas*, 285; Billingsley, *1840 Saline County, Arkansas, Census* (as a U.S. deputy marshal, George W. Rutherford was the enumerator for the census in this county in 1840); and "Saline County Commissioned Officers," 115.

48. Baptist, "The Migration of Planters," 527–54, 529 (first quotation), 553 (second quotation). For an expanded version of this article, see Baptist's dissertation, "Creating an Old South."

49. Billingsley, *1850 Saline County, Arkansas, Census*, 9, 72, 187, 189; and McLane and Allen, *1850 Census of Southern Arkansas*, 110 (slave schedule).

50. McLane and Hubbard, *Saline County, Arkansas Marriage Records*, 29, 72, 76; Henderson, *Arkansas Gazette Index*, 203, announcement of the marriage of Peter Smith to Mary Calvert on 28 December 1848, 3, col. 4; Morgan, *Arkansas Marriage Notices*, 40, George Washington Rutherford and Miss Lucy Calvert, eldest daughter of Col. Robert Calvert, both of Saline County, on Thursday, 28 September 1843, Saline County by Rev. William Wharton as noted in the *Arkansas Banner*, 7 October 1843, and the *Arkansas Times and Advocate*, 2 October 1843; McLane and Allen, *1850 Census of Southern Arkansas*, 100, which shows William and Alabama residing in Union County, Johnson Township, Dwelling 419, and states that the marriage was recorded in Book A, 95. Also see 104: Alabama's father is enumerated in Union County, Wilmington Township, Dwelling 691; and 1850 U.S. Census, Population Schedule, Union County, Arkansas, 255-B, Dwelling 419, Johnson Township—the census column "Married within the year" was checked.

51. For Robert Calvert's buying and selling of Benton town lots, see Saline County, Arkansas, Deed Book A, 347, Book B, 9–10, 205, Book C, 214–16, 231, 265, and Book E, 273–74, 284, Office of the Saline County Clerk, Benton, Arkansas. For William Calvert's business enterprise, see Saline County, Arkansas, Deed Book B, 9–10, in which James Moore as Saline County commissioner, along with surviving partner William Calvert of the firm Smith and Calvert, sells two town lots to Robert Calvert after the death of Smith (1839). For Robert Calvert sending some of his slaves

to Union County with his son William, see 1850 U.S. Census, Slave Schedule, Union County, Arkansas (Johnson Township), for fifteen slaves under the name "Robt. Calvert." For quotation, see McNeilly, *The Old South Frontier,* 68.

52. Saline County, Arkansas, Deed Book B, 9–10, Office of the Saline County Clerk, Benton, Arkansas.

53. Saline County, Arkansas, Deed Book A, 349, Office of the Saline County Clerk, Benton, Arkansas.

54. Crawford, *Saline County, Arkansas, County Court Record Book, Vol. 1,* 61, 63, 67, 69, 71, 79–80. Note that in 1839 Saline County paid Hicks $4.00 for the black-smithing job, $47.00 for the repairs to the jail, $1.50 for services as a justice of the peace, and $10.00 for his duties as associate justice of the county court.

55. Milton was enumerated in Saline County in 1840, was on a jury there in August 1841, but was listed as having "left the county" on the 1842 tax list. In 1848 Union County Democrats nominated him for a position in the Arkansas House of Representatives. He was not enumerated there at the time of the 1850 census, however. See Billingsley, *1840 Saline County, Arkansas, Census,* 10; Landreth, *Abstract,* 1 (1837), 14 (1839), 55 (August 1841, defendant in debt case, failed to appear), 56 (August 1841, served on jury); and Crawford, *Saline County, Arkansas, County Court Record Book, Vol. 2,* 62 (Milton Keesee is on the delinquent tax list for 1842). For service in Arkansas General Assembly in 1848–49, see Harper, ed., *Historical Report,* 259.

56. "From Alabama to Arkansas," *Grassroots* 8 (July 1988): 8–9.

57. Bolton, *Territorial Ambition,* 54–55.

58. McLane and Allen, *1850 Census of Southern Arkansas,* 95–110.

59. Robertson County, Texas, Deed Book M, 311–12, judgment for *Milton Keesee v. Robt. Calvert as Adm. of Wm. M. Webb,* citing to original deed in Deed Book I, 31, 34; and Robertson County, Texas, Deed Book L, 74–75, all in Robertson County Court-house, Franklin, Texas.

60. Baker, *A History of Robertson County, Texas,* 129; and Parker, *Historical Recollections,* 137–38.

61. Robertson County, Texas, Tax Lists, 1853 and 1860, Robertson County Court-house, Franklin, Texas.

62. Calvert, in fact, was the executor of Wharton's estate when he died in Robertson County in 1862. For Wharton's residence in Saline County, Arkansas, see Billingsley, *1840 Saline County, Arkansas, Census,* 9 (census p. 209, Saline Township). For Wharton's residence in Robertson County, see 1860 U.S. Census, Population Schedule, Washington County, Texas, 176B, Dwelling 406, Precinct 3, P.O. Sterling, Texas. For more on the relationship between Wharton and Robert Calvert, see chapter 3.

63. Parker, *Historical Recollections,* 80, 137–38; and "Contract—Houston & Texas Central Railway Company to and with Robert Calvert and James S. Hanna," Robertson County, Texas, Deed Book N, 211–18, Robertson County Courthouse, Franklin, Texas.

64. *Central Arkansas,* 235; Baker, *A History of Robertson County, Texas,* 445; and Parker, *Historical Recollections,* 137–38. Note that his tombstone is adorned with a Masonic symbol; survey of Sterling Cemetery by the author, 28 March 1997. For his selling town lots and land, see, for example, Robertson County, Texas, Deed Book O, 480–81, Robertson County Courthouse, Franklin, Texas. For his business partnership with Rutherford, see G. W. Rutherford Probate, particularly "J. T. Garrett admr, Petition filed Oct. 31 1859, Succession of G. W. Rutherford," Robertson County, Texas, Loose Probate Files, Robertson County Courthouse, Franklin, Texas.

65. "Amended Petition for Letters of Administration, R. Calvert, Succession of Milton Keesee, Robertson County, Texas," filed 26 June 1860, Milton Keesee Probate, Robertson County, Texas, Loose Probate Files, Robertson County Courthouse, Franklin, Texas.

66. The sale bill in the Milton Keesee Probate, filed 29 April 1862, lists only horses and mules, sold mostly to family members at an estate sale held in Sterling, for a total of $3,018.50. An inventory of the estate filed in 1860 also lists "500 Acres of Land on the West Bank of Brazos River in Milam County" at $1.50 an acre for a total valuation of $750. Even if Milton Keesee had "no fixed domicile" and was "a nonresident . . . of any county in the state," his account with the merchant J. J. Hodge and Company, paid by his estate, listed only items obviously for his family's use, for example, reticule, scissors, garters, beads, ribbon, hose, thimble, silk, gingham, calico, buttons, candy, and Swiss muslin. For quotations, see "R. Calvert's Amended Petition for Letters of Administration," filed 26 June 1860, Milton Keesee Probate.

67. Milton Keesee Probate.

68. 1860 U.S. Census, Population Schedule, Falls County, Texas, Dwelling 202.

69. Various vouchers, Milton Keesee Probate.

70. Baker, *A History of Robertson County, Texas,* 480; and Brown, *Indian Wars and Pioneers of Texas,* 638–39 (quotation).

71. Report of auditor and list of claims, estate of Robert Calvert, 3 March 1869, Robertson County, Texas, Loose Probate Files, Robertson County Courthouse, Franklin, Texas.

72. His wife, Mary "Polly" (Keesee) Calvert, died on 16 December 1873 in Robertson County, also of yellow fever during a local epidemic. Baker, *A History of Robertson County, Texas,* 639; and survey of Sterling Cemetery by the author, 28 March 1997, photographs of tombstones in possession of the author. See also Sterling Cemetery, Texas Historical Commission Marker, Robertson County, Texas: "Burial place of some 400 Texas pioneers and descendants. On land granted (1835) to A. J. Webb, bought in 1850 by Judge Robert Calvert, a civic leader in Sterling, a town named for empresario Sterling C. Robertson. Calvert dedicated 11.1-acre cemetery and built adjacent Cumberland Presbyterian Church of his own plantation timber. In 1867, Judge Calvert died and was buried near cemetery gate. The church building was moved by

oxen to new town of Calvert (1 mi. E). In 1868, his wife, Mary Keesee Calvert, and their three daughters deeded cemetery site to the Cumberland Presbyterians." The marker was erected in 1973. Site visit by the author, 6 March 1997.

73. *Texas State Travel Guide,* 95; Brown, *Indian Wars and Pioneers of Texas,* 638; and survey of Sterling Cemetery by the author, 28 March 1997.

74. Estate of Robert Calvert.

75. Brazy, "An American Planter," 3–4.

Chapter Five. The Kinship Group in the Postbellum Era

1. Faust, "The Peculiar South Revisited," 107 (quotation).

2. "Last Will and Testament of Thomas Keesee Sr.," written 16 December 1858, proved 1861, Will Record 1, 157–59, Abstract Office Volume, Ashley County, Arkansas. One puzzling element in this document is Thomas Keesee Sr.'s mention of his daughters Jane Jenkins and Agnes Clardy, who had died several years previous to Keesee's writing of his will. Although Jane and her husband were prosperous planters in Choctaw County, Mississippi, separated from most of the rest of her family, and Agnes was among the group who stayed behind in Saline County, Arkansas, we would expect Keesee to have known about the death of his own daughters and the fate of his grandchildren. Either he did not know of their deaths, which is an anomaly in this closely bound kinship group, or he simply listed them as an alternative to listing all their heirs. By saying he had provided for them already, he was, in effect, avoiding any claims against his estate by Jane's or Agnes's immediate families, preferring to allocate his estate to his other children. Since he named *two* deceased daughters, the latter scenario seems most likely. However, his son Gideon's exclusion from inheritance is more puzzling, since Gideon was still alive.

3. Benton Keesee enlisted in Company B, Third Arkansas Infantry, C.S.A., National Archives, *Civil War Compiled Military Service Records,* Provo, Utah, 1999, <http://ancestry.com>, accessed 14 September 2002.

4. Spencer, *Marriage Bonds,* 137, D. H. Thornton, twenty-four, to Miss Virginia Keesee, fourteen, on 18 December 1855, by Joab B. Pratt, MG of Baptist Church, as transcribed from Union County Marriage Book B, 141 (second page).

5. 1860 U.S. Census, Population Schedule, Saline County, Arkansas, Saline Township, Dwelling 984.

6. Isaac N. Keesee, as administrator of the estate of George Keesee, assessed and paid taxes for the year 1868 on over 2,000 acres of land; affidavit, Unity Keesee, administratrix, estate of George Keesee, filed 14 September 1865 (this document reported the value of the estate to be "about the sum of Four Thousand"); affidavit, Finis Leech, administrator de bonis non, estate of George Keesee, filed 18 December 1865 (reported the value of the estate to be "about the sum of Four Thousand"); application for letters of administration, I. N. Keesee, filed 5 February 1866 (assessing a value for the estate of about $5,500); and claim of A. F. Mitchell against the estate of

George Keesee, dated 29 September 1868—all contained in George Keesee Probate, Loose Probate Files, Office of the Saline County, Arkansas, County Clerk, Benton, Arkansas. For Aaron Keesee, see Orr-Hickey, transcriber, *1880 Census*, 46. Note that Grant County was created from Saline County in 1867.

7. 1860 U.S. Census, Population Schedule, Saline County, Arkansas, Davis Township, P.O. Prattville, 6 June 1860, 11, Dwelling 63 (Isaac N. Keesee); and Rowan, "1860 Saline County, Arkansas Slave Schedule Summary."

8. Application to compromise debt, estate of George Keesee (Daniel Leech note), filed 1 November 1867, George Keesee Probate.

9. William E. Bedinger <webed@emial.msn.com> to author, 23 December 1998. Bedinger is the great-great-grandson of Daniel Leech. J. Leech, also a descendant, provided much information on this family.

10. Manford Eugene Jones, "A History of Cotton Culture along the Middle Brazos River," master's thesis, University of New Mexico, 1939, <http://www.rootsweb .com/~txrober2/>.

11. "Inventory & Appraisement of Estate of Milton Keesee, Dec'd," filed 31 December 1860, Milton Keesee Probate, Robertson County, Texas, Loose Probate Files, Robertson County Courthouse, Franklin, Texas. The land in Milam County was valued at $1.50 per acre.

12. "Amended Petition for Letters of Administration, R. Calvert, Succession of Milton Keesee," filed 26 June 1860, Milton Keesee Probate.

13. "Rob't Calvert Annual Exhibit as Adm'or, Succession of Milton Keesee, Dec'd," filed 31 December 1861, Milton Keesee Probate.

14. "Receipt, Succession of M. Keesee," filed 31 August 1863, Milton Keesee Probate. This document represents the final settlement to the heirs of Milton Keesee. Those signing the receipt were Mary Keesee (widow); F. A. Thomson for his wife, L. R. Thomson; Nannie C. Keesee; and Mary M. Garrett (the latter three were daughters of the deceased and his only surviving children).

15. Mary Keesee and the remainder of her family are found on the 1870 U.S. Census, Population Schedule, Robertson County, Texas, P.O. Calvert, 181B, 182A, Dwelling 274. Mary and her daughters are "House Keepers," while her orphaned grandson William Keesee is a "Bank Teller." Mary is the only one in the household who reports any real or personal property.

16. Family Bible of Mary Keesee Sims, daughter of Milton Keesee and Mary Calvert: "Mary Calvert Keesee, died of yellow fever 11 Oct 1873, age 67" (transcribed by Lucy Foster Miller, copies in possession of Carolyn Earle Billingsley).

17. *A Memorial and Biographical History of McClennan, Falls, Bell, and Coryell Counties, Texas*, 770.

18. Milton's daughter Lucy Rogers Keesee, named for her maternal grandmother, Lucy (Rogers) Calvert, married the brother of her aunt Martha Wooding (Chappell) Keesee, the wife of Milton Keesee's brother Gideon Keesee.

19. Saline County, Arkansas, Marriage Book A, 35, Marriage Records, Office of

the Saline County Clerk, Benton, Arkansas; and "1860 Union County Slave Schedules." G. W. Murphy had eight slaves, three males and five females. See also 1860
U.S. Census, Slave Schedule, Union County, Arkansas, El Dorado Township, dated
25 September 1860.

20. List of lands patented to George W. Murphy, Government Land Office
Records, U.S. Department of the Interior, Bureau of Land Management, <http://
www.glorecords.blm.gov/>, accessed 16 September 2000.

21. Marriage Book A, 35, for marriage of James Moore and Saryan Clardy; and
Gantrud, *Alabama Records*, 47, for the marriage of James Moore and Lucy Calvert.

22. Billingsley, *1840 Saline County, Arkansas, Census*, 10.

23. Childs and Ross, *North Louisiana Census Reports*, 3:38; G. W. Murphy was enumerated in Dwelling 332 and James Moore in Dwelling 334.

24. Ibid., 3:164, 219, Dwellings 594 and 1098, respectively; and "1860 Union County
Slave Schedules," 31.

25. Austin, *Twigs and Branches*, 20, citing 1870 U.S. Census, Population Schedule,
Union Parish, Louisiana, Ward 6, 136, Dwelling 26. Austin is the great-great-great-
great-great-grandson of Thomas Keesee Sr. through the Clardy-Moore line.

26. 1870 U.S. Census, Population Schedule, Union Parish, Louisiana, Ward 6, 136,
Dwelling 24. Sarah A. Moore is listed on the same page in Dwelling 26.

27. See Louisiana Division of Historic Preservation, Cherokee Plantation, <http://
www.crt.state.la.us/nh12/search_results.asp?search_type=historicname&value=
Cherokee+Plantation&pageno=1>, accessed 24 September 2002.

28. For more information about Charles H. Murphy Jr., see the editorials and obit-
uaries published at the time of his death in 2002, for example, "Obituary: Charles
Murphy," *Arkansas Democrat-Gazette* (Little Rock), Thursday, 21 March 2002: B6;
"The Practical Mariner: Charles Murphy Makes Port" (editorial), *Arkansas Democrat-Gazette*, 25 March 2002; and Young's Funeral Directors of Distinction, <http://
www.youngs.plan4ever.com>, accessed 31 March 2002, which contains the most
complete information.

29. 1830 U.S. Census, Tuscaloosa County, Alabama, 334; 1840 U.S. Census, Saline
County, Arkansas; 1850 U.S. Census, Slave Schedule, Union County, Arkansas,
Johnson Township; and 1860 U.S. Census, Slave Schedule, Union County, Arkansas,
Johnson Township, 9 July 1860.

30. Armour, comp., "From Union County, Arkansas Court Record Book E," 38;
and 1861 Union County, Arkansas, Home Guard Roster, <http://www.couchgenweb
.com/civilwar/unionco.html>, accessed 7 December 2000.

31. *A Memorial and Biographical History of Ellis County, Texas*, 476. Works of this
type and from this era are known to present their subjects in a laudatory manner.

32. Ibid., 476 (quotation); and John Hill Spain, "The Keesee Family," in Ovilla
Historical Society, *Ovilla, Texas History Book*, 111–13. Ovilla is a small community,
centered on the Shiloh Cumberland Presbyterian Church, where the Keesees and related families lived in Ellis County, Texas. It is in the vicinity of Waxahachie.

33. *A Memorial and Biographical History of Ellis County, Texas,* 477. Eleanor was already dead when this article was published.

34. Confederate pension application of Thomas J. Keesee (Texas 2915), Texas Confederate Pension Application Files, Texas State Archives, Austin, Texas.

35. Billingsley, *1840 Saline County, Arkansas, Census,* 3, 12; Landreth, "1850 Saline County, Arkansas Slave Schedule Summary"; and 1860 U.S. Census, Population Schedule, Washington County, Texas, 175B, Dwelling 392, Precinct 3, P.O. Sterling, Texas.

36. For more information on Robert Calvert and family, see Billingsley, "Antebellum Planters."

37. Petition of Mary M. Quaite for divorce from W. G. L. Quaite, filed originally in Fourteenth Judicial District Court, Ellis County, Texas; see also testimony of J. M. Strong. Due to a change in venue, the case was tried in Dallas County; see *Quaite v. Quaite,* Dallas County, Texas, District Court, Case 3000, Dallas County District Court Civil Case Papers, Cases 2995–3029, Microfilm 2057306, Dallas History and Archives Division, Dallas Public Library. The over four hundred pages of testimony offer incredible stories about the lives of the principals in the case.

38. 1830 U.S. Census, Tuscaloosa County, Alabama, 335; 1860 U.S. Census, Slave Schedule, Washington County, Texas, 590A–590B; and 1860 U.S. Census, Population Schedule, Washington County, Texas, 219–20, Dwelling 1060.

39. Nieman, "Black Political Power"; and *Burning of Brenham, Texas: Letter from the Secretary of War, in Relation to the Burning of the Town of Brenham, Texas, by United States Soldiers, as Alleged, in the Year 1866,* House of Representatives, 41st Cong., 3rd sess., Ex. Doc. 145. Brenham is the county seat of Washington County.

40. 1840 U.S. Census, Choctaw County, Mississippi, 74, l. 25.

41. Jane is alive on the 1850 census, taken 23 October; Elias Jenkins remarried in 1852. 1850 U.S. Census, Population Schedule, Choctaw County, Mississippi, Western Division, 4, Dwelling 48; and Jonathan Kennon Thompson Smith, *Death Notices from the Christian Advocate, Nashville, Tennessee, 1874–1876,* 2000, <http://www.tngenweb.org/madison/smith/nca6-08.htm>, accessed 10 July 2002: "June 17, 1876—Colonel Elias Jenkins, native of Wilson Co., Tenn., died near Aberdeen, Miss., Mar. 31, 1876 in the 74th year of his age; married Jane Keesee, Dec. 22, 1831 and moved from Tuscaloosa, Ala. to Choctaw Co., Miss. where he farmed; married Sue McNamora, 1852; located at Aberdeen in 1871."

42. 1860 U.S. Census, Population Schedule, Ashley County, Arkansas, Extra Township, P.O. Hamburg, 48, printed page 152, dated ——— July 1860.

43. I greatly appreciate Bethany L. Johnson's contributions to developing this view.

44. McPherson, *Ordeal by Fire,* 493 (quotation).

45. For the shattering of southern society after the war, see, for example, ibid., 493–95, 577, 582.

46. See, for example, Woodman, "Economic Reconstruction," 301–2; and Boswell, *Her Act and Deed.*

47. Bolsterli, *A Remembrance of Eden,* 101 (first and second quotations), 112 (third, fourth, and fifth quotations).

48. Thomas G. Dyer, "Education," in Wilson and Ferris, eds., *Encyclopedia of Southern Culture,* 1:400–402.

49. McPherson, *Ordeal by Fire,* 488.

50. For a larger discussion and overview of the issues of continuity versus change and the persistence of the planter elite, see Woodman, "Economic Reconstruction," 254–307; and Cobb, *Redefining Southern Culture,* esp. 5–24.

Conclusion: The Prospects for Kinship Studies

1. I would like to express my appreciation to Francelle Pruitt, Rice University, 2002, whose input helped me clarify some of these points.

2. McMillen, *Motherhood in the Old South,* 6 (quotation).

3. Williamson, *New People,* 55 (quotation). In a less explicit but no less powerful way, two books use the lens of family ties to focus and illuminate issues of race and gender: Alexander, *Ambiguous Lives;* and Leslie, *Woman of Color, Daughter of Privilege.*

4. Williamson, *New People,* 43–48.

5. Ibid., 44 (first quotation), 45 (second quotation).

Appendix: A Neighborhood Study of Kin in Union County, Arkansas

1. McLane and Allen, *1850 Census of Southern Arkansas.* My thanks to McLane and Allen for supplying me with the book's data file, from which these listings were copied. For the population figures, see DeBow, *The Seventh Census of the United States,* 545.

BIBLIOGRAPHY

Abernethy, Thomas Perkins. *The Formative Period in Alabama, 1815–1828.* Tuscaloosa: University of Alabama Press, 1965.

Akins, George, and Leon Rowland Moore, transcribers. *Saline County, Arkansas, Marriage Records, Books A-B-C-D-E. 1836–1885.* Benton, Ark.: Saline County History and Heritage Society, 1999.

Alexander, Adele Logan. *Ambiguous Lives: Free Women of Color in Rural Georgia, 1789–1879.* Fayetteville: University of Arkansas Press, 1991.

Allen, Albert H. *Arkansas Imprints: 1821–1876.* New York: R. R. Bowker Company for the Bibliographical Society of America, 1947.

Allen, Desmond Walls. "Mama's Baby, Daddy's Maybe." *Heritage Quest* (January–February 2002): 50–55.

Allen, Desmond Walls, and Carolyn Earle Billingsley. *Beginner's Guide to Family History Research.* 3rd ed. Conway, Ark.: Research Associates, 1997.

Allen, Desmond Walls, and Bobbie Jones McLane. *Arkansas Land Patents: Grant and Saline Counties.* Conway, Ark.: Arkansas Research, 1991.

Anderson, Benedict. *Imagined Communities: Reflections on the Origin and Spread of Nationalism.* London: Verso, 1983. Reprint, 1991.

Armour, Jamie Rhyan, comp. "From Union County, Arkansas Court Record Book E, 1853–1866." *Tracks and Traces* 5, no. 1 (1979): 38.

Austin, Roy L. *Twigs and Branches: A Reunion of Family Clardy.* Houston: Published by the author, ca. 1998.

Bailyn, Bernard, with the assistance of Barbara DeWolfe. *Voyagers to the West: A Passage in the Peopling of America on the Eve of the Revolution.* 1986. Reprint, New York: Vintage Books, 1988.

Baker, J. W. *A History of Robertson County, Texas.* Waco, Tex.: Texian Press, 1971.

Baker, Russell P., comp. "A List of the Taxable Property of the County of Saline for the Year 1836, as Taken by the Sheriff of Said County." *Saline* 1 (December 1984): 87–90.

Ball, Edward. *Slaves in the Family.* New York: Ballantine Books, 1998.

Baptist, Edward Eugene. "Creating an Old South: The Plantation Frontier in Jackson and Leon Counties, Florida, 1821–1860." Ph.D. diss., University of Pennsylvania, 1997.

————. "The Migration of Planters to Antebellum Florida: Kinship and Power." *Journal of Southern History* 62, no. 3 (August 1996): 527–54.

Bardaglio, Peter W. *Reconstructing the Household: Families, Sex, and the Law in the Nineteenth Century South.* Chapel Hill: University of North Carolina Press, 1995.

Barefield, Marilyn Davis. *Old Tuscaloosa Land Office Records and Military Warrants, 1821–1855.* Easley, S.C.: Southern Historical Press, 1984.

Barnhart, John D. "Sources of Southern Migration into the Old Northwest." *Mississippi Valley Historical Review* 22, no. 2 (June 1935): 49–62.

Bennett, Robin L., et al. "Genetic Counseling and Screening of Consanguineous Couples and Their Offspring: Recommendations of the National Society of Genetic Counselors." *Journal of Genetic Counseling* 11, no. 2 (April 2002): 97–119. Online at Lippincott Williams & Wilkins, <http://www.lww.com>, article ID 368835. Accessed 10 April 2002.

Billingsley, Carolyn Earle. "Antebellum Planters: Communities of Kinship on the Cotton Frontier." *East Texas Historical Quarterly* 39, no. 2 (2001): 58–74.

————, comp. *Early Saline County, Arkansas, Records: Transcriptions of the 1840 Federal Census and 1846 Tax Book.* 1987. Reprint, Conway, Ark.: Arkansas Research, 2000.

————. *1840 Saline County, Arkansas, Census.* Alexander, Ark.: Saline Research, 1987.

————. *1850 Saline County, Arkansas Census, Photocopied from the Original Microfilmed Census: Schedules 1, 2, 3, 4, 5, and 6, with Full-Name Index.* Alexander, Ark.: Saline Research, 1988.

————. "Settlement Patterns in Early Saline County, Arkansas." *Arkansas Historical Quarterly* 52, no. 2 (summer 1993): 107–28.

Billington, Ray Allen. *America's Frontier Heritage.* 1963. Reprint, Albuquerque: University of New Mexico Press, 1974.

Biographical and Historical Memoirs of Pulaski, Jefferson, Lonoke, Faulkner, Grant, Saline, Perry, Garland, and Hot Spring Counties, Arkansas: A Condensed History of the State, a Number of Biographies of Distinguished Citizens of the Same; a Brief Descriptive History of Each of the Counties Above Named, and Numerous Biographical Sketches of Their Prominent Citizens. Chicago: Goodspeed Publishing Company, 1889. Reprint, Easley, S.C.: Southern Historical Press, 1978.

Biographical and Historical Memoirs of Southern Arkansas. Chicago: Goodspeed Publishing Company, 1890. Reprint, Easley, S.C.: Southern Historical Press, 1978.

Blaisdell's 1919 Atlas of Arkansas. Little Rock: F. L. Blaisdell, 1919. Located at the Arkansas History Commission, Little Rock.

Boles, John B. *Black Southerners: 1619–1869.* Lexington: University Press of Kentucky, 1984.

————. *The Great Revival: Beginnings of the Bible Belt.* Religion in the South Series, ed. John B. Boles. 1972. Rev. ed., Lexington: University Press of Kentucky, 1996.

Bolsterli, Margaret Jones, ed. *A Remembrance of Eden: Harriet Bailey Bullock Daniel's*

Memories of a Frontier Plantation in Arkansas, 1849–1872. Fayetteville: University of Arkansas Press, 1993.

Bolton, S. Charles. *Territorial Ambition: Land and Society in Arkansas, 1800–1840*. Fayetteville: University of Arkansas Press, 1993.

Boswell, Angela. *Her Act and Deed: Women's Lives in a Rural Southern County, 1837–1873*. Sam Rayburn Series on Rural Life. College Station: Texas A&M University Press, 2001.

Boucher, Morris Raymond. "Factors in the History of Tuscaloosa, Alabama, 1816–1846." M.A. thesis, University of Alabama, 1947.

Brazy, Martha Jane. "An American Planter: Slavery, Entrepreneurship, and Identity in the Life of Stephen Duncan, 1787–1867." Ph.D. diss., Duke University, 1998.

Brown, John Henry. *Indian Wars and Pioneers of Texas*. Austin: L. E. Daniel, 1880.

Brown, Marie L. "A Social History of Tuscaloosa from 1816–1850." M.A. thesis, University of Alabama, 1930.

Burrus, Ben M., Milton L. Baughn, and Thomas H. Campbell. *A People Called Cumberland Presbyterians*. Memphis: Frontier Press, 1972.

Burton, Orville Vernon. *In My Father's House Are Many Mansions: Family and Community in Edgefield, South Carolina*. Chapel Hill: University of North Carolina Press, 1985.

Busch, Ruth C. *Family Systems: Comparative Study of the Family*. American University Studies, Series 11, Anthropology and Sociology, vol. 2. New York: Peter Lang, 1990.

Campbell, Randolph B. "Family History from Local Records: A Case Study from Nineteenth Century Texas." *East Texas Historical Journal* 19, no. 2 (1981): 13–26.

Campbell, Thomas H. *History of the Cumberland Presbyterian Church in Texas: Centennial Volume*. Nashville: Cumberland Presbyterian Publishing House, 1936.

Carp, W. Wayne. *Family Matters: Secrecy and Disclosure in the History of Adoption*. Cambridge, Mass.: Harvard University Press, 1998.

Carr, Lois Green, Russell R. Menard, and Lorena S. Walsh. *Robert Cole's World: Agriculture and Society in Early Maryland*. Chapel Hill: University of North Carolina Press for the Institute of Early American History and Culture, 1991.

Casey, James. *The History of the Family*. New Perspectives on the Past Series, R. I. Moore, gen. ed. Oxford: Basil Blackwell, 1989.

Cash, W. J. *The Mind of the South*. New York: Alfred A. Knopf, 1941. Reprint, New York: Vintage Books, 1991.

Cashin, Joan E. *A Family Venture: Men and Women on the Southern Frontier*. New York: Oxford University Press, 1991.

———. "The Structure of Antebellum Planter Families: 'The Ties That Bound Us Was Strong.'" *Journal of Southern History* 56, no. 1 (February 1990): 55–70.

Censer, Jane Turner. *North Carolina Planters and Their Children, 1800–1860*. Baton Rouge: Louisiana State University Press, 1984.

———. "Southwestern Migration among North Carolina Planter Families: 'The

Disposition to Emigrate.'" *Journal of Southern History* 57, no. 3. (August 1991): 407–26.

————. "What Ever Happened to Family History? A Review Article." *Comparative Studies in Society and History* 33, no. 3 (July 1991): 528–38.

Chappell, Phil E. *A Genealogical History of the Chappell, Dickie, and Other Kindred Families of Virginia, 1635–1900.* Rev. ed. Kansas City, Mo.: Hudson Kimberly Publishing, 1900.

Childs, Marleta, and John Ross. *North Louisiana Census Reports.* Vol. 2, *1830 and 1840 Schedules of Caddo, Claiborne, and Natchitoches Parishes;* vol. 3, *1850 and 1860 Schedules of Union Parish.* New Orleans: Polyanthos, 1977.

Clinton, Matthew William. *Tuscaloosa, Alabama: Its Early Days, 1816–1865.* Tuscaloosa, Ala.: Zonta Club, 1958.

Cloud, Opal. "Early Devotion in Saline County." *Arkansas Democrat* (Little Rock), 17 September 1961, *Magazine.*

Cobb, James C. *Redefining Southern Culture: Mind and Identity in the Modern South.* Athens: University of Georgia Press, 1999.

Collier, J. F., and S. J. Yanagisako, eds. *Gender and Kinship: Essays toward a Unified Analysis.* Stanford, Calif.: Stanford University Press, 1987.

Corliss, Richard. "Cousins: A New Theory of Relativity." *Time*, 15 April 2002: 60.

Crawford, Sybil, comp. *Saline County, Arkansas, County Court Record Book Vol. 1: 1836–1839.* Bryant, Ark.: Saline County History and Heritage Society, 1988.

————. *Saline County, Arkansas, County Court Record Book Vol. 2: 1840–1843.* Bryant, Ark.: Saline County History and Heritage Society, 1988.

Cremin, Lawrence A. *American Education: The Colonial Experience, 1607–1783.* New York: Harper and Row, 1970.

Crisman, E. B. *Biographical Sketches of Living Old Men of the Cumberland Presbyterian Church.* Vol. 1. St. Louis, Mo.: Perrin and Smith, 1877.

————. *Origin and Doctrines of the Cumberland Presbyterian Church.* St. Louis, Mo.: Perrin and Smith, 1877.

DeBow, J. D., Superintendent of the U.S. Census. *The Seventh Census of the United States.* 1853. Reprint, New York: Arno Press, 1976.

"1860 Union County Slave Schedules." *Tracks and Traces* 6, no. 2 (November 1984): 31.

Ellison, Rhonda Coleman. *Bibb County, Alabama: The First Hundred Years, 1818–1918.* Tuscaloosa: University of Alabama Press, 1984.

Encyclopedia of the New West Containing Fully Authentical Information of the Agricultural, Mercantile, Commercial, Manufacturing, Mining and Grazing Industries, and Representing the Character, Development, Resources and Present Condition of Texas, Arkansas, Colorado, New Mexico and Indian Territory. Also, Biographical Sketches of Their Representative Men and Women. Marshall, Tex.: United States Biographical Publishing Company, Hodge and Jennings Bros., Proprietors, 1881.

Faragher, John Mack. *Daniel Boone: The Life and Legend of an American Pioneer*. New York: Henry Holt and Company, 1992.

Faust, Drew Gilpin. *John Henry Hammond and the Old South: A Design for Mastery*. Southern Biography Series. Baton Rouge: Louisiana State University Press, 1982.

————. "The Peculiar South Revisited: White Society, Culture, and Politics in the Antebellum Period, 1800–1860." In John B. Boles and Evelyn Thomas Nolan, eds., *Interpreting Southern History: Historiographical Essays in Honor of Sanford W. Higgenbotham*. Baton Rouge: Louisiana State University Press, 1987. 78–119.

Fields, Barbara J. "Ideology and Race in American History." In J. Morgan Kousser and James M. McPherson, eds., *Region, Race, and Reconstruction: Essays in Honor of C. Vann Woodward*. New York: Oxford University Press, 1982. 143–77.

Flynt, Wayne. *Alabama Baptists: Southern Baptists in the Heart of Dixie*. Tuscaloosa: University of Alabama Press, 1998.

Gantrud, Pauline Jones. *Alabama Records*, vol. 8. Shreveport: J&W Enterprises, 1996.

Gewehr, Wesley M. *The Great Awakening in Virginia*. Durham, N.C.: Duke University Press, 1930.

Gies, Frances, and Joseph Gies. *Marriage and the Family in the Middle Ages*. New York: Harper and Row, 1987.

Glover, C. N., LeRoy Polk, and Russell P. Baker. *Pine Bluff Missionary Baptist Association, 1974 Minutes and Yearbook*. Little Rock: Pine Bluff Missionary Baptist Association, 1975.

Glover, Lorri. *All Our Relations: Blood Ties and Emotional Bonds among the Early South Carolina Gentry*. Baltimore, Md.: Johns Hopkins University Press, 2000.

Goody, Jack. *The Development of the Family and Marriage in Europe*. 1983. Reprint, Cambridge: Cambridge University Press, 1994.

Gore, Matthew Harry. *A History of the Cumberland Presbyterian Church in Kentucky to 1988*. N.p.: Joint Heritage Committee of Covenant and Cumberland Presbyteries, 2000.

Green, Jack P. "Foundations of Political Power in the Virginia House of Burgesses, 1720–1776." *William and Mary Quarterly*, 3rd ser., 16, no. 4 (October 1959): 485–506.

Gross, Robert A. *The Minutemen and Their World*. 1976. Reprint, New York: Hill and Wang, 1995.

The Handy Book for Genealogists: United States of America. 8th ed. Logan, Utah: Everton Publishers, 1991.

Harper, C. Armitage, ed. *Historical Report of the Secretary of State*. Little Rock: C. G. Hall, Secretary of State, 1958.

Hartog, Hendrik. *Man and Wife in America: A History*. Cambridge, Mass.: Harvard University Press, 2000.

Hatcher, Patricia Law. *Producing a Quality Family History*. Salt Lake City: Ancestry Incorporated, 1996.

Headstone History: Cemetery Inscriptions, Hot Spring County, Arkansas. Vol. 3. Malvern, Ark.: Hot Spring County Historical Society, 1979.

Henderson, Shannon J. *Arkansas Gazette Index: An Arkansas Index, 1840–1849.* Russellville: Arkansas Tech University Library, 1979.

Hendrix, Ge Lee Corley, comp. *Pendleton County, S.C., Deed Books A & B.* Greenville, S.C., 1980.

Heyrman, Christine Leigh. *Southern Cross: The Beginnings of the Bible Belt.* New York: Alfred A. Knopf, 1997.

Hill, Samuel S., ed. *Encyclopedia of Religion in the South.* 1984. Reprint, Macon, Ga.: Mercer University Press, 1997.

Holy, Ladislav. *Anthropological Perspectives on Kinship.* London: Pluto Press, 1996.

Hughes, Robert. "The Real Australia." *Time,* 11 September 2000: 104.

Isaac, Rhys. *The Transformation of Virginia, 1740–1790.* Chapel Hill: University of North Carolina Press for the Institute of Early American History and Culture, 1982.

Jackson, Ronald Vern, ed. *Arkansas Tax Lists: 1830–1839.* Bountiful, Utah: Accelerated Indexing Systems, 1980.

Jones, J. Wayne. "Seeding Chicot: The Isaac J. Hilliard Plantation and the Arkansas Delta." *Arkansas Historical Quarterly* 59, no. 2 (summer 2000): 149.

Keesee, Vincent A. *A History of the Keesee Family.* Rev. ed. Tifton, Ga.: By the author, 2000.

Kenzer, Robert C. *Kinship and Neighborhood in a Southern Community: Orange County, North Carolina, 1849–1881.* Knoxville: University of Tennessee Press, 1987.

Kulikoff, Allan. *Tobacco and Slaves: The Development of Southern Cultures in the Chesapeake, 1680–1800.* Chapel Hill: University of North Carolina Press for the Institute of Early American History and Culture, 1986.

Kurtz, Donn M., II. *Kinship and Politics: The Justices of the United States and Louisiana Supreme Courts.* Baton Rouge: Louisiana State University Press, 1997.

Lambert, Alton. *History of Tuscaloosa County, Alabama.* Vol. 2. Centre, Ala.: Stewart University Press, 1978.

Landreth, Eddie G. *Abstract of the Saline County, Arkansas, Circuit Court Common Law Book "A," 1836–1842.* Bryant, Ark.: Saline County History and Heritage Society, 1990.

———. "1850 Saline County, Arkansas Slave Schedule Summary." *Saline* 5, no. 1 (March 1990): 35–36.

Lee, Jean B. *The Price of Nationhood: The American Revolution in Charles County.* New York: W. W. Norton and Company, 1994.

Leslie, Kent Anderson. *Woman of Color, Daughter of Privilege: Amanda America Dickson, 1849–1879.* Athens: University of Georgia Press, 1995.

Lévi-Strauss, Claude. *The Elementary Structures of Kinship.* Ed. Rodney Needham, trans. James Harle Bell and John Richard von Sturmer. Boston: Beacon Press, 1969.

Lockridge, Kenneth A. "Land, Population, and the Evolution of New England Society, 1630–1730." *Past and Present* 39 (1968): 62–80.

Loveland, Anne C. *Southern Evangelicals and the Social Order, 1800–1860.* Baton Rouge: Louisiana State University Press, 1980.

MacKethan, Lucinda H., ed. *Recollections of a Southern Daughter: A Memoir by Cornelia Pond Jones of Liberty County.* Athens: University of Georgia Press, 1998.

Mann, Ralph. "Mountains, Land, and Kin Networks: Burkes Garden, Virginia, in the 1840s and 1850s." *Journal of Southern History* 58, no. 3 (August 1992): 411–34.

Mathews, Donald G. *Religion in the Old South.* Chicago: University of Chicago Press, 1977.

Maynes, Mary Jo, Ann Waltner, Birgitte Soland, and Ulrike Strasser, eds. *Gender, Kinship, Power: A Comparative and Interdisciplinary History.* New York: Routledge, 1996.

McDonnold, B. W. *History of the Cumberland Presbyterian Church.* Nashville: Board of Publication of Cumberland Presbyterian Church, 1888.

McLane, Bobbie Jones. *Hot Springs County, Arkansas, 1860 United States Census.* Hot Springs, Ark.: Arkansas Ancestors, 1989.

McLane, Bobbie Jones, and Desmond Walls Allen. *1850 Census of Southern Arkansas: Ashley, Bradley, Clark, Dallas, Drew, Hempstead, Lafayette, Ouachita, Pike, Polk, Sevier, and Union Counties.* Conway, Ark.: Arkansas Research, 1995.

McLane, Bobbie Jones, and Margaret Harrison Hubbard. *Saline County, Arkansas Marriage Records: Books A-B-C, 1836–1875.* Hot Springs, Ark.: Arkansas Ancestors, 1978.

McMillen, Sally G. *Motherhood in the Old South: Pregnancy, Childbirth, and Infant Rearing.* Baton Rouge: Louisiana State University Press, 1990.

McNeilly, Donald P. *The Old South Frontier: Cotton Plantations and the Formation of Arkansas Society, 1819–1861.* Fayetteville: University of Arkansas Press, 2000.

McPherson, James M. *Ordeal by Fire: The Civil War and Reconstruction.* New York: Alfred A. Knopf, 1982.

A Memorial and Biographical History of Ellis County, Texas. Chicago: Lewis Publishing Company, 1892. Reprint, Waxahachie, Tex.: Ellis County Historical Museum and Art Gallery, 1972.

A Memorial and Biographical History of McClennan, Falls, Bell, and Coryell Counties, Texas. Chicago: Lewis Publishing Company, 1893.

Mills, Elizabeth Shown. "Academic Discrimination." *National Genealogical Society Quarterly* 90, no. 1 (March 2002): 3.

———. *Evidence! Citation and Analysis for the Family Historian.* Baltimore, Md.: Genealogical Publishing Company, 1997.

———. "Working with Historical Evidence: Genealogical Principles and Standards." *National Genealogical Society Quarterly* 87, no. 3 (September 1999): 165–84.

Moneyhon, Carl H. *Arkansas and the New South, 1874–1929.* Histories of Arkansas, Elliott West, gen. ed. Fayetteville: University of Arkansas Press, 1997.

Moore, Henry Campbell. *Black's Law Dictionary*, 5th ed. St. Paul, Minn.: West Publishing Company, 1979.

Morgan, James Logan. *Arkansas Marriage Notices, 1819–1845.* Newport, Ark.: Morgan Books, 1984.

Morris, Christopher. *Becoming Southern: The Evolution of a Way of Life, Warren County and Vicksburg, Mississippi, 1770–1860.* New York: Oxford University Press, 1995.

Murray, Joyce Martin, comp. *Austin County, Texas, Deed Abstracts, 1837–1852, Republic of Texas and State of Texas.* N.p., 1987.

———. *Washington County, Texas, Deed Abstracts, 1834–1841, Republic of Texas and State of Coahuila and Texas (Mexico).* Dallas: By the compiler, 1986.

Murray, Nicholas Russell. *Tuscaloosa County, Alabama, Marriages, 1821–1860.* Hammond, La.: Hunting for Bears, 1986.

Nieman, Donald G. "Black Political Power and Criminal Justice: Washington County, Texas, 1868–1884." *Journal of Southern History* 55 (August 1989): 391–420.

Oakes, James. *The Ruling Race: A History of American Slaveholders.* New York: Alfred A. Knopf, 1982.

Ogburn, W. F. "The Family and Its Functions." In Bryan S. Turner, ed., *Readings in the Anthropology and Sociology of Family and Kinship.* London: Routledge/Thoemmes Press, 1998.

Orr-Hickey, Johnny Elizabeth, transcriber. *1880 Census, Grant County, Arkansas.* San Antonio: By the author, n.d.

Ottenheimer, Martin. *Forbidden Relatives: The American Myth of Cousin Marriage.* Urbana: University of Illinois Press, 1996.

Otto, John Solomon. "The Migration of the Southern Plain Folk: An Interdisciplinary Synthesis." *Journal of Southern History* 51, no. 2 (May 1985): 183–200.

Ovilla Historical Society. *Ovilla, Texas History Book.* Dallas: Taylor Publishing Company, 1996.

Ownby, Ted. *Subduing Satan: Religion, Recreation, and Manhood in the Rural South, 1865–1920.* Fred W. Morrison Series in Southern Studies. Chapel Hill: University of North Carolina Press, 1990.

Owsley, Frank L. *Plain Folk of the Old South.* Baton Rouge: Louisiana State University Press, 1949. Reprint, Chicago: Quadrangle Books, 1965.

Parker, Richard Denny. *Historical Recollections of Robertson County, Texas, with Biographical and Genealogical Notes on the Pioneers and Their Families.* Salado, Tex.: Anson Jones Press, 1955.

Pasternak, Burton, Carol R. Ember, and Melvin Ember. *Sex, Gender, and Kinship: A Cross-Cultural Perspective.* Upper Saddle River, N.J.: Prentice-Hall, 1997.

Payne, Jennifer M. "Independent Minds and Shared Community: Married Women's Wills in Amite County, Mississippi, 1840–1919." M.A. thesis, Rice University, 1996.

Peterson, Merrill D. *Thomas Jefferson and the New Nation.* 1970. Reprint, London: Oxford University Press, 1975.

Phelan, Macum. *A History of Early Methodism in Texas, 1817–1866.* Nashville: Cokesbury Press, 1924.

Phillips, Ulrich Bonnell. *American Negro Slavery: A Survey of the Supply, Employment and Control of Negro Labor as Determined by the Planter Regime.* 1918. Reprint, Baton Rouge: Louisiana State University Press, 1990.

Raboteau, Albert J. *Slave Religion: The "Invisible Institution" in the Antebellum South.* New York: Oxford University Press, 1978.

Radcliffe-Brown, A. R., and Daryll Forde, eds. *African Systems of Kinship and Marriage.* London: Oxford University Press for the International African Institute, 1950.

Ragsdale, William Oates. *They Sought a Land: A Settlement in the Arkansas River Valley, 1840–1970.* Fayetteville: University of Arkansas Press, 1997.

Ray, Worth S. *Austin Colony Pioneers, Including History of Bastrop, Fayette, Grimes, Montgomery and Washington Counties, Texas.* 1949. Reprint, Austin: Pemberton Press, 1970.

Reese, June O., transcriber. *Overseers of the Poor, 1818–1833, Tuscaloosa County, Alabama.* Tuscaloosa, Ala.: N.p., 1982.

Rose, Christine. *Genealogical Proof Standard: Building a Solid Case.* San Jose, Calif.: Rose Family Association, 2001.

Rosengarten, Theodore. *Tombee: Portrait of a Cotton Planter, with the Journal of Thomas B. Chaplin, 1822–1890.* New York: William Morrow and Company, 1986.

Rosenthal, Joel T. *Patriarchy and Families of Privilege in Fifteenth-Century England.* Philadelphia: University of Pennsylvania Press, 1991.

Rowan, Marilyn G. "1860 Saline County, Arkansas Slave Schedule Summary." *Saline* 6, no. 1 (March 1991): 12–15.

Royce, Charles C. *Indian Land Cessions in the United States.* Washington, D.C.: Government Printing Office, 1900. Reprint, Arno Press, 1971.

Rundell, William, Jr. "Southern History from Local Sources: A Survey of Graduate History Training." *Journal of Southern History* 34, no. 2 (May 1968): 214–26.

Rutman, Darrett B. "Assessing the Little Communities of Early America." *William and Mary Quarterly,* 3rd ser., 43, no. 2 (April 1986): 163–78.

Rutman, Darrett B., and Anita H. Rutman. *A Place in Time: Explicatus.* New York: W. W. Norton and Company, 1984.

———. *A Place in Time: Middlesex County, Virginia, 1650–1750.* New York: W. W. Norton and Company, 1984.

Salmon, Marylynn. *Women and the Law of Property in Early America.* Chapel Hill: University of North Carolina Press, 1986.

Schneider, David M. *American Kinship: A Cultural Account.* 1968. Reprint, Chicago: University of Chicago Press, 1980.

Schweiger, Beth Barton. *The Gospel Working Up: Progress and the Pulpit in Nineteenth-Century Virginia.* New York: Oxford University Press, 2000.

Shoumatoff, Alex. *The Mountain of Names: A History of the Human Family.* New York: Simon and Schuster, 1985.

Sistler, Barbara, Byron Sistler, and Samuel Sistler. *Tennessee Land Grants: Surnames I–K.* Nashville: Byron Sistler and Associates, 1997.

Smith, Daniel Blake. *Inside the Great House: Planter Family Life in Eighteenth-Century Chesapeake Society.* Ithaca, N.Y.: Cornell University Press, 1980.

Smith, Daniel Scott. "'All in Some Degree Related to Each Other': A Demographic and Comparative Resolution of the Anomaly of New England Kinship." *American Historical Review* 94, no. 1, supplement to vol. 94 (February 1989): 44–79.

———. "Child-Naming Practices, Kinship Ties, and Change in Family Attitudes in Hingham, Massachusetts, 1641–1880." *Journal of Social History* 18 (summer 1985): 541–66.

Smith, William C. "Daddy No More: Ex-Husband Contests Presumption of Paternity with DNA Results Proving He Has No Biological Ties." *American Bar Association Journal* 85 (July 1999): 30.

Snydor, Charles S. *Gentlemen Freeholders: Political Practices in Washington's Virginia.* Chapel Hill: University of North Carolina Press, 1952.

Spencer, Annie Laurie. *Marriage Bonds and Ministers Returns of Union County, Arkansas, 1829–1870.* Privately published, 1962.

Stevenson, Brenda E. *Life in Black and White: Family and Community in the Slave South.* New York: Oxford University Press, 1996.

Stone, Elizabeth. *Black Sheep and Kissing Cousins: How Our Family Stories Shape Us.* New York: Times Books, 1988.

Stone, Lawrence. *The Family, Sex and Marriage in England, 1500–1800.* 1977. Abbreviated ed., New York: Harper Colophon Books, 1979.

Sturdevant, Katherine Scott. *Bringing Your Family History to Life through Social History.* White Hall, Va.: Betterway Publications, 2000.

Suddath, Maggie Hubbard. *Tuscaloosa County, Alabama Records.* Vol. 1, *1837 Tax List and Probate Records.* Tuscaloosa: By the author, 1988.

Tebbenhoff, Edward H. "Tacit Rules and Hidden Family Structures: Naming Practices and Godparentage in Schenectady, New York, 1680–1800." *Journal of Social History* 18 (summer 1985): 567–85.

Texas State Travel Guide. Austin: State Department of Highways and Transportation, n.d. (annual publication).

Thorndale, William, and William Dollarhide. *Map Guide to the U.S. Federal Censuses, 1790–1920.* 1987. Reprint, Baltimore, Md.: Genealogical Publishing Company, 1988.

Turner, Bryan S., ed. *Readings in the Anthropology and Sociology of Family and Kinship.* London: Routledge/Thoemmes Press, 1998.

Turner, Frederick Jackson. *The Frontier in American History*. New York: H. Holt, 1920.

Ulrich, Laurel Thatcher. *A Midwife's Tale: The Life of Martha Ballard, Based on Her Diary, 1785–1812*. New York: Vintage Books, 1991.

Vos Savant, Marilyn. "Ask Marilyn." *Parade Magazine*, 14 December 1997: 20.

Wagner, Roy. "Incest and Identity: A Critique and Theory on the Subject of Exogamy and Incest Prohibition." *Man*, n.s., 7, no. 4 (December 1972): 601–13.

Walsh, Lorena. *From Calabar to Carter's Grove: The History of a Virginia Slave Community*. Colonial Williamsburg Studies in Chesapeake History and Culture, Cary Carson, series ed. Charlottesville: University Press of Virginia, 1997.

"Walter Scott's Personality Parade." *Parade Magazine*, 14 January 2001.

Walz, Robert Bradshaw. "Migration into Arkansas, 1820–1880: Incentives and Means of Travel." *Arkansas Historical Quarterly* 17, no. 4 (winter 1959): 309–24.

———. "Migration into Arkansas, 1834–1880." Ph.D. diss., University of Texas, 1958.

Weber, Max. *The Protestant Ethic and the Spirit of Capitalism*. Trans. Talcott Parsons. 1930. Reprint, London: Routledge, 1992.

West, Anson. *A History of Methodism in Alabama*. 1893. Reprint, Spartanburg, S.C.: Reprint Company, 1983.

Williamson, Joel. *New People: Miscegenation and Mulattoes in the United States*. 1980. Reprint, Baton Rouge: Louisiana State University Press, 1995.

Wilson, Charles Reagan, and William Ferris, eds. *Encyclopedia of Southern Culture*. Chapel Hill: University of North Carolina Press, 1989. Reprint, New York: Anchor Books, Doubleday, 1991.

Winfield, Nathan, and Judy Winfield. *All Our Yesterdays: A Brief History of Chappell Hill*. 1969. Reprint, Waco, Tex.: Texian Press, 1986.

Woodman, Harold D. "Economic Reconstruction and the Rise of the New South, 1865–1900." In John B. Boles and Evelyn Thomas Nolan, eds., *Interpreting Southern History: Historiographical Essays in Honor of Sanford W. Higgenbotham*. Baton Rouge: Louisiana State University Press, 1987. 254–307.

———. *King Cotton and His Retainers: Financing and Marketing the Cotton Crop of the South, 1800–1925*. 1968. Reprint, Columbia: University of South Carolina Press, 1990.

Woodward, C. Vann, ed. *Mary Chesnut's Civil War*. New York: Book-of-the-Month Club, 1994.

Wright, Robert. "Sin in the Global Village." *Time*, 19 October 1998: 130.

Census Records

1790 U.S. Census, Greenville District, South Carolina. National Archives and Records Administration (hereafter cited as NARA) M637, R11.

1800 U.S. Census, Spartanburgh District, South Carolina. NARA M32, R50.

1830 U.S. Census, Tuscaloosa County, Alabama. NARA M19, R3. Online at <http://www.ancestry.com>.

1840 U.S. Census, Choctaw County, Mississippi. NARA M704, R215. Online at <http://www.ancestry.com>.

1840 U.S. Census, Saline County, Arkansas. NARA M704, R20.

1850 U.S. Census, Population Schedule, Choctaw County, Mississippi, Western Division. NARA M432, R370. Online at <http://www.ancestry.com>.

1850 U.S. Census, Population Schedule, Union County, Arkansas. NARA M432, R30.

1850 U.S. Census, Slave Schedules: Union County, Saline County, Hot Spring County, and Ouachita County, Arkansas. NARA M432, R32.

1860 U.S. Census, Population Schedule, Ashley County, Arkansas. NARA M653, R37.

1860 U.S. Census, Population Schedule, Falls County, Texas. NARA M653, R1293.

1860 U.S. Census, Population Schedule, Saline County, Arkansas. NARA M653, R50.

1860 U.S. Census, Population Schedule, Washington County, Texas. NARA M653, R1307. Heritage Quest Digital Microfilm.

1860 U.S. Census, Slave Schedule, Ashley County, Arkansas. NARA M653, R53.

1860 U.S. Census, Slave Schedule, Columbia County, Arkansas. NARA M653, R53.

1860 U.S. Census, Slave Schedule, Falls County, Texas. NARA M654, R1309.

1860 U.S. Census, Slave Schedule, Hot Spring County, Arkansas. NARA M653, R53.

1860 U.S. Census, Slave Schedule, Robertson County, Texas. NARA M654, R1312.

1860 U.S. Census, Slave Schedule, Saline County, Arkansas. NARA M653, R54.

1860 U.S. Census, Slave Schedule, Union County, Arkansas. NARA M653, R54.

1860 U.S. Census, Slave Schedule, Washington County, Texas. NARA M653, R1312. Heritage Quest Digital Microfilm.

1870 U.S. Census, Population Schedule, Robertson County, Texas. NARA M93, R1602. Heritage Quest Digital Microfilm.

1870 U.S. Census, Population Schedule, Union Parish, Louisiana. Online at <http://www.rootsweb.com/~usgenweb/la/census/1870>. Accessed 22 November 2002.

INDEX

Page numbers in italics refer to figures. Page references for a woman are listed under her married name, unless she was married more than once, in which case she is listed under her maiden name or the surname of her first husband.

CREDITS

The sources for the chapter epigraphs are as follows.

Introduction. Antoine de Saint-Exupéry, *Flight to Arras,* trans. Lewis Galantiére (New York: Reynal and Hitchcock, 1942).

Chapter 1. David Thackery, "Editor's Note," *Ancestry* 17 (May/June 1999):7. Used with permission.

Chapter 2. Jane Howard, *Families* (New York: Simon and Schuster, 1978).

Chapter 3. C. S. Lewis, *Mere Christianity* (1943).

Chapter 4. Maya Angelou, quoted in the *New York Times,* 16 April 1972. Used with permission.

Chapter 5. Marcus Tullius Cicero, 106 B.C.–43 B.C.

Conclusion. George Santayana, *The Life of Reason* (Amherst, N.Y.: Prometheus Books, 1998), 104.